*The*
# LOCHABER
# EMIGRANTS
# TO GLENGARRY

*Front cover*

Oil painting (1960) by Stuart McCormick depicting three brigs, the *Friends*, the *Helen* and the *Jane* entering Montreal harbour 1802. Painting courtesy Sybil MacMillan Barbour, Kitchener, Ontario. Photograph courtesy of Michael Albano, Acton, Ontario. Stuart McCormick (1906-1992) painted the heart and soul of Glengarry. His more than 3,000 pieces, most of them oils, are prized by collectors, who include Her Majesty Queen Elizabeth II.

*Inside cover*

Harriet (Kennedy) McMillan's paisley shawl. The shawl travelled with her to Canada in 1802. Harriet married Duncan Ban McMillan, who died before the family, three sons and eleven daughters, left Scotland. She managed to preserve the shawl through pioneer days on lot 27, concession 8, Lochiel Township, Glengarry. Since Harriet's death in 1839, the shawl has travelled to Seattle and California. It returned home to Glengarry in 1992, and it is in the collection of Hugh Allan MacMillan, Dalkeith, Ontario. Photograph courtesy of Bryan Thompson Photography, Alexandria, Ontario.

Allan 'Glenpean' McMillan (1752-1803), co-organizer of the Lochaber migration of 1802. Photograph in Hugh P. MacMillan Collection, Guelph, Ontario. The original oil painting has been lost.

# *The* LOCHABER EMIGRANTS TO GLENGARRY

RAE FLEMING, *Editor*

NATURAL HERITAGE / NATURAL HISTORY INC.

The Lochaber Emigrants to Glengarry
Rae Fleming, Editor

Published by Natural Heritage / Natural History Inc.
P.O. Box 95, Station "O", Toronto, Ontario M4A 2M8

Design and typesetting: Robin Brass Studio
Printed and bound in Canada by Hignell Printing Limited, Winnipeg, Manitoba

**Canadian Cataloguing in Publication Data**

Main entry under title:

Lochaber emigrants to Glengarry

Includes bibliographical references and index.
ISBN 0-920474-96-9

1. Glengarry (Ont.) – Emigration and immigration – History.  2. Lochaber (Scotland) – Emigration
and immigration – History.  3. Immigrants – Ontario – Glengarry – History.  4. Scots – Ontario –
Glengarry – History.  5. Lochaber (Scotland) – History.  I. Fleming, Rae Bruce, 1944-    .

FC3095.G5L6 1994      971.3´77´0049163
FI059.G5L6 1994               C94-932440-X

Natural Heritage / Natural History Inc. gratefully acknowledges the assistance of the Canada
Council, the Ontario Arts Council, and the Government of Ontario through the Ministry of
Culture, Tourism and Recreation.

# CONTENTS

# LIST OF ILLUSTRATIONS

# FOREWORD

RAE FLEMING

*A*cting as editor for this volume reminded me of excursions in the 1980s led by Hugh MacMillan and Ted Cowan as part of the Canadian Association for Scottish Studies annual meetings. During these trips – through Glengarry or the Bruce, where Scots migrants had settled – participants often wondered if we would have some place to rest our weary heads that evening. During one lunch break, a Scottish academic from Stirling leaned forward onto a picnic table, gazed over his glasses at some distant point and mumbled that Ted and Hugh should found a travel company called Kamikaze Tours.

Once the trips were over, however, small inconveniences were overlooked. Fondly remembered were new friends lasting years and the pleasure in learning about an area of Canada from the inside out. Who can forget Tony Mackenzie's stories of Cape Breton and outport Newfoundland? Who did not benefit from new contacts for scholarly or genealogical research?

Once or twice while editing this book, I wondered whether we would reach our destination. The editor, part passenger and part driver, must make the best of the trip while following an itinerary set by promoter and contributors. The editor can tinker and polish, cajole and sympathize, but he cannot choose a new route or fire the promoter. Several times along the route of this project, I held my breath. What was to be done when the promoter missed final deadlines? Or when an overseas contributor retreated into misty silence as we anxiously awaited an amended version of his chapter, four months late? How, I often wondered, would authors react upon discovering that the editor had eviscerated a paragraph or two of his/her treasured work? One contributor made his feelings clear. 'You do not understand the difference between editorial discretion and editorial interference,' he fumed in a fax from Glasgow.

The journey has now been completed, and I can say that I am pleased with the finished work. I have made new friends, and kept old ones. In addition to telephone conversations with people whose faces remained a mystery – Stan Barrett, Heather Devine, Ken McKenna, David Anderson, Duncan MacDonald and Graeme Mackenzie, I also had the pleasure of dealing with people I have known for years – Ted

Cowan; Ian MacMillan; Hugh MacMillan, without whose faith and persistence this book would not exist; and Marianne McLean, whose introduction has tied together the book's themes. As editor, I valued Marianne's generous advice on aspects of Glengarry County. It has also been my pleasure to deal with publisher Barry Penhale, and Robin Brass, design and layout artist. I want to thank Microage Computers in Peterborough, Ont. and Lindsay Computer Centre for advice on diskette/computer problems; and my neighbour, Lisa Burton, for use of her fax machine.

I'm sure that the reader will derive as much pleasure and learning from reading this book as I have in editing it.

## NOTE TO READERS

The spelling of Scottish Highland surnames varies, partly because they were spelled and spoken originally in Gaelic then later translated into English. The difference between 'Mc' and 'Mac' seemed to matter little until the twentieth century. Many people today assume that 'Mac' implies Prostestant and Scottish; and that 'Mc' is Catholic and Irish or Scottish. It's never that simple. Documents indicate that Archibald 'Murlaggan,' a Presbyterian, preferred 'McMillan.' Members of the same family today prefer 'Mac-Millan.' There is also some variation in the choice of small or large 'm.' The editor and contributors have chosen to respect the variety of spellings of surnames. Readers will also note spelling irregularities in documents. As much as possible, we have respected the original spelling. We have added [sic] after the error to indicate that we have decided to leave it intact. In the few cases where unusual spelling, punctuation and grammar have created imprecision, we have added correctives in square brackets.

# PREFACE

HUGH P. MacMILLAN

*T*he several authors in this book were asked to write about the Lochaber emigration from their own perspective, based on research of their own and also material that I had assembled over many years. My role has been that of facilitator, promoter and contributor. The book, which evolved from family history to emigration story, demonstrates how those two themes can be combined.

Many of us maintain contacts with friends at home and abroad. There is no reason why we cannot do the same for some of the relatives we meet through this book. We often find it difficult to maintain contact with close relatives, never mind fourth or fifth cousins. I am not suggesting we rush out and try to meet them all, but rather pick and choose whom to contact when we are travelling. An annual or biannual gathering might be held in Glengarry and tied to the 'Highland Feis' held in the county every summer. Family gatherings of all sizes go on all over the world. Why do we not have one? I am not just thinking of

our Glenpean and Murlaggan line, but also descendants of other migrants. We can learn from the wide range of people and relatives we meet. Joining the Glengarry Highland Society may be the best way to accomplish this. The Mayflower Society has been going many years so why not a Lochaber Emigrants branch of the Highland Society?

The Highland Society of Glengarry and descendants of the emigrants can also play a role in helping promote such research by universities involved in Scottish emigration studies. They can lobby Scottish Studies programmes, and they can contribute to fundraising projects such as the Scottish Studies Foundation at the University of Guelph.

It has been an interesting and enjoyable experience to help organize this book. I hope you get equal pleasure from reading it. Special thanks to my network of contacts who have provided invaluable research information over many years.

# INTRODUCTION

MARIANNE McLEAN

Lochaber is not a Highland placename immediately recognizable to most North Americans. Yet many visitors to the western Highlands of Scotland pass through Lochaber, which stands astride the western outlet of the Great Glen and on the famous road to the Isles. Lochaber is likely best known for the town of Fort William and for Ben Nevis, the highest mountain peak in Great Britain. The region's massive hills and its many valleys radiating out from the Great Glen are remarkable for their beauty and, in the twentieth century, for their wilderness character.

Few clansmen whose names are traditionally associated with Lochaber remain in its glens and valleys today. Camerons, McMillans and Macdonalds have for many years been found in much larger numbers in Canada and Australia than in their Gaelic homeland. The social and economic forces that transformed the Highlands of Scotland in the 200 years after Culloden

MARIANNE McLEAN is a descendant of Duncan McLean, a member of Archibald McMillan's 1802 emigrant party. Marianne holds a PhD in history from the University of Edinburgh and is the author of the award-winning book, *The People of Glengarry*. She works as an archivist at the National Archives of Canada in Ottawa.

had the ironic effect of creating a wilderness in many Lochaber glens at the same time as the migrant clansmen created farms, towns and cities in the wilderness of the New Worlds. The clansmen of the late eighteenth and early nineteenth centuries responded to change by seeking new ways of making their living and new communities to support their extended families. Faced with powerful forces threatening their standard of living and their communal life, the conservative clansmen took the radical step of emigrating to North America.

Emigration from Lochaber was given a North American focus by reports brought back to Scotland by officers and men of Highland regiments after service in the colonial wars of the mid-eighteenth century. Lochaber clansmen came to the colony of New York in the decade before the American Revolution both as individuals and as members of the 1773 emigrant party led by the Macdonells of Leek, Collachie and Aberchalder. After 1783, the defeat of British forces brought the clansmen loyal to the Crown north to Canada where they established a new community, later called Glengarry County. Emigration from Lochaber was now directed to Canada. Individual

1

McMillan families were among the Glen Garry and Knoydart emigrations of 1785 and 1786, while Alexander McMillan of Glenpean brought some fifteen families from Lochaber in 1792. When the cessation of war with revolutionary France again permitted large-scale emigration in 1802, Archibald McMillan of Murlaggan organized the departure of 448 clansmen to Canada; of these perhaps 160 were either McMillan or other Lochaber clansmen. One year later another twenty-one men from Lochaber received land in Finch township, adjacent to Glengarry County.

The Lochaber emigration to Glengarry forms part of the mass emigration from Europe to North America that is usually associated with the settling of the west and the development of our cities. Highland emigration of the period 1770 to 1804 offers a preview of the dense movement of people that depopulated regions and minimized European population growth over the last one hundred and fifty years. Historians analysing emigration point out the variety of experiences, from individual departures without family or friends to group departures of both. A majority of the Lochaber emigrants came in groups. While some emigrants travelled alone, others were members of groups organized both by their own clan leaders and by Macdonell tacksmen. The Lochaber community itself seems to have been divided by the departures, as the early migrants, principally McMillans, settled in Glengarry County or adjacent districts, while later migrants chose Nova Scotia or western Ontario.

In this volume the Lochaber story is surveyed from its origins hundreds of years before emigration, through the migration experience, and into the present day. Graeme Mackenzie provides a genealogy of the McMillans, particularly the Glenpean and Murlaggan families, while Edward Cowan and Kenneth McKenna present the social and economic context behind the departures. The tales of two individual emigrants indicates the range of fates which awaited the clansmen in the New World. Hugh MacMillan writes of Duncan Ban McMillan who settled in the Glengarry district, while Heather Devine describes James McMillan and his life in fur trade posts in Western North America. Today's events provide Stanley Barrett with the subject of his article which hints at the possibilities for genealogical research and ethnocultural analysis within a single family history. Finally Hugh MacMillan sums up a lifetime's interest in family history with an account of how *The Lochaber Emigrants to Glengarry* came to be.

The stars of this book may just be its original documents, assembled by Ian MacMillan, David Anderson and Kenneth McKenna. Archibald McMillan preserved a few of the records created in organizing the departure in 1802, as well as letter books kept after his settlement in Canada. Passenger lists are rare for pre-Confederation Canada, so Archibald McMillan's list of the 448 people who travelled to America under his leadership is of great value, especially for the detail about the composition of the emigrant party: the number of women and children, family relationships, and the farms from which they originated. All these pieces of information are usually hard to come by. Archibald McMillan's letters are also well worth close reading for the information, both factual and interpretative, about McMillan's new life in Canada, as well as for the occasional reference to his fellow emigrants' experiences. Duncan MacDonald's charts, the result of detailed research, provide useful genealogical information for McMillans who settled in Glengarry.

One note of caution to the reader. The legal boundaries of Glengarry County extend over four townships some twenty-nine kilometres by forty-three kilometres in extent. Beyond this physical reality, the cultural community of Scottish Highlanders extends west of Glengarry into Stormont and north into Prescott counties in Ontario, and east into Soulanges and south into Beauharnois counties in Quebec. And yet even beyond these social boundaries, Glengarry was also an idea – that there could be Gaelic communities in British North America – and it was this idea that attracted people from Lochaber and the rest of the Highlands to Glengarry County and to other Highland settlements in Ontario and Nova Scotia.

# PART I

# PASSENGERS 1802

# CHAPTER 1

# SHIPS' LISTS OF LOCHABER IMMIGRANTS 1802

## DAVID G. ANDERSON

*T*he ships' lists for the three ships, the *Friends*, the *Helen* and the *Jane* are located in the Archibald 'Murlaggan' McMillan Papers, National Archives of Canada (NA), MG 24 I 183. These lists form one of the key documents for a study of the Lochaber migration.

Originally we had thought to publish a reproduction of the original ship lists that are part of the Archibald McMillan papers. Because the writing is so faded, it was decided to do a new transcription from the primary source document. We have reproduced one page so that the reader may see the original. It is interesting to note that the families came from all parts of Lochaber – Laddy, Livisie, Munergy and many other places noted in the lists. The husband-wife-children groups are obvious but it is more difficult to tell about the rest. Many groups would be sister-brother combinations, or just close friends. By all accounts they had a much better time at sea than was

the lot of most emigrants. Judging by Archibald's concerns as expressed in his writings, it seems likely that he was responsible for seeing to their welfare at sea and on land. The logistics of assembling so many people in one place (Fort William) on a certain date must have been formidable. Roads and communications were limited.

The initial list of passengers (numbers 1 to 299) boarded in Fort William. The addendum at the end of the list as published below is a list of passengers added by Somerled MacMillan in his *Bygone Lochaber*, and seems to include names of people who boarded the ships in Saltcoats on the Clyde River, the last stop before the Atlantic crossing. Archibald 'Murlaggan' McMillan, his wife and family are included in this second list. Over a period of several weeks before going south, McMillan had enlisted over 250 passengers. At number 254 (John McMillan), the handwriting changes, signalling a second compiler. Archibald McMillan apparently had departed Fort William for Glasgow in order to stock up on provisions and water. He, his wife and family then boarded one of the ships at Saltcoats.

DAVID ANDERSON, U.E. is a tenant of the Bethune-Thompson House in Williamstown, Glengarry. He is past president of the Glengarry Historical Society.

Passenger list of one page ship's lists of Lochaber immigrants 1802, showing names such as Cameron, Grant and Stewart. (Courtesy National Archives of Canada, Manuscript Division, Archibald McMillan and Family Papers, MG 24, I 183, p. 6)

*MacDonell* and *Macdonald* are anglicized variants of the Gaelic word *Dhomniull* for all those bearing the name of clan Donald. It was the compiler of the original list who made the choice. Other lists from this period show that some writers consistently used 'Mc' as opposed to 'Mac' while others employed 'Donell' as opposed to 'Donald.' The stress is on the first syllable in Gaelic. However one notable exception occurs in Catholic Jacobite families where the second language was French and the stress on the last syllable would be employed as in French. The few instances of the spelling 'McDonald' in this list are cases where the line was crowded and the abbreviation 'McDon:d' is employed. The single case which is spelled out as such is entry 284 (Don: McDonald), which is in a different hand. In other words, the spelling variants are not important – they are all simply *dhomniull* in the Gaelic.

The compilers of the 1802 list wrote with a fine clear hand and there is rarely an ambiguity in the spelling. A case in point is *Leck*; although most English-speakers use the spelling *Leek*, the Gaelic pronunciation is better represented as *Leck* as the list compiler has done.

*Broy:r* as an abbreviation for Brother is an instance of the old convention of representing the diphthong 'th' by the old Anglo-Saxon letter *thorn* for which English typographers usually substituted the roman letter 'y.' Readers of the time would know by context and pronounce the word correctly, reading 'ye' as 'thee', for instance.

Strike-outs in the lists are as they appear in the original (for example number 10). The line numbers occur in the original and are a running tally of the number of adult passengers.

## NAMES OF PASSENGERS IN ORDER OF APPEARANCE ON THE LISTS

| | |
|---|---|
| Alex McPhee | Aberchalder |
| Alex McPhee | Do. |
| Catherin McAlpin | " |
| Mary McPhee | " |

| | | |
|---|---|---|
| 5 | Marg: McPhee | " |
| | Anny McPhee & 1 child | |
| | ===== | |
| | Donald McPhee | |
| | Anne Kennedy | |
| | Janet Marshall | |
| 10 | McPhee's wife ~~& 1 child~~ | |
| | ===== | |
| | Ewen Kennedy | Aberchalder |
| | his Wife | |
| | Don: Kennedy | Kinlochlochy |
| | 4 children | |
| | ===== | |
| | Don: Cameron | Drimnasallie |
| 15 | his Wife | |
| | ===== | |
| | John Corbet | Ardachy |
| | Mrs Corbet | |
| | ~~Mary Corbet~~ | |
| | William Corbet | |
| 20 | Christy Corbet & 1 child | |
| | ===== | |
| | John McDonald | Inchlagan |
| | his Wife | |
| | Don: McDonell & 2 children | |
| | ===== | |
| | Donald Scot | Aberchalder |
| 25 | his Wife | |
| | Alex Scot | |
| | Dun: Scot | |
| | Janet Scot | |
| | Mary Scot & 2 children | |
| | ===== | |
| 30 | Dun: Kennedy | Aberchalder |
| | his Wife & 3 children | |
| | ===== | |
| | Don: Kennedy | Achluachrach |
| | Mrs Kennedy | |
| | ~~Mary McDonell~~ & 5 children | |
| | ===== | |
| 35 | Alex McDonell | Laggan |
| | Mrs McDonell & 2 children | |
| | ===== | |
| | John McDonell | Leck |
| | ===== | |
| | Don: Kennedy | Laddy |
| | Mrs Kennedy & 2 children | |
| | ===== | |
| 40 | Don: McDonell | Laddy |

|    |                                    |              |    |                                  |            |
|----|------------------------------------|--------------|----|----------------------------------|------------|
|    | John McDonell                      |              | 80 | Peggy McDonell                   |            |
|    | Dun: McDonell                      |              |    | Allan McDonell & 4 children      |            |
|    | Catherine McDonell                 |              |    | =====                            |            |
|    | Mary Kennedy                       |              |    | Alexander McDonell               | Boline     |
|    | =====                              |              |    | his Wife                         |            |
| 45 | Allan McDonell                     | Munergy      |    | Dun: McDonell                    |            |
|    | Mrs McDonell                       |              | 85 | Donald McDonell                  |            |
|    | Margaret McDonell taken in no. 298 |              |    | Cath: McDonell & 4 children      |            |
|    | Catherin McDonell                  |              |    | =====                            |            |
|    | Donald McDonell & 2 children       |              |    | John McDonell                    | Invervigar |
|    | =====                              |              |    | Dugald McDonell                  |            |
|    | Donald McDougald                   | Ft Augustus  |    | Catherin McDonell                |            |
| 50 | Mrs McDougald                      |              | 90 | Flory McDonell                   |            |
|    | Marjery McDougald                  |              |    | Peggy McDonell                   |            |
|    | Alex McDougald                     |              |    | Donald McDonell & 1 child        |            |
|    | John McDougald                     |              |    | =====                            |            |
|    | =====                              |              |    | Arch'd McLean                    | Lady [sic] |
|    | Alexander Stewart & 1 child        | Ft Augustus  |    | ~~Alex~~ Angus McLean            | Do.        |
| 55 | Donald Fraser                      | Leck         |    | =====                            |            |
|    | Mrs Fraser & 1 child               |              | 95 | John Kennedy                     | Invervigar |
|    | =====                              |              |    | his Wife                         |            |
|    | Mary McAlpin                       | Greenfield   |    | Dun: Kennedy                     |            |
|    | Mary Cameron                       | Letterfinlay |    | Alexander Kennedy                |            |
|    | Catherin McAlpin                   | Do.          |    | =====                            |            |
| 60 | Eliz: Grant                        | Drimdrochil  |    | Donald Kennedy                   | Inchlagan  |
|    | =====                              |              | 100| Angus Kennedy                    |            |
|    | Alexander Grant                    | Achnaconern  |    | Alex Kennedy                     |            |
|    | Mrs Grant                          |              |    | Allan Kennedy                    |            |
|    | John Grant & 4 children            |              |    | Mrs Kennedy & 2 children         |            |
|    | =====                              |              |    | =====                            |            |
|    | Donald Grant                       | Dalcattaig   |    | John Kennedy                     | Inchlagan  |
| 65 | Mrs Grant                          |              | 105| his Wife                         |            |
|    | =====                              |              |    | Ewen Kennedy                     |            |
|    | Mary Grant                         | Duldregan    |    | Mary Kennedy                     |            |
|    | Flory Grant                        |              |    | Alex Kennedy                     |            |
|    | Isabella Grant                     |              |    | Janet Kennedy                    |            |
|    | Anne Grant                         | Livisie      | 110| Angus Kennedy & 3 children       |            |
| 70 | John Grant & 1 child               |              |    | =====                            |            |
|    | =====                              |              |    | John McDonell                    | Ardnabie   |
|    | James McDonell                     | Balmean      |    | his Wife & 1 child               |            |
|    | Mrs McDonell                       |              |    | Alex Cameron                     | Do.        |
|    | Kath: McDonell                     |              |    | his wife                         | Do.        |
|    | Allan McDonell & 4 children        |              |    | =====                            |            |
|    | =====                              |              | 115| John Stewart                     | Boline     |
| 75 | Don: McDonell                      | Inchlagan    |    | Mary Stewart                     |            |
|    | his Wife                           |              |    | Catherin Stewart                 |            |
|    | Mary McDonell                      |              |    | =====                            |            |
|    | Janet McDonell                     |              |    | Ranald McDonell                  | Achteraw   |
|    | Catherin McDonell                  |              |    | Alex McKinzie                    | Urquhart   |

| | | |
|---|---|---|
| 120 | John McDonell | Divach |
| | Alex Scot | Urquhart |
| | ===== | |
| | Chas. McArthur | Inverskilroy |
| | John McArthur | |
| | Sarrah McArthur | |
| 125 | Lizie McArthur | |
| | Donald McArthur | |
| | ===== | |
| | Dun: McKinnon | Donie |
| | his Wife & 6 children | |
| | ===== | |
| | Effy Kennedy | Caum |
| 130 | Archy McMillan | |
| | Mary McMillan | |
| | Kath: McMillan | |
| | Miles McMillan | |
| | Dun: McLean & Wife | |
| 135 | Alex McKinnon | |
| | his Wife & 3 children | |
| | Dun: McKinnon | |
| | ===== | |
| | James McIntosh | Kerrowdoun |
| | Catherin McIntosh | |
| 140 | Mary McDonell | |
| | Mary McDonell | |
| | ===== | |
| | Donald Kennedy | Lewiston |
| | Marg: Kennedy & 3 children | |
| | ===== | |
| 145 | John Cameron | Glenturret |
| | Angus Cameron & his broy:r | |
| | Catherin Cameron | Leck |
| | Mary Gillis | |
| | Mary Cameron | |
| 150 | Marjery Cameron 2 children | |
| | ===== | |
| | Donald Cameron | Kenlocharkaig |
| | his Wife & 2 children | |
| | ===== | |
| 155 | John Cameron | Kenmere |
| | his Wife | |
| | John Cameron | |
| | Donald Cameron | |
| | Ewen Cameron | |
| | ===== | |
| | Dun: McMillan | Shanvall |
| | his Wife | |
| 160 | Catherin McMillan | |

| | | |
|---|---|---|
| | Effy McMillan | |
| | 4 children | |
| | ===== | |
| | John McMillan | Shanvall |
| | his Wife | |
| | Alex McKay & 3 children | |
| | ===== | |
| 165 | Kath: McMillan | Shanvall |
| | Mary McMillan | Do. |
| | Peggy McMillan | Do. |
| | & 1 child | |
| | ===== | |
| | Angus McPhee | Crieff |
| 170 | his Wife & 3 children | |
| | ===== | |
| | John McDonald | Kenlochnadale |
| | his Wife | |
| | Alex. McDonald | |
| | Donald McDonald | |
| 175 | Peggy McDonald | |
| | Mary McGilvray | |
| | ===== | |
| | Donald McMillan | Tomdoun |
| | his Wife & 4 children | |
| | ===== | |
| | E. McMillan | Corrybuy |
| 180 | his Wife & 4 children | |
| | Arch'd McMillan | |
| | ===== | |
| | Ewen McMillan | Craigalachie |
| | his Wife & 1 child | |
| | ===== | |
| | John McMillan | Corsuck |
| | his Wife | |
| 185 | Ewen McMillan | |
| | 5 children | |
| | ===== | |
| | John McMillan | Muick |
| | his Wife | |
| | Mary McMillan | |
| 190 | Marg: McMillan | |
| | Catherin McMillan | |
| | ===== | |
| | Ewen McMillan | Coinich |
| | his Wife & 3 children | |
| | ===== | |
| | John McMillan | Glenpean |
| 195 | his Wife | |
| | Dun: McMillan | |

|     |                             |            |
| --- | --------------------------- | ---------- |
|     | Dugald McMillan             |            |
|     | Bell McMillan               |            |
|     | Alex McMillan               |            |
|     | 1 child                     |            |
|     | =====                       |            |
| 200 | John McMillan               | Camusein   |
|     | 3 children                  |            |
|     | =====                       |            |
|     | John McMillan               | Coinich    |
|     | his Wife                    |            |
|     | Dun: McMillan               |            |
|     | Betty McKinnon              |            |
| 205 | Alex McDonell               |            |
|     | Mary McMillan               | Munergy    |
|     | 3 Children                  |            |
|     | =====                       |            |
|     | Alex: McMillan              | Callich    |
|     | his Wife & 1 child          |            |
|     | =====                       |            |
|     | Ewen McMillan               | Quarter    |
| 210 | Cath: McMillan              |            |
|     | =====                       |            |
|     | Angus McMillan              | Arkaig     |
|     | his Wife & 2 children       |            |
|     | =====                       |            |
|     | Angus McDonell              | Invervigar |
|     | his Wife                    |            |
| 215 | Duncan McDonell             |            |
|     | Katherin McDonell           |            |
|     | Mary McDonell               |            |
|     | Alex: McDonell              |            |
|     | John McDonell               |            |
|     | =====                       |            |
| 220 | Donald McMillan             | Achintore  |
|     | his Wife                    |            |
|     | =====                       |            |
|     | John McDonald               | Doers      |
|     | =====                       |            |
|     | John McDon'd for his Broy:r | Inchlagan  |
|     | =====                       |            |
|     | Donald McDonell             | Leck       |
| 225 | his Wife                    |            |
|     | =====                       |            |
|     | Dun: Gillis                 | Aberchalder |
|     | Moread McMillan             |            |
|     | Mary Kennedy                |            |
|     | Mrs Gillis                  |            |
|     | 4 children                  |            |
|     | =====                       |            |

|     |                             |            |
| --- | --------------------------- | ---------- |
| 230 | Don: McDonell               | Aberchalder |
|     | his Wife                    |            |
|     | Anne McDonells              |            |
|     | Dun: McDonells              |            |
|     | Ewen McDonells              |            |
|     | 2 children                  |            |
|     | =====                       |            |
| 235 | William Fraser              | Ft Augustus |
|     | his Wife & 2 children       |            |
|     | =====                       |            |
|     | Alex Fraser                 | Ft Augustus |
|     | his Wife                    |            |
|     | =====                       |            |
|     | Alex Rankin                 | Carnach    |
| 240 | his Wife                    |            |
|     | X                           | [blank]    |
|     | & ~~2~~ 1 children          |            |
|     | =====                       |            |
|     | Archibald Henderson         | Glencoe    |
|     | his Wife                    |            |
| 245 | [blank]                     |            |
|     | ~~1 child~~                 |            |
|     | =====                       |            |
|     | Ewen McLean                 | Aberchalder |
|     | his Wife                    |            |
|     | Donald McLean               |            |
| 250 | Cath: McLean                |            |
|     | Mary McLean                 |            |
|     | 4 children                  |            |
|     | =====                       |            |
|     | Don: McMillan               | Aberchalder |
|     | his Wife                    |            |
|     | John McMillan               |            |
| 255 | Marg: McMillan              |            |
|     | Mary McDonell & 3 children  |            |
|     | =====                       |            |
|     | Donald McDonell             | Thornhill  |
|     | his Wife & 3 children       |            |
|     | =====                       |            |
|     | Alexander Cameron           | Thornhill  |
| 260 | his Wife & 2 children       |            |
|     | =====                       |            |
|     | Arch'd McDonell             | Paisley    |
|     | his Wife                    |            |
|     | =====                       |            |
|     | Mary McLean                 | Laddy      |
|     | Katherin McLean             | Do.        |
|     | =====                       |            |
| 265 | Dun: McLean                 | Munergy    |

his Wife
Angus McLean
Duncan McLean
Janet McLean & 1 child
=====
270  Mary McMaster          Glenpean
Anne Cameron           Muick
=====
Ewen McMillan          Lubriach
his Wife
Mary McMillan
275  Peggy McMillan
Donald McMillan
Ewen McMillan
=====
Cath: McLean           Caum
=====
John Cameron           Achnacary
280  his Wife
Dun: Cameron
=====
Mary Chislom [sic]     Strathglass
Anne Chislom [sic]     Do.
=====
Don: McDonald          Inchlagan
285  his Wife & 2 children
=====
Dugald McMillan        Inchlagan
his Wife & 1 child
=====
Ewen Kennedy           Invergarry
his Wife
290  ~~Christy McLean~~
Peggy Kennedy
=====
Don: McMillan          Paisley
his Wife & 2 children
=====
Annie McMillan         Paisley
=====
295  Alex: Kennedy          Laddy
his Wife & 2 chidren
=====
Alex: Cameron          Lochielhead
=====
Marg: McDonell         Munergy
see no 45 omitted in that family
=====
Dun: McLean's Wife No 134 omitted

ADDENDUM
**(Additional passengers not in above lists. See introductory note.)**

Archibald McMillan Murlaggan
his Wife & 5 children
Thamasina Gray                         Maryburgh
=====
Allan McMillan                         Glenpean
his Wife Margaret & children
Ewen, John, Alexander, James,
Donald, Archibald, Helen,
Janet
=====
Alexander Cameron        Gortenorn
Alexander Cameron        Sallachan
Alexander Cameron        Arkaigside
Donald Cameron           Kirkton
Duncan Cameron           Drimnasallie
John Cameron             Kinlochiel
John Cameron             Muick
Margaret Cameron         Glengarry
John Campbell            Glenelg
Alex:McDonald            Moy, GlenSpean
Duncan McDonell          Aviemore
Angus McKay              Shanvall
Kenneth McLean           Mull
Donald McLellan          Glenelg
Mary McMaster            Oban
Alex McMillan     Late Soldier, Lochaber Regiment
Angus McMillan           Callich
Don:MacMillan       Callop, Glenfinnan
Donald McMillan          Rellen
Dugald McMillan          Oban
James McMillan           Knoydart
John McMillan            Callich
Murdoch McPherson     Noid, Badenoch
Dun:McRae             Glenshiel, Kintail
Gilchrist McRae       Lianish, Kintail
Norman Morrison          Glenelg
John Wright        millwright from Ayrshire

## FAMILY GROUPS IN ALPHABETICAL ORDER

The following indexed listing, ordered alphabetically by head of family, is from two sources: the original manuscript 'List of Emigrants per Mr Archibald MacMillan' (NA, MG 24, I 183); and the listing in Somerled MacMillan's *Bygone Lochaber* (Glasgow, 1971). The two lists have been merged, retaining details from both. The family grouping is preserved intact by entering each family under the name of the head of the family. As to the relationships within the groups, it appears to adhere to the following format: husband, wife, children thirteen and over, servants or in-laws, children (under thirteen). In two instances, Alexander Stewart of Fort Augustus and Effy Kennedy of Caum, other entire families were listed within their families. These intrusive families have been cross-entered in this present revised listing.

Cameron, Alex: (Gortenorn)
Cameron, Alex: (Lochielhead)
Cameron, Alex: (Sallachan, Arkaigside)
Cameron, Alex: (Thornhill), wife, children (2)
Cameron, Donald (Drimnassalie), wife
Cameron, Donald (Kenlocharkaig), wife, children (2)
Cameron, Donald (Kirkton)
Cameron, Duncan (Drimnasallie), wife
Cameron, John (Achnacary), wife, Duncan
Cameron, John (Glenturret), Angus (his brother), Catherin (Leck), Mary, Margery, children (2), Mary Gillis
Cameron, John (Kenmere), wife, John, Donald, Ewen
Cameron, John (Kinlochiel)
Cameron, John (Muick)
Cameron, Margaret (Glengarry)
Campbell, John (Glenelg)
Chisholm, Mary (Strathglass), Anne
Corbet, John (Ardachy), wife, Mary, William, Christy, 1 child
Fraser, Alex: (Fort Augustus), wife
Fraser, Donald (Leck), wife, 1 child [travelling with Alex: Stewart family, below]
Fraser, William (Fort Augustus), wife, children (2)
Gillis, Duncan (Aberchalder), wife, Moread McMillan, Mary Kennedy, children (4)
Grant, Alex: (Achnaconern), wife, John, children (4)
Grant, Donald (Dalcattaig), wife
Grant, Mary (Duldregan), Flory, Isabella; John & Anne Grant (Livisie), 1 child
Henderson, Archibald (Glencoe), wife, 1 child
Kennedy, Alex: (Laddy), wife, children (2)
Kennedy, Donald (Achluachrach), wife, Mary McDonell, children (5)
Kennedy, Donald (Inchlagan), wife, Angus, Alex:, Allan, children (2)

Kennedy, Donald (Laddy), wife, children (2)
Kennedy, Donald (Lewiston), Margaret, children (3)
Kennedy, Duncan (Aberchalder), wife, children (2)
Kennedy, Effy (Caum), Archy McMillan, Mary, Katherine, Miles [see Duncan McLean & Alex: McKinnon families]
Kennedy, Ewen (Aberchalder), wife, Donald Kennedy (Kenlochlochy), children (4)
Kennedy, Ewen (Invergarry), wife, Christy, Peggy
Kennedy, John (Inchlagan), wife, Ewen, Mary, Alex, Janet, Angus, children (3)
Kennedy, John (Invervigar), wife, Duncan, Alex:
McAlpin, Mary (Greenfield), Mary Cameron (Letterfinlay), Catherin McAlpin (Letterfinlay), Eliz: Grant (Drimdrochil)
McArthur, Charles (Inverskilroy), John, Sarrah, Lizie, Donald
McDonell, Alex: (Boline), wife, Duncan, Donald, Catherin, children (4)
McDonell, Alex: (Laggan), wife, children (2)
McDonald, Alex: (Moy, Glenspean [sic])
McDonell, Allan (Munergy), wife, Catherin, Margaret, Donald, children (2)
McDonell, Angus (Invervigar), wife, Duncan, Katherine, Margaret, Alex:, John
McDonell, Archibald (Paisley), wife
McDonell, Donald (Abercalder), his wife, Anne, Duncan, Ewen, children (2)
McDonell, Donald (Inchlagan), wife, Mary, Janet, Catherin, Peggy, Allan, children (4)
McDonald, Donald (Inchlagan), wife, children (2)
McDonell, Donald (Laddy), John, Duncan, Catherin, Mary Kennedy
McDonell, Donald (Leck), wife
McDonell, Donald (Thornhill), wife, children (3)
McDonell, Duncan (Aviemore)
McDonell, James (Balmean), wife, Allan & Katherine McDonell, children (4)
McDonell, John (Ardnabie), wife, 1 child, Alex: Cameron & wife
McDonald, John (Doers)
McDonald, John (Inchlagan), wife, Donald McDonell, children (2)
McDonald, John (for his brother, Inchlagan)
McDonell, John (Invervigar), Dugald, Catherin, Flory, Peggy, Donald, 1 child
McDonald, John (Kenlochnasale), wife, Alex, Donald, Peggy, Mary McGilvray
McDonell, John (Leck)

McDonell, Ranald (Achteraw), Alex: McKinzie (Urquhart), John McDonell (Divach), Alex: Scot (Urquhart)

McDougald, Donald (Fort Augustus), wife, Marjery, Alex, John

McIntosh, James (Kerrowdoun), Catherin, Mary McDonell, Mary McDonell

McKay, Angus (Shanvall)

McKinnon, Alex: (Caum), wife, Duncan, children (3) [travelling with Effy Kennedy and family, above]

McKinnon, Duncan (Donie), wife, children (6)

McLean, Angus (Munergy), Duncan, Janet, 1 child

McLean, Archibald (Laddy), Angus

McLean, Duncan (Caum), wife (travelling with Effy Kennedy and family)

McLean, Duncan (Munergy), wife, Angus, Duncan, Janet, 1 child

McLean, Ewen (Aberchalder), wife, Donald, Catherin, Mary, children (4)

McLean, Catherin (Caum)

McLean, Kenneth (Mull)

McLean, Mary (Laddy), Katherin

McLellan, Donald (Glenelg)

McMaster, Mary (Glenpean), Anne Cameron (Muick)

McMaster, Mary (Oban)

McMillan, Alex: (late soldier, Lochaber Regiment)

McMillan, Alex: (Callich), wife, 1 child

McMillan, Allan (Glenpean), Margaret (his wife), Ewen, John, Alex:, James, Donald, Archibald, Helen, Janet

McMillan, Angus (Arkaig), wife, children (2)

McMillan, Angus (Callich)

McMillan, Annie (Paisley)

McMillan, Archibald (Murlaggan), wife, children (5), Thamasina Gray (Maryburgh, his sister-in-law)

McMillan, Donald (Aberchalder), wife, John, Margaret, children (3), Margaret McDonell

McMillan, Donald (Achintore), wife

McMillan, Donald (Callop, Glenfinnan)

McMillan, Donald (Paisley), wife, Annie, children (2)

McMillan, Donald (Rellen)

McMillan, Donald (Tomdoun), wife, children (4)

McMillan, Dugald (Inchlagan), wife, 1 child

McMillan, Dugald (Oban)

McMillan, Duncan (Shanvall), wife, Catherin, Effy, children (4)

McMillan, Ewen (Coinich), wife, children (3)

McMillan, Ewen (Corrybuy), wife, Archibald, children (4)

McMillan, Ewen (Craigalachie), wife, 1 child

McMillan, Ewen (Lubriach), Mary, Peggy, Donald, Ewen

McMillan, Ewen (Quarter), Catherin

McMillan, James (Knoydart)

McMillan, John (Callich)

McMillan, John (Camusein), children (3)

McMillan, John (Coinich), wife, Duncan, Betty, Alex, Mary McMillan (Munergy), children (3)

McMillan, John (Corsuck), wife, Ewen, children (5)

McMillan, John (Glenpean), wife, Duncan, Dugald, Bell, Alex:, 1 child

McMillan, John (Muick), wife, Mary, Margaret, Catherin

McMillan, John (Shanvall), wife, Alex: McKay, children (3)

McMillan, Katherin (Shanvall), Mary, Peggy, 1 child

McMillan, Mary (Laddy), Catherin McLean

McPhee, Alex: (Aberchalder), Alex:, Catherin McAlpin, Mary, Margaret, Anny, 1 child

McPhee, Angus (Crieff), wife, children (3)

McPhee, Donald (Aberchalder), wife, Anne Kennedy, Janet Marshall

McPherson, Murdoch (Noid, Badenoch)

McRae, Duncan (Glenshiel, Kintail)

McRae, Gilchrist (Lianish, Kintail)

Morrison, Norman (Glenelg)

Rankin, Alex: (Carnach), wife, children (2)

Scot, Donald (Aberchalder), wife, Alex, Duncan, Janet, Mary, children (2)

Stewart, Alex: (Fort Augustus), wife, 1 child; [travelling with Donald Fraser family, above]

Stewart, John (Boline), Mary, Catherin

Wright, John (Ayrshire, 'a millwright')

# PART II

# THE SCOTTISH BACKGROUND

# CHAPTER 2

# THE LOOTING OF LOCHABER

E.J. COWAN

TED COWAN is Professor of Scottish History and Literature at the University of Glasgow. He has taught at the University of Edinburgh, and from 1979-1993 was Professor of History and Chair of Scottish Studies at the University of Guelph. He is the author of *Montrose, For Covenant and King* and *The People's Past, Scottish Folk in Scottish History*, as well as numerous articles on various aspects of Scottish History. He is currently researching the Vikings in Scotland, Scottish popular culture 1500-1800, and Scottish emigration to Canada. He has no McMillan connection whatsoever.

[ADDRESS OF BEELZEBUB] [1]

To the Rᵗ Honᵇˡᵉ JOHN, EARL OF BREDALBANE, President of the Rᵗ Honᵇˡᵉ the HIGHLAND SOCIETY, which met, on the 23ᵈ of May last, at the Shakespeare, Covent garden, to concert ways and means to frustrate the designs of FIVE HUNDRED HIGHLANDERS who, as the Society were informed by Mʳ McKenzie of Applecross, were so audacious as to attempt to escape from their lawful lords and masters whose property they are emigrating from the lands of Mʳ MᶜDonald of Glengary to the wilds of CANADA, in search of that fantastic thing — LIBERTY —

But, hear me, my lord! Glengary, hear!
Your HAND'S OWRE LIGHT ON THEM, I fear:
Your FACTORS, GREIVES [overseers], TRUSTEES an' BAILIES [bailiffs],
I canna say but they do gailies [tolerably];
They lay aside a' tender mercies
An' tirl [strip] the HALLIONS [rascals] to the BIRSIES [bristles];
Yet, while they're only poin'd [distressed], and herriet [plundered],
They'll keep their stubborn Highlan spirit.
But smash them! crush them a' to spails [splinters]!
An' rot the DYVORS [bankrupts] i' the JAILS!
The young dogs, swinge [flog] them to the labour,
Let WARK an' HUNGER mak them sober!
The HIZZIES, if they're oughtlins fausont [at all decent],
Let them in DRURY LANE be lesson'd!
An' if the wives, an' dirty brats,
Come thiggan [begging] at your doors an' yets [gates],
Flaffan [flapping] wi' duds [rags], an' grey wi' beese
Frightan awa your deucks an' geese;
Get out a HORSE-WHIP, or a JOWLER [hound],
The langest thong, the fiercest growler,
An' gar [make] the tatter'd gipseys pack
Wi' a' their bastarts on their back!

Thus in 1786, in excerpt from his only poem linking Scotland and Canada, Scotland's national bard, Robbie Burns, encapsulated the great debate on emigration which raged throughout his own short lifetime (1759-1796), and beyond it to 1820, the year of the 'Radical War' when the 'lower orders' of Scotland were allegedly on the brink of revolution. During these years, the British establishment such as Breadalbane and Glengarry frowned upon emigration since it reduced the number of bodies contributing to the economy and the military. West Inverness-shire emigrants, the subject of this book, thus departed from their native land when such activity was discouraged.

Rare is the historian of Highland history who is uninfluenced by the mythos of the *Gaidhealtachd* (Gaelic-speaking Scotland). It requires a considerable effort of will to put aside the various prisms through which the Highlands have long been viewed, from the primitivism of James MacPherson whose famed translations of the legendary poet Ossian brought about the Romantic revival in the aftermath of the last Jacobite Rising of 1745-6; to the tartan-tinted spectacles of Sir Walter Scott, obsessed as he was with the clash between tradition and technology. The brutality of the Clearances when people were replaced by sheep, and subsequently deer, contrasts painfully with the image of empty scenery peddled by the Scottish Tourist Board. The desolation of modern Loch Arkaig is a powerful monument to a human tragedy that was part of a profound historical process.

The Glengarry of Burns' poem, Alastair MacDonnell, the 'Highland devil', was himself a glorious, if dangerous, anachronism with a head full of Ossianic nonsense. He swaggered around in full Highland regalia topped off with a Glengarry bonnet invented by its wearer, as well as a light sporran. He was remembered as 'a man of excitable disposition, desirous to be considered the type of an old chief, absolute in his commands, litigious, and sometimes hurried by his ungovernable temper into acts of the most serious nature.' He killed an innocent man in a duel, and a gamekeeper; and he was involved in 'several bloody assaults.' At the Invergarry Highland Gathering, he invented the sport of twisting the four legs off a cow, first prize being a fat sheep. His own life ended impetuously in 1828 when a steamer was wrecked on rocks south of Fort William. All the passengers were safely landed, except for Glengarry who 'jumped off the plank, or fell off on his head on the rocks and was killed.'[2] He left debts of £80,000 which presumably would have been higher had not some of his tenants and clansfolk been considerate enough to depart for Ontario.

Although many of those who remained were proud of their chief's behaviour, Glengarry typified the unreality infecting many contemporaries. He craved the profits of modern economic management in order to bolster a pre-industrial lifestyle and value system; he sought shelter from modernity in a semi-mystical past; and he lived a Highland legend while knowing little of the real world. Even someone as pragmatic as the Rev. James Robertson was fascinated by the mystique of clanship. Of the inhabitants of Inverness-shire Robertson wrote:

They have uniformly proved themselves to be warm in their attachments, true to the cause they espouse, steady in their engagements, prudent under many privations, vigorous in their constitution, inured to toil, active in their motives, indefatigable in exertion and fearless in the hour of danger. Descended, or conceiving themselves to be descended, from some renowned leader of their tribe, and counting kindred with the Chieftain of their own time, they feel the impulse of honour, natural to such blood, and becoming such connexion; and disdain to bring a stain upon their Clan, by bringing a stain upon themselves. This pride of clanship affects their manners, their habits, their conversation, their sentiments, their address, and their prospects in life. It inspires them with a certain elevation of mind, which is perhaps unfriendly to the drudgery of continued labour, while untutored by experience

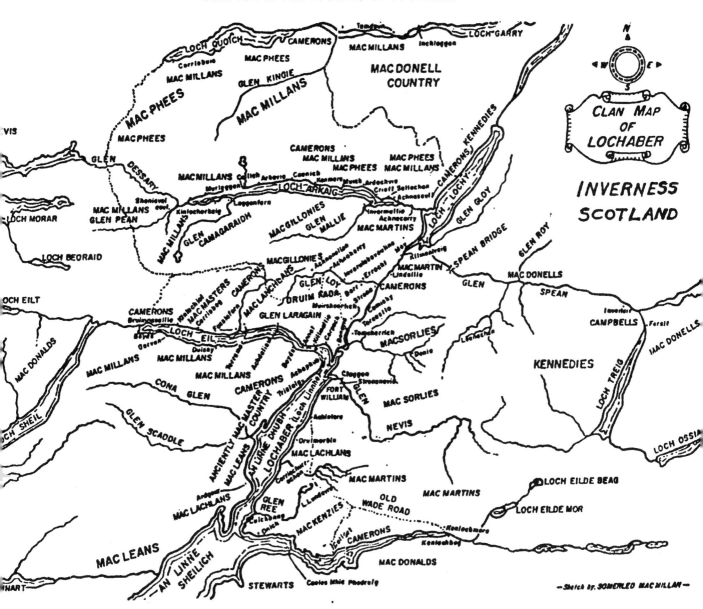

Clan map of Lochaber, Scotland, by Somerled McMillan for his *Bygone Lochaber* (1971).

or not supported by clear views of interest. It gives them, however, consequence in their own eyes, and they aspire to obtain the same consequences in the opinion of others.[3]

While Robertson's assertions contain some truth, the clan system itself was over in many parts of the Highlands by the early seventeenth century when sev-eral of the great clans such as the McDonalds, the Macleans and the Mackenzies were in the process of self destructing through fragmentation, internecine strife and intra-clan rivalry. The Camerons were drowned in debt, their estates largely held in wadset (mortgage) by the Campbells and the Gordons. There is little sign that the McMillans had functioned as a clan since the fourteenth century, if ever.

Clan survival was a myth perpetuated by lingering clan rivalries. During the hundred years between the Montrose wars of 1644-45 and Bonnie Prince Charlie's Jacobite Rising of 1745-46, the so-called 'Loyal Clans' fought for the Stewart cause again and again, motivated by contempt for Clan Campbell, the most successful of all clans. The lesser clans hoped to regain territory and estates. Their victories during Montrose's 'Glorious Year' were not to be repeated, the apparent successes, for example, at Killiecrankie (1689) or Prestonpans (1745), being mere flashes in the heather. British armies enjoyed superior technology and the military function of the clan was becoming redundant. While individual participants showed bravery, clan sentiment was cynically exploited in a doomed cause.

At the same time the chiefs were becoming alienated from their kinsfolk and tenants. The Statutes of Iona (1609) had insisted that the sons of chiefs be educated in the Lowlands, as many of them had been for over a century. By 1620 the heirs of the Earl of Sutherland were attending schools in England. The Jacobite fiasco of 1745-46 forced several chiefs into exile. The abolition of heritable jurisdictions in 1748 (first mooted by James VI in 1597), which effectively removed a chief's powers over his clanspeople, legislated what was already a reality in many parts of the Highlands and Islands.

When Cameron of Lochiel, the major landowner in Lochaber and feudal superior of the McMillans, set out to meet Charles in 1745, he was determined to block the Prince's rash attempt. The 'Gentle' Lochiel's brother, John Cameron of Fassiefern, was suspicious. 'I know you better than you know yourself,' he told Lochiel. 'If this Prince once sets his eye on you, he will make you do whatever he pleases.'[4] Fassiefern's instinct was correct. Lochiel fell for Charles, and was forced to flee into exile.

After the battle of Culloden on 16 April 1746, the looting of Lochaber began in earnest. The victorious Duke of Cumberland pillaged and burned the property of Jacobite supporters. Particular ferocity was reserved for the Lochiel estates as well as for those of MacDonnell of Glengarry and the Macdonald estates of Knoydart and Moidart, the homelands of most of the emigrants who would find their way to Canada some fifty or sixty years later. Some of those who had followed Cameron to join Prince Charles were reluctant recruits. It has even been asserted that some of Lochiel's own tenants assisted the Duke of Cumberland's troops when they burned Achnacarry Castle in 1746. There is also the legend that when the Prince sought refuge in the heather after Culloden, not one Highlander would play Judas by betraying him for a reward of £30,000. Somerled MacMillan, however, has pointed out that two out of three Lochaber men willing to claim the reward were McMillans.[5]

When Lochiel fled to the Continent, his estates were forfeited and administered by strangers, to the detriment of tenants and kindred alike. Tenants were forced to pay double dues, to Lochiel in exile, and to the crown. It was such irritants that led to the murder of Colin Campbell of Glenure – the Red Fox – in nearby Appin in 1752, the central episode in Robert Louis Stevenson's novel *Kidnapped*. A similar event took place on the shores of Loch Arkaig in 1746 when an unnamed assailant shot Captain Munro of Culcairn. There is, however, little record of resistance, even though large numbers of livestock were looted from Lochaber, and substantial numbers of men on the forfeited estates were conscripted into the British army. At times, parts of the Highlands, including west Inverness-shire, were occupied territory, and the culture and the economy of the *Gaidhealtachd* were transformed. The clan system, already in decline for over a century, was forever shattered. A rental of the Lochiel estate for 1787 lists sixty-five Camerons and sixty-two others including McMasters, Macdonalds, Macintoshes, Mackinnons, Macphees, MacLachlans, Malcolms, Mackenzies, a Macinnes, a Rankin and a Robertson, as well as McMillans. By that date any bond or affection that had once tied the clansfolk to their chiefs had evaporated. Yet such realities did not prevent commentators on the Highlands at the time of the migrations from evoking concepts such as chieftainship and clanship. People tend to romanticise cultures on the edge of extinction and the romantic haze which descended upon the Highlands in the aftermath of the Jacobite rebellions has not since lifted. It has often served to camouflage a way of life far from romantic.

Although the Rev. Robertson was mightily upset by the 'sneering remarks' directed against the impoverished dwellings of the Inverness-shire folk by travellers from the south, even he had to admit that such slights were well observed. Commentators assumed that the inhabitants of 'mean, dirty and inconvenient houses' must be 'poor, spiritless and indolent, and what is worst of all, perhaps, oppressed.' Like many others, Robertson found their earthen structures 'beyond description.' He added that 'the huts of the Indians bordering on the Lakes of the St Laurence cannot be worse, in point of structure and accommodation.'[6] For such appalling conditions he blamed the landlords. Joseph Mitchell, in his *Reminiscences*, concurred. When the Highlanders 'did not dwell in common with their animals, their byres and stables were in close and offensive proximity,' and the houses of the tacksmen, who managed the chief's lands and were responsible for the clans' military organization, were often little better, according to Mitchell. The McMillans of Glenpean and Murlaggan were tacksmen of Cameron of Lochiel.

The average tenant was less distracted by military matters than by the daily struggle for existence. Diet was adequate if somewhat monotonous. During the summer, 'a season of contentment, of feasting, of health and joy,' dairy products, produced at the shielings (upland pastures), formed the major part of the diet. Otherwise the people depended upon meal and the invaluable (and recently introduced) potato, accompanied by fish or a little meat. Salmon and herring were plentiful. Fuel was generally peat, sometimes wood. Ceilidhs were joyous occasions, the Gaels, then as now, having a great fondness and talent for music, song and poetry.

Before the advent of sheep, the main crop was black cattle. Glenpean was described as 'a beautiful green grazing' region, and Glenelg as 'the richest spot both in grass and corn.' Thomas Telford's map of the Great Glen marked the large forests of fir on both sides of Loch Arkaig. Lochiel owned more plantations than anyone else in Lochaber, he and his brother taking great care, unlike other proprietors in the county, to enclose their valuable oak woods. It is not surprising that Archibald McMillan became involved in the timber industry of the Ottawa valley. He and his tenants had acquired some expertise in forestry in Lochaber.

The parish of Kilmallie where the Lochiel estate was situated was part of the Synod of Glenelg, as was the parish of the Small Isles – Muck, Eigg and Rhum – whence some of the emigrants were drawn in 1802. It was this ecclesiastical organization that embraced the large area (including Moidart and Knoydart) supplying emigrants in the period under review. Information about emigration schemes, as about cattle sales and military recruitment, was communicated through the parish churches.

Excellent detailed investigations of the McMillan migrations, such as Jack Bumsted's *The People's Clearances* and Marianne McLean's *The People of Glengarry*, already exist. Historians, however, have not focused on the outrage and despair with which government officials and church ministers greeted the craze for emigration. The Rev. Robertson asked, 'Is there no remedy to prevent this voluntary exile of the inhabitants? Are the Highlands to be depopulated?' Every effort was to be made 'to render emigration unnecessary … to prevent the Highlands from becoming a desert.' Robertson's book was conceived as a solution to a problem no less prevalent today than in 1802.

Much to his shame and indignation, Robertson lived in an age that valued money more than people. Estate managers had discovered that 'the rearing of bestial in place of men, was the most lucrative speculation.' 'The sordid passion of accumulation' was ruining the Highlands, and its consequence was emigration. 'This outrage against the human race,' Robertson railed,

> when it prevailed hath invariably produced its natural consequence upon their minds – aversion, hatred, indignation, contempt. Some of the Chieftains themselves have given the death-blow to Chieftainship; they have cut the cords of affection, which tied their followers to them and to one another; and with their own hands, have torn to pieces the bonds of consanguinity betwixt them and their tribes, which, with their eyes open, they have driven from them![7]

Robertson well understood the pressures that lay behind emigration, namely the steep increase in rents. He claimed that in some instances grasslands had risen tenfold in rent between 1748 and 1808. In some places a shepherd and two under-shepherds could displace between one hundred and one hundred and twenty people. While townships were in ruins, short or nonexistent leases were also a disincentive to tenants. The devastation of depopulation would have been even greater were not populations actually increasing, because of women marrying younger, better child care including increased smallpox vaccinations, and improved diet, thanks to the potato. Nevertheless, Robertson noted, 'the monster of depopulation has traversed almost every corner: his gigantic strides have ventured from sea to sea, overthrowing cottage and farmhouse, and without mercy driving the miserable inhabitants before him, whenever he has appeared.' Robertson was, undoubtedly, allowing his rhetoric to carry him away, and statistics show that emigration was actually less than he implied, and that population increase was substantially greater. However, in historical investigation, popular perceptions are just as important as the so-called 'reality' recreated by historians.

Some light is shed on the problems besetting the Camerons, and thus their estate and tenants, by court documents. The family of Allan Cameron of Erracht had a rival claim to the chiefship of Clan Cameron dating back to the sixteenth century. The colourful Allan, so legend has it, took part in the last duel to be fought with broad swords. Cameron drove the blade of his opponent, Fear Muirshearlich, into the latter's brain. Cameron fled to Mull and eventually to America to serve in the Royal Highland Emigrant Corps. He had several adventures which led his American opponents to charge him with 'the unmilitary proceeding of tampering with the native Indians in their loyalty to American interests.' He was rewarded with two years imprisonment in Philadelphia as a common felon. He escaped and returned to Britain where he fought battles on behalf of the Highland Society of London, notably to restore the wearing of Highland attire. He wrote what remains the most eloquent defence of the kilt, in response to a suggestion that the Highland regiment should be clad in trews or 'tartan pantaloons,' as he called them. Allan was to enjoy a distinguished career which would take him to the rank of General.

In 1784, the Camerons of Lochiel regained control of the Lochaber estates when the whole property was restored to Donald (Lochiel's grandson) on payment of a fine of £3,432. However, while still a minor and without ever visiting the estates, Donald sold a substantial chunk to Allan. The legality of the transaction was questionable, though Allan later protested that he was well aware of Donald's age and that he had simply intended to alleviate the latter's financial embarrassment.

In 1790, Donald of Lochiel visited Scotland for the first time. He attempted to keep the transaction a secret from his guardians, knowing full well that he had no right to 'suffer the estate to be dismembered in such a manner, immediately upon its being restored by the benignity and liberality of government, to the heir of a very ancient and respectable family, and before that heir was of age to enter into a possession of an estate which he was bound by so many ties to preserve entire and undiminished.' However, Allan's brother began to boast that Allan was 'now laird of part of the estate of Lochiel,' and the whole business was made public. A court case followed.

During proceedings, Allan contrasted himself – 'born on the farm of Erracht' worked by his father until his death – with Donald of Lochiel who had been educated at Westminster School and abroad, and who 'in consequence of some youthful dissipation … had got into some pecuniary embarrassment from which he wished to be relieved.'

The case was finally settled in 1792. Allan lost, and on 6 March 1792 the sale was declared null and void. Three years later the Lyon Court reduced and annulled Erracht's patent as Chief of Clan Cameron.

Not by coincidence, 1792 was the year that Alexander McMillan of Glenpean departed Lochaber for Upper Canada. The tensions revealed by the case no doubt contributed to Glenpean's decision to emigrate. For example, the first action of Lochiel's curators after the restoration of the estate to Donald in 1784 had been to demand additional rent from the tenants to pay off the fine. 'From the natural and well-known attachment of Highlanders to the place of their nativity and connections, the tenants in general agreed upon this occasion to pay one third of additional rent,' a hefty increase. In addition, Lochiel's factor 'assumed the absolute management, and, by his residence on the estate, obtained arbitrary sway among the tenantry,' obliging some of them 'to seek a retreat in the wilderness of America.' During the trial, Allan had declared himself the champion of the Camerons, arguing that if he had not bought the lands in question they might have been acquired by strangers. He claimed to deplore the renting of *sheilings* as separate farms, which effectively raised farm rents. Allan described sheep farming as 'the curse and scourge of the poor ill-fated Highlander.'[8]

Allan of Erracht projected himself defender of the clan, opposed to economic innovation, invoking the bond between people and lands in opposition to an ignorant, spendthrift young chief. Beneath Allan's gentlemanly exterior lurked the Gaelic warrior prepared to push claymores into heads to advance his claims to be chief. The young chief's own close relatives, the *doine-vaisle* or tacksmen, were involved in a power play familiar to their ancestors. Tacksmen were known to depose a weak or hopelessly inept leader and in the ensuing struggle for power, the clan sometimes fragmented, witness the best known case, the great Clan Donald. When a financially strapped chief could sell his lands, and possibly even peddle his chiefship, then the writing was clearly on the rocks and it was only a matter of time before the snows would leave Ben Nevis. When that happened, everyone knew that it was time for the Camerons to leave Lochaber.

Such considerations lay behind Alexander McMillan of Glenpean's emigration, with Macdonnell of Greenfield, to Glengarry, Ontario, in 1792. These men and their people, and those who came afterward, sought to preserve a way of life perceived to be on the very verge of disintegration.

Although he had won back the Cameron estates, Donald of Lochiel did not linger in Lochaber. Around 1800, he moved to Achnacarry where he started to build a fine new house costing £9,000 at the very moment that the Lochaber emigrants were heading out to the Ottawa valley. 'With his French training and education and want of acquaintance with the old clan, and the customs of the country, it can easily be imagined how distasteful a Highland life must have been to him,' observed Joseph Mitchell.[9]

There were other economic factors encouraging migration at the turn of the nineteenth century in Lochaber. In 1804, Thomas Telford commenced construction of the Caledonian Canal. Ninety-six kilometres long, of which some sixty-four kilometres were lochs, the canal required the construction of twenty-eight locks at a cost of £1.25 million. The project employed three thousand Highlanders over a twenty year period thus fulfilling one of its remits – 'to prevent that emigration which will deprive the country of its hardiest and bravest protectors, who have distinguished themselves most conspicuously by land and sea.'[10] In fact some of those involved later worked on the Trent and Rideau systems in Ontario. Telford envisaged a network of roads throughout the

Highlands. The old military road of General Wade from Fort Augustus to Bernera Barracks in Glen Elg followed a tortuous route and was frequently impassable. New roads were built from Fort William to Arisaig, from Invergarry to Kinlochhourn and from Invermoriston to Glen Sheil and Loch Duich, thus rendering redundant the old road that struck west of Loch Arkaig to the coast, further isolating the area. The provision of good communications further facilitated emigration.

Two years after the McMillan migration of 1802, Duncan Cameron of Fassiefern informed Archibald 'Murlaggan' McMillan that 'every single tenant' on both sides of Loch Arkaig was to be dispossessed' and 'everything is turned upside down since you left Lochaber…. Families who have not been disturbed for 4 or 500 years are turned out of house and homes and their possessions given to the highest bidders. So much for Highland attachment between Chief and clans.' But then he added that in his opinion the landlords were responsible for 'a general good without any intention of doing so, by driving those people to desperation and forcing them to quit their country'.[11] He was articulating a sentiment often enunciated in the decades to come and reiterated in the sterile rhetoric of modern planners on both sides of the Atlantic.

Cameron's letter confirmed McMillan's suspicion that there would soon be more Highlanders in Canada than in the Old Country. 'I never spoke more Gaelic any winter in Lochaber than I did last winter [in Glengarry, Upper Canada], the Highlanders powering down every day in most astonishing numbers.' In 1806 he petitioned to have the name of Suffolk Township changed to Lochaber, 'which will be an inducement to those from that part of the old Country to settle in it who are every year arriving.'

To suggest, as does Jack Bumsted,[12] that such emigration was voluntary, is misleading. Closer to the mark were the well chosen, if oft quoted, words of Archibald 'Murlaggan': 'We cannot help looking to our native spot with sympathy and feelings which cannot be described, yet I have no hesitation in saying that considering the arrangements that daily take place and the total extinction of the tyes twixt Chief and clan, we are surely better off to be out of the reach of such unnatural tyranny.'

So the Lochaber emigrants, like their countrymen of 1786, went in search of 'that fantastic thing – Liberty.' Whether they found it is for Canadian historians to judge.

## APPENDIX

Since *The Statistical Account of Scotland* is not readily available in most North American libraries, the following description of the people of Kilmallie is appended from Volume XVII, page 155 in order that descendants of the Lochaber migrations can reflect upon the fine ancestral stock. It was appended to his account by the Rev. Alexander Fraser of Kilmallie, who said that 'the following character of the people, drawn up by a friend of the incumbent's, does not seem to err, on, what is too commonly the case, the side of partiality; and is therefore given, as in general the clergy are accused of having transmitted accounts, rather too favourable, of the manners and morals of their parishioners.'

CHARACTER OF THE PEOPLE. They are sometimes accused of being given to change; but many instances of steady and unshaken friendship are not wanting. In professions of kindness they are profuse; and their sincerity, in general, is more to be depended on, than is usual on such occasions. They are inquisitive, but (more especially after having had the advantage of some intercourse with the world at large), distinguished by the politeness of their manners, and the insinuation of their address: Fond of sauntering in idleness, but less addicted to a roving life than heretofore: Though poor, inclined to indolence; and though naturally sagacious and intelligent, yet not in general learned: Less revengeful and implacable than formerly, and, now, more disposed to determine matters by litigation, than by arms; family dissensions imbitter not their lives, as in the feudal times: Impatient of restraint; yet, when under a proper leader, in whom they have confidence, invincible by fatigue, cold, or hunger: Intrepid, equal to any race of men ever known, in the midst of the greatest dangers: Less hospitable than of old, (indeed the old exertions of hospitality are not now so necessary as formerly;) but when feasts are prepared, the cheer is good: Spirited in a high degree to promote works of public utility: Charitable and willing to relieve the distressed, as far as their circumstances will admit of: Though no strangers to the power and influence of religion, yet rather apt to undervalue its holy ordinances: Fond of spiritous liquors, yet seldom habitual drunkards: They deserve praise for their continence; but are rather addicted to swearing – These are some of the predominant traits; and though there must be a great variety of character among 4,225 persons, yet there are, in this district, no inconsiderable proportion of persons, distinguished by their generosity, humanity, disinterestedness, benevolence, hospitality, temperance, piety, and religion.

### NOTES

1. *The Poems and Songs of Robert Burns*, 3 Vols. (Oxford: Oxford University Press 1968), Vol. I, no. 108, 255.

2. Joseph Mitchell, *Reminiscences of My Life in the Highlands*, 2 Vols. (London: Gresham Press 1884), Vol. I, 73-7.

3. James Robertson, *General View of the Agriculture in the County of Inverness* (London: Board of Agriculture 1808), 5.

4. Alexander Mackenzie, *History of the Camerons* (Inverness: A. & W. Mackenzie 1884), 218-9.

5. Somerled McMillan, *Bygone Lochaber* (Glasgow: K. & R. Davidson 1971) 167.

6. Robertson, *General View of the Agriculture in the County of Inverness*. 56 and 373.

7. Robertson, *General View of the Agriculture in the County of Inverness*, 187 and 327-9.

8. Mackenzie, *History of the Camerons*, appendix 2.

9. Mitchell, *Reminiscences of My Life in the Highlands*, 255. Allan never finished the house. When Mitchell visited Achnacarry in 1837 he found that it 'was all but finished when [Lochiel] became disgusted with the place, left it and never returned. We found that the plaster ornaments of the ceiling lay all that time on the floor ready to be fixed, and doors of the rooms, of beautiful Highland pine, gone brown with age, leaned against the wall ready to be screwed on. They had remained in position for thirty-five years.'

10. Mitchell, *Reminiscences of My Life in the Highlands*, 20-2.

11. National Archives of Canada, Archibald 'Murlaggan' McMillan & family papers, MG 24, I 183. These letters have been consulted in photocopies supplied by Hugh MacMillan. They are also printed in Somerled McMillan's *Bygone Lochaber*, 182-3. I am also indebted to the late Don McOuat who kindly presented me with a copy of his collected materials on the Inverskilavulin Emigration.

12. Jack Bumsted, *The People's Clearance* (Edinburgh: Edinburgh University Press 1982) xi, 229 and *passim*.

# ORIGINS OF THE LOCHABER MACMILLANS

## AND THE DESCENT OF THE FAMILIES OF MURLAGGAN AND GLENPEAN

GRAEME M. MACKENZIE

*'Clann 'Ic 'illemhaoil bho thaobh Loch Airceig nach robh tais no mi-thapaidh.'*[1]

## TRADITIONS OF THE EARLY LOCHABER MACMILLANS

*Clann MhicGhillemhaoil nan toitean*
*A thainig air tir's a'Chorpaich.*
Clan Macmillan of the roasted collops
Who came ashore at Corpach.[2]

Thus local folklore retains the tradition that the ancestors of the Murlaggan and Glenpean families landed at Corpach, near Fort William, with rations consisting of nothing more than roasted collops (slices of meat). The circumstances that brought them to the district were first recorded by Buchanan of Auchmar in 1723:

> A son of the great MacMillan of Knap, who resided in a certain place in Kintyre, called Kilchammag, having killed one Marallach Moir … was with six of his friends, his associates in that action, obliged to take boat, and flee to Lochaber, and in this exigency having recourse to the laird of Locheal, he was received into his protection, and allowed possessions in his lands….[3]

The Reverend Somerled MacMillan assumed 'the great MacMillan of Knap' to be the chief named 'Malcolm Mor' (Malcolm the Great) in the 1467 genealogy of the clan. However, because 'MacMhaolain Mor a' Chnaip' (The Great MacMillan of Knap) was a title probably used by all the Knapdale chiefs, this identification of the refugee's father must be open to question.[4] The same caution must be applied to the date given by the late clan historian to this event (ca. 1360), which is based on the questionable assumption that the refugee's father was Malcolm Mor (whose dates are in any case uncertain), and the even more dubious assumption that the refugee's son was the leader of the Lochaber Macmillans at the Barrier Battle at Perth in 1396.

Somerled MacMillan was undoubtedly right in his assertion that the Lochaber Macmillans were one of the clans that duelled at Perth.[5] It is unlikely, however, that their leader on that momentous day was the son of the refugee from Knapdale. Local tradition has always suggested there was a separate, and at one time very important branch of the clan in Lochaber and Badenoch, linked to the original Clan Chattan.[6] Important new evidence has recently come to light confirming that link; and suggesting, therefore, that it was this family who fought, and died, at Perth in 1396. It would seem, furthermore, that this defeat was the first of a series of disasters to befell the old Clann 'ic 'illemhaoil Abrach – in the course of which this original chiefly family was extinguished.[7] This left a vacuum in the Macmillans' most ancient homeland, which was in due course filled by the family of the refugee from Knapdale.

The elimination of the original Lochaber Macmillans after 1396 is supported by the fact that given names associated with the earlier clan are not to be found among the Murlaggan and Glenpean families.[8] This would be surprising in any circumstances if they were the descendants of the fourteenth century chieftains – given the Scottish custom of commemorating ancestors by handing their names on from generation to generation. It would be especially so, however,

among the heirs to families involved in a legendary encounter like the Barrier Battle.

This being the case, one clearly cannot identify the Knapdale ancestor of the Murlaggan and Glenpean families from the name of the Macmillan's leader at Perth – as Somerled MacMillan appears to have done in concluding he was called John (from the 'Cristy Johne sone' of 1396). There appears to be no evidence whatever as to the refugee's name, and no way therefore – given the present state of our knowledge – of identifying the individuals that connect the later Lochaber Macmillans with the Macmillans of Knap. There is no reason, however, to doubt the tradition that links the two branches; and from the middle of the sixteenth century, the genealogy of the Murlaggan family can be traced in the public records.

### THE MACMILLANS OF MURLAGGAN

The unnamed ancestor of the Murlaggan and Glenpean Macmillans must have arrived in Lochaber from Kintyre sometime before 1505 (when 'The Great MacMillans' ceased to be Lairds of Knap). His descendants, retaining the old Gaelic name of MacGhillemhaoil, were settled in one of the wildest and most beautiful parts of the Western Highlands. In 1723, Buchanan of Auchmar noted:

> The MacGilveils of Lochaber are mostly placed upon both sides of Locharkek in Lochaber, and live generally under and are close dependants upon the laird of Locheal, and upon all expeditions make up a company of an hundred men, with officers, of all of that sept; not reputed the worst of Locheal's regiment, being generally employed in any desperate enterprise that occurs.[9]

Desperate enterprises were the stock in trade of the Lochaber Macmillans, and their reputation as cattle lifters reached the farthest counties of the north:

> *Tha Maolanaich ann an Arcaig,*
> *Bu mhaith air slaodadh na creich iad,*
> *'S fhad's a mhaireas ni aig Cataich*
> *Cha bhi ac' ach leum air.*[10]

GRAEME M. MACKENZIE was born in London in 1951, and educated in his mother's home town of Cambridge. He won a scholarship to Emmanuel College, and graduated from the University with an honours degree in history, which he taught for some years. His interest in rock music, about which he wrote in local papers, and eventually in his own magazine, led him into work for local radio there. A major historical series produced for the BBC included a considerable genealogical element; and it was a growing interest in this aspect of history that led him to move back to his father's native Scotland in the mid-1980s. Though suffering from the neglect of Scottish history that is common in English universities, Graeme has read extensively in the subject since settling in Inverness – and eventually starting working as a professional genealogist, specialising in Highland Scots families. His detailed research into his grandmother's family, the Macmillans of Glen Urquhart, has led to his present role as Archivist and Genealogist at the MacMillan Clan Centre in Finlaystone (home of the Clan Chief), where he is setting up 'Project MAOL' (Macmillan Ancestry On Line), an attempt to put all the known genealogy of the clan and its septs on computer so that it can be tapped into by clanspeople interested in tracing their ancestors, and their distant cousins around the world.

Loch Arkaig in 1993, almost two centuries after most of its inhabitants migrated to Canada. Hugh P. MacMillan Collection.

(In Arkaig are MacMillans
Who drive the herds from shealing.
In Sutherland they're the villains,
So bent are they on stealing.)

Though reiving (cattle stealing) was not considered a heinous crime among Highlanders, it was looked at in a very different light among the Lowlanders who were so frequently on the receiving end of their forays. Their views were echoed by the official who reported to the government on the inhabitants of Lochaber in 1750:

> That part of Lochiel's Estate that runs along the Side of Locharkeg is a Den of Thieves ... instructed in this Villanous Trade from their Cradles ... and tho' the rest of the Camerons are not so Infamous as the Locharkeg people yet few of them are free from either Theft Receipt or Concealment.[11]

That the Macmillans were not much worse than the Camerons is evident from the nickname proudly born by the late fifteenth century 'Captain of Clancameroun,' 'Allan Dubh nan Creach' (dark Allan of the Forays), and from the official accounts of his clan's mass misdemenours. It is in these royal records that we find the first contemporary evidence about the Macmillans of Murlaggan.

The earliest mention of an identifiable member of the family is in 1547 when *Duncane Beane McFinlay*, residing in the Lordship of Lochiel, is listed among 361 followers of the Cameron chief indicted for (amongst other things) 'tresonable inbringing and assistence ... to oure auld inymeis of Ingland in the invasioun of this realme and liegis thairof in tyme of weir ... and for the tresonable assegeing and taking of oure soverane ladyis hous and castell of Urquhard.'[12]

In 1588 'Allan M'Conill Dow, captain of

# CHAPTER 3: ORIGINS OF THE LOCHABER MACMILLANS...

Clanchamron in Lochabir' and a smaller number of confederates were charged that they 'daily and nightly go abroad in bands, oppressing and sorning on the lieges, committing murders, thefts, and other crimes.'[13] Among Lochiel's followers on this occasion was a family group of Macmillans: *Duncan Bane M'Finlay in Crewe; Duncan, his son there; William M'Coniche Bane; John M'William, his son, in Ballache.*

The inconsistency of spelling in those days, along with the difficulty of interpreting medieval handwriting, are all too apparent in these, and later quotes from the printed copies of the original records. In this case, the above entry can be interpreted as: Duncan 'Ban' (the fair) son of Finlay, in Crieff; Duncan his son in the same place; William son of Duncan Ban; John son of William, in Callich (Ballache in the original should probably read Callache; in 1661 Callich is recorded as Calloch).

Two further records prove the connection of this group with the holding known to be the seat of the later Lochaber Macmillans. In 1598, *Williame McCondoquhy Bane, Midlygane* (the first mention of Murlaggan) was among 200 'brokin hieland men and sorneris, all bodin in feir of weir, with bowis, darlochis and tua handit swordis, steilbonnettis, haberschonis, hacquebutis and pistolettis ... undir cloude and silence of nicht, be way of briggancie.'[14]

In 1617, among those associated with 'Allan Cameroun of Lochyall' in 'delyting in nothing els bot in cruell and detestable murthouris fyre raisingis Sorcery's and utheris insolencys offensive to God and onworthie to be hard of in ony Kingdome subject to a Prince law and justice' was *Wm. McConochie in Moir Lagane, Jon McWm. his sone in the head of Locherkaik*, which is defined in the same document by this entry: *Johnne McWilliame VcCondochie Vane in Glenpeane.*[15] William's grandson *John vic (son of) Ewen vic Wm.* is on record as tenant of *Murligan* (the spelling varies) in 1642; and in 1663, when he and his son were named among Lochiel's leading lieutenants as *Jon Cameron alias McEwin in Muirlagan*, and *Ewin Cameron alias McEan there*. His final appear-

ance in the record, in 1684, is the first with the clan name. *John McGilliveille in Muirlaggan in Locharclack*, along with the other Lochaber 'landlords, chieftains and branches of clans,' is accused of having followers who 'dailly infest, trouble and molest the peace of the Highlands and particularlie the lands and duellings of the laird of McIntosh by dailly incursions thereon.'[16]

In 1717 the tenant of *Muirlagan* was John's grandson *Archibald Mac Ewen vic Ian*; and in 1761 it was another John (assumed to be Archibald's son), who gave the following deposition to the government:

> John McMillan, in Murlaggan ... depones that he is Head of the tribe of McMillans or McIllywouls and he and his ancestors have been kindly tenants or possessors of Murlagan for more than 300 years past. That he himself possessed them for many years preceding the year 1745, when, falling low in circumstances, he was obliged to give up holding lands.[17]

John of Murlaggan is said to have lost both his sons to the Jacobite cause in 1746 – his eldest, Ewen, leading the clan to Culloden as a Captain in Lochiel's regiment. Having also been ruined by the depredations of Cumberland's troops, he moved to Ardgour, where it is said his great grandson John was born in 1769. From this John is descended the present 'Murlaggan,' William G.M. MacMillan who now lives in Aberdeen.[18]

## THE MACMILLANS OF GLENPEAN

When recorded in 1588, Murlaggan's earliest documented ancestor was living at Crieff, further east on the northern shore of Loch Arkaig, where a branch of the clan continued to reside down to at least 1661. It was the Crieff branch that the Reverend Somerled MacMillan believed to be the ancestors of the later Glenpean and Murlaggan families, the promoters of the 1802 emigration to Canada. While there is insufficient evidence for now to come to any firm conclusions on the matter, it would be unusual for the new

29

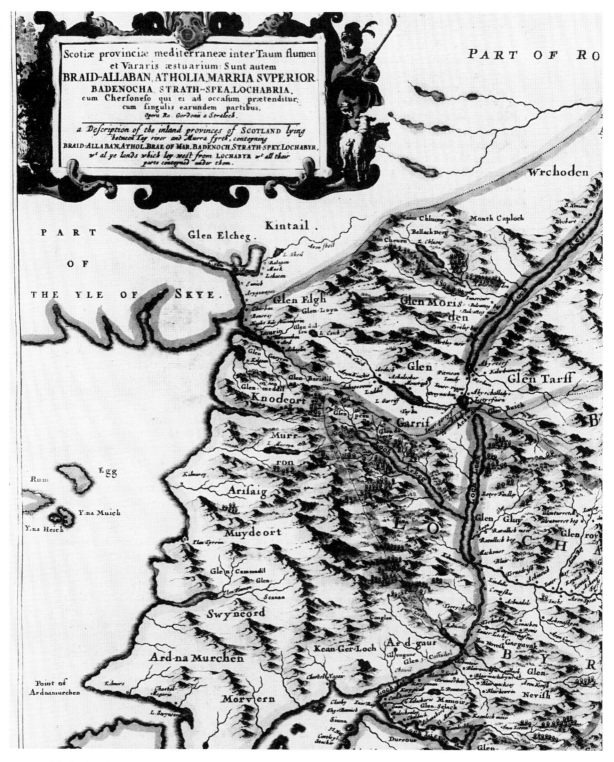

Portion of the earliest known map of Glenpean and Loch Arkaig, taken from Blau Atlas (1662), published in Holland. (Courtesy of Scottish Collection, McLaughlin Library, University of Guelph)

Glenpeanmor River, at head of Loch Arkaig, Scotland. (Hugh P. MacMillan Collection)

leaders of a clan to have been as distantly related to the old chieftains as the descendants of the Crieff Macmillans would by then have been to the Murlaggan family.

There was a tradition among old Murlaggan's descendants that the new leading family made its fortune by helping themselves to some of the Jacobite gold buried on the shores of Loch Arkaig. The story, however, is probably the result of envy at the achievements of this more dynamic branch of the clan.[19] Their success would have been built on the confidence that comes from a sound education (such as it was in the Highlands in those days) and the sort of relatively secure economic base that was only available to the close relatives of a clan chieftain.

It was the practice of chiefs and chieftains to place their closest relatives on their most profitable farms,

so the more distant cousins who were previous tenants became either subtenants or had to seek land elsewhere. Significantly, in 1723, long before any treasure was buried on the shores of Loch Arkaig, Buchanan of Auchmar reported that 'The principal persons of this sept are the MacGilveils of Murlagan, of Caillie (Callich) and Glenpean'; and that in 1745, the tacksman of Glenpean was Ewan, father of Allan 'Glenpean'; and the tacksman of Callich was Alexander, father of Archie 'Murlaggan.'

It is probable therefore that Ewan and Alexander's father was the brother of Archibald mac Ewan vic Ian of Murlaggan. This conjecture is supported by the fact that Ewan was the eldest son of the family; and as such would have been named (according to Scottish custom) after his paternal grandfather, in this case, the Ewan Macmillan in Murlagan in 1661.

## THE GLENURQUHART MACMILLANS

After the Glenpean branch, the closest family to that of Murlaggan would have been the descendants of Duncan mac Ewan vic Ian – who in 1717 was living with his brother Archibald at Murlaggan. Until recently nothing else was known about Duncan; but it would now appear that he had at least one son, who left Lochaber to seek his fortune elsewhere.

In 1745 Lieutenant Finlay McGilvaile of Buntait in Glen Urquhart joined the Buchanan Society in Glasgow, along with Captain Ewan McGilvaile the Younger of Murlaggan, and Dougald McGilvaile from Loch Arkaig (thought to have been of the Glenpean family).[20] In 1754 Finlay was repaid 500 marks[21] by Roderick Chisholm of Comar; which sum had been lent to the Chisholm chief by his father in 1746/47 – the name of Finlay's father being identified in the discharge as Duncan.[22]

As the only other recorded officer of the Macmillan Company in 1745/46, it is clear that Finlay Macmillan was a close relative of the clan chieftain, a fact reinforced by his marriage to a daughter (albeit an illegitimate one) of another clan chieftain, Mackenzie of Applecross.[23] In the circumstances, the conclusion that his father was Duncan mac Ewan, brother of Archibald of Murlaggan is inescapable.

Finlay not only fought at Culloden, but was something of a hero, at least in the eyes of the officer who believed his life was saved by the gallant Highlander. When the Chevalier Johnstone lost his horse in the midst of the battle, Finlay 'Cameron' liberated a spare horse and bodily threw the shaken Lowlander on to it, before disappearing into the mist of battle, never to be seen again by the Chevalier. We know that he survived the battle, however, as he lived on in Glen Urquhart until at least 1781.[24]

There is an intriguing snippet from one of the many collections of tales about Bonnie Prince Charlie's last days in Scotland, which mentions a Finlay Macmillan as being among those who bade farewell to the Young Pretender when he sailed from Arisaig at the conclusion of his adventures. As the tale comes

from a Chisholm who claimed to be there in person – and dined out on it for decades thereafter, including in the company of Sir Walter Scott – and as Finlay was a relatively unusual name in the clan, it is not impossible that this was also the gallant Lieutenant from Buntait.[25]

At least one of Finlay Macmillan's sons (Duncan) is known to have emigrated to Ontario – though whether in 1802 or later is not clear. Alexander, another son, went to Augusta, Georgia, and two sons ended up in England, where one of them became an important and influential member of London society. Buchanan Macmillan was Printer to the House of Commons, and then to the King. He had his wife's portrait painted by Gainsborough, and left a substantial fortune when he died in 1822 near Inverness.

One of Buchanan's descendants, who lives close to the Scottish border in northern England, has a note written by her grandfather which reports that Buchanan thought himself the Head of the Macmillans. This is perhaps not surprising if he was indeed the grandson of Murlaggan's brother – given that the Glenpean family had disappeared overseas, and the original Murlaggan line had sunk into obscurity (and for all Buchanan knew, had died out entirely).[26]

Macmillans had been arriving in Glen Urquhart for perhaps 200 or more years before Buchanan's father settled there – though the fifteenth century individual once said to have been the progenitor of all the Macmillans in the Inverness area was not actually a member of the clan at all.[27] In Glen folklore the clan's name-father is said to have been a Cameron who in the mid-1500s fled from a murder charge in Lochaber and disguised himself from his pursuers by shaving his head – so becoming 'An Gille Maol'[28] ('the shaven-headed lad'). And his children became known as 'Mac Ghille Mhaol' (one of the Gaelic forms of Macmillan).[29]

There are many other colourful tales in the folklore of the Glen and the neighbouring areas about the Clan MacGhillemhaoil; not all of whom in fact came from Lochaber. When the Campbells acquired the estate of Cawdor (to the east of Inverness) they seem to have planted some of their Macmillan tenants from Argyll in the area. Some of these are reported to have come from Inverary, and yet to have been closely related to the Loch Arkaigside Macmillans.[30] This suggests they were some of the MacGilveils who are said to have returned to Argyll from Lochaber, and settled at the head of Loch Fyne – and who later had their name 'Englished' to Bell.

The whole question of surnames becomes very complicated for those MacGilveils who settled outside Lochaber. In parts of Argyll and the southwestern islands they accepted the name Bell, knowing that their clan identity would remain certain among their fellow Gaels. Some members of the same families, however, seem to have insisted on Macmillan when emigrating to Glasgow – presumably for fear of losing that identity among the English-speaking Lowlanders.[31]

Lochaber Macmillans, as followers of Lochiel, were also called Cameron in many parts of the Highlands. Local traditions in Strathspey in Inverness-shire, and the Black Isle in Ross-shire, mention settlements of Lochiel's followers called by the natives 'Clann Ghille Mhaoil Dubh' – but described by some later historians instead as bald, bonnetless or steel-helmeted Camerons.[32] Even in Glen Urquhart in the early nineteenth century one couple had successive children baptised as Macmillan, Cameron, Macmillan, and Cameron; while as late as the 1850s, around Dingwall, a man married with children under the name of Macmillan, had parents and siblings living nearby as Camerons.[33]

### LOCHABER MACMILLANS
### ELSEWHERE IN THE HIGHLANDS

As well as the major branch of the MacGilveils in the Glen Urquhart area, the northward spread of the clan took them all the way to the Outer Hebrides, where today there are more Macmillans living than anywhere else in the northern Highlands. Among these are thought to be descendants of medieval priests from the Kintyre clan, as well as of some Lochaber

Macmillans employed, according to local tradition, to row parties of nuns across The Minch. There were some Lochaber Macmillans too on the inner isles, such as Skye – from whence came the noted Australian explorer Angus Macmillan – and further south, MacGilveils (later Bells) lived alongside Kintyre Macmillans on both Islay and Colonsay.[34]

There was a particular concentration of MacGilveils in Ardnamurchan. Having expelled the MacIans from the peninsular, the Campbells leased it to a branch of the Camerons, who brought with them a considerable number of Macmillan subtenants, one family of whom now live near the lighthouse, in the most westerly farm on the Scottish mainland. MacGilveils in neighbouring Morvern were often tenants of the Macleans, who also owned Ardgour, and had their seat across the water in Mull. There is a tradition among the Macgillivray chieftains on Mull that they inherited their one-time estate of Glencannel from Macmillans.[35]

Mid-seventeenth century rent rolls do show Macmillans living alongside the Macgillivrays on Mull – with 'MacGilveils' (the spelling varies) even then distinguished from 'Macmillans.' The 'Macmillans' may once again have been descendants of the priests whom we know were on the island in the fifteenth century, and who probably came from elsewhere in Argyle.[36] As this Mull evidence shows, far from being cut off from the rest of the clan, the Lochaber MacGilveils often coexisted in other parts of Scotland with their distant cousins from Kintyre, Knapdale and Inverary.

Buchanan of Auchmar informs us that he got much of his information on the Macmillans from the contemporary clan chief in southern Knapdale, Macmillan of Dunmore. The Dunmore family were engaged in the seventeenth century in cattle-droving which took them to the Isle of Skye.[37] This must have entailed frequent involvement with the MacGilveils on the nearby mainland, for whom the island was a favourite cattle-lifting ground; and Auchmar may also have got his information on the Lochaber clan through these contacts. Later, when Dunmore's descendants moved to be merchants in Campbeltown in the late eighteenth century, they found themselves living alongside Macmillans from Lochaber, as well as from Kintyre.[38]

While some MacGilveils on the mainland went south, others went north through Inverness-shire to Easter Ross, sometimes by a very circuitous route. One Macmillan family now living in the Dingwall area is descended from a customs officer who worked in Sutherland at the beginning of this century – whose ancestor a century before was a policeman in Kintail. His ancestors no doubt came originally from Lochaber; though in this case they cannot be traced that far back.[39]

Another Macmillan now living in nearby Invergordon – and again with family at one time in Kintail

– can, however, be traced that far back, and it turns out that his great-great-great-grandparents from Loch Arkaigside were among those who emigrated in 1802 to Ontario. Their Canadian descendants today form one of the best documented of Macmillan families from Lochaber.[40] It is to be hoped that further systematic research among the clan scattered on both sides of the Atlantic will lead to further such links being established between the far-flung cousins of the historic Clann 'ic 'illemhaoil Abrach.

### NOTES

1. 'Clan Macmillan from Loch Arkaigside that were not soft or backward,' quoted by Somerled MacMillan, *The Macmillans and their Septs* (Glasgow: Private Publication, 1952), 79.

2. Somerled MacMillan, *Bygone Lochaber* (Glasgow: K. & R. Davidson, 1971), 56. This valuable work contains

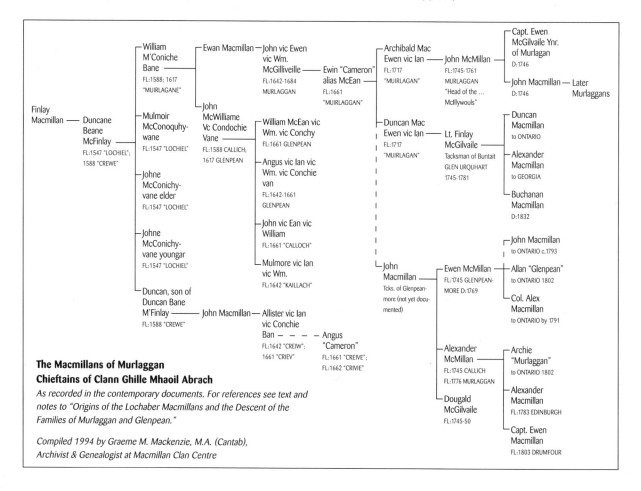

**The Macmillans of Murlaggan**
**Chieftains of Clann Ghille Mhaoil Abrach**
As recorded in the contemporary documents. For references see text and notes to "Origins of the Lochaber Macmillans and the Descent of the Families of Murlaggan and Glenpean."

Compiled 1994 by Graeme M. Mackenzie, M.A. (Cantab), Archivist & Genealogist at Macmillan Clan Centre

many traditions about the Lochaber Macmillans, including most of those quoted here, presumably gathered by MacMillan as a Minister in the district in the 1950s. Unfortunately the late clan historian rarely provides detailed references, but it is clear that much of this work, including many of the genealogies, are based on oral accounts, which therefore need to be approached with care, however true the traditions may be.

3. William Buchanan of Auchmar, 'An Account of the Macmillans,' in Buchanan of Auchmar, *An Inquiry into the Genealogy … of the Ancient Scottish Surnames* (Glasgow: John Wylie & Co., 1820), 281.

4. Somerled MacMillan, *The MacMillans and their Septs*, 74 and 15-29 which deals with the chiefs and the history of the clan prior to their settlement in Knapdale, which may need substantial revision on the basis of my ongoing research into the very early history of the clan in Lochaber and Badenoch. For the 1467 genealogy, see William F. Skene, *Celtic Scotland*, Vol. III, appendix viii, section v (Edinburgh: David Douglas, 1880), 489.

5. For the original accounts of the battle, see David Laing, ed., *Andrew of Wyntoun, Orygynale Cronykil of Scotland*, Vol. III (Edinburgh: William Paterson, 1879), 63; D.E.R. Watt, ed., *Walter Bower, Scotichronicon*, Vol. VIII (Aberdeen: Aberdeen University Press, 1987), 6-11. For Somerled MacMillan's arguments identifying the Macmillans as one of the participating clans see *The MacMillans*, 75-7; and *Bygone Lochaber*, 56-7. For proof that he was right about the clan there, see Sir Iain Moncrieffe of that Ilk, *The Highland Clans, (London: Haarlem Press, 1967), 175.*

6. The traditions linking the Macmillans with Clan Chattan (the original families of whom lived in Lochaber long before Murlaggan's ancestors came to Knapdale, let alone Loch Eil) were twice reported in the mid-eighteenth century. See "A Memoriall anent the true state of the Highlands as to their Chieftenries, followings and dependances before the late rebellion," in Col. James Allardyce, ed., *Historical Papers Relating to the Jacobite Period,* (Aberdeen: New Spalding Club, 1895), Vol. I, paper no. 17, 166; and Andrew Lang, ed., *The Highlands of Scotland in 1750* (Edinburgh: William Blackwood & Sons, 1898), 87-90.

7. For the key new evidence confirming the link between these original Lochaber Macmillans and Clan Chattan, see Scottish Records Office (SRO), Edinburgh,

Macpherson of Cluny Collection, GD.80/965, Murdoch Mackenzie of Ardross, 'The origin of the haill tribes of the Clan Chattan,' 1687. For the extinguishing of 'Clan Kauel' (another form of 'Qwhewyl,' the name used by the Lowland chroniclers of the Barrier Battle for the Macmillans), see Johannes Major, *Historia Majoris Brittaniae* (Paris: J.B. Ascensio, 1521).

8. The names in question being Shaw (Sythach MacMallon, recorded in Badenoch ca. 1228, was probably clan chief; 'Sythach' = 'Shaw') and either Farquhar or Gilchrist – depending on which of the 'chifftanys twa' named by Wyntoun ('Shaw son of Farquhar' or 'Gilchrist son of John') was the Macmillan leader at Perth.

9. Buchanan of Auchmar, 'An Account of the Macmillans,' 282.

10. Somerled MacMillan, *The MacMillans*, 83.

11. Lang, ed., *The Highlands of Scotland in 1750*, 83.

12. *Register of Privy Seal of Scotland (RPS)*, Vol. III, no. 2204, 354.

13. Henry Paton, ed., *The Mackintosh Muniments*, no. 50 (Edinburgh: Private Publication, 1903), 43.

14. RPC, Vol. V, 498.

15. RPC, Vol. XI, 204-5.

16. C. Fraser Mackintosh, *Celtic Magazine*, Vol. XIII, no. 154, 1888, 469; RPC, 3rd Series, Vol. I, 55, 179 and 411; and SRO/GD.80/168.

17. Mackintosh, *Celtic Magazine*, Vol. XI, no. 131, 1886, 526; and SRO, *Forfeited Estate Papers quoted in S. MacMillan, Bygone Lochaber*, 64.

18. S. MacMillan, *Bygone Lochaber*, 65.

19. S. MacMillan, *Bygone Lochaber*, 66.

20. R.M. Buchanan, *Notes on the members of the Buchanan Society* (Glasgow: Jackson, Wylie & Co., 1931).

21. The mark was a denomination of weight for gold and silver, and therefore a unit of accounting in Britain. One mark was worth about 2/3 of £1.

22. Jean Munro, ed., 'Inventory of Chisholm Writs,' Scottish Record Society, New Series, Vol. XVIII, no. 951, 1992, 137.

23. William Mackay, *Urquhart and Glenmoriston* (Inverness: Northern Counties Publishing Co., 1914), 409.

24. Chevalier James de Johnstone, *Memoirs of the Rebellion in 1745 & 1746* (London: Folio Society, 1970), 139.

25. Alexander Mackenzie, *History of the Chisholms* (Inverness: A. & W. Mackenzie, 1891), 223.

26. PRO/PROB.11/1805/Folio 312 for Buchanan's will, which names his brothers abroad; and Macmillan Clan Centre (Buchanan Macmillan file), letters from his descendant, Mrs. Rosemary Green.

27. 'Tearlach mac Ewen Vic Volan,' whom Somerled MacMillan believed to have been the ancestor of the earliest Macmillans in the Inverness area (*Bygone Lochaber*, 94) was actually a Maclean, and progenitor of the Dochgarroch family – whose present Chieftain lives in Glen Urquhart. Although the eponymous (progenitor or namefather) of Clann Thearlaich, Tearlach mac Eachainn vic Iain, is fully identified in all the Maclean and Clan Chattan histories, the Reverend Mr. MacMillan's mistake comes from the 'Vic Volan' appended to this mistranscription of Tearlach's patronymic (it appearing to be the phonetic form of 'Mhic Mholan' or 'MacMhaolain'). This comes from the printed texts of Mackintosh of Kinrara's 'The Epitome of the Origin and Increase of the Mackintoshes' in *Macfarlane's Genealogical Collections*, Scottish History Society, Vol. I, no. 33, 1900, 144, where it appears thus in both the modern English and the old Latin texts. But see A.M. Mackintosh (aka A.M. Shaw), *The Mackintoshes and Clan Chattan* (Edinburgh: Private Publication, 1903), who says that the Latin version was a translation of an original English MS, which in this case read 'Tearlich macEachin vicWolan.' While 'macEachin' (son of Hector) is the correct patronymic for Tearlach (Charles), who was son of Hector 'Reaganach' Maclean, 'vicWolan' appears to be a mystery. Since, however, Hector Reaganach's father was called John, the probability is that 'Wolan' was a mistranscription – from one of the even older MSS that Kinrara is known to have used – of 'Jhohan,' a nice illustration of the perils facing the modern clan historian using sources that have been so often transcribed and/or translated over the centuries.

28. Mackay, *Urquhart and Glenmoriston*, 102.

29. While 'Gille' came to mean a 'boy' in medieval times, it often meant a servant of God, and is sometimes translated as 'devotee.' In the context of MacMillan ('MacMhaolain' or 'son of the little shaven-headed one,'), 'maol' means 'tonsured' – with the head shaved at the front from ear to ear (as favoured by the old Celtic Church) rather than a circular patch on the crown (as favoured by the Roman Church). Such a tonsure makes a man look bald (which is the modern meaning of 'Maol'). The alternate version of the clan name in Gaelic, as favoured by the Lochaber and Glen Urquhart Macmillans, was 'MacGhilleMhaoil' or 'son of the tonsured servant,' pronounced something like 'Mac'ilveuil.' With two Gaelic versions, many local pronunciations and various transcriptions into English, it is not surprising that there are at least 158 recorded variants of the name.

30. Inverness Public Library, and Macmillan Clan Centre (Glen Urquhart genealogical file), Duncan Macmillan, family history manuscript ca. 1902.

31. One such family was that of the late clan historian, Rev. Somerled MacMillan, whose father was born as McMillan in 1880 in Glasgow, though his grandfather had married 8 years before in Oban as Bell; see 'The Macmillan Bells' information sheet, available from Macmillan Clan Centre, Finlaystone, Langbank, Renfrewshire PA14 6TJ, Scotland.

32. For Strathspey see Rev. W. Forsyth, *In the Shadow of Cairngorm* (Inverness: Northern Counties Publishing Co., 1900), 82; and Alexander Mackenzie, *History of the Camerons* (Inverness: A. & W. Mackenzie, 1884), 57. For the Black Isle, see John Maclean, *Historical & Traditional Sketches* (Inverness: John Noble, 1895), 125.

33. Inverness Public Library (Highland Family History Society Archives) and Macmillan Clan Centre, Graeme M. Mackenzie, 'Glen Urquhart Macmillans,' sheet 33C; 'Ross-shire Macmillans,' sheet 3.

34. S. MacMillan, *The MacMillans*, 66.

35. Robert McGillivray and George B. Macgillivray, *History of Clan Macgillivray* (Thunder Bay: Privately Published, 1973), 73.

36. S. MacMillan, *The MacMillans*, 70; some later 'Macmillans' may have been imported as tenants by the Campbells from their mainland estates.

37. Buchanan, *Notes*, 278-79; T.G.S.I., Vol. XLV, 277.

38. Macmillan Clan Centre, New Zealand genealogical file, family of Margaret Pool.

39. Mackenzie, 'Ross-shire Macmillans,' sheet 4.

40. Mackenzie, 'Ross-shire Macmillans,' sheet 2, which links with genealogy in 'MacMillan,' Glengarry (Canada) and District Branch of the Clan MacMillan Society, 1977, Vol. I, 22.

# CHAPTER 4

# DÈ CHO FADA'S A THA GU CANADA? – HOW FAR IS IT TO CANADA?

KENNETH J. McKENNA

'We're Scotch, you know,' is a common refrain in the Canadian Glengarry. The phrase refers to the Gaelic-speaking Highlanders who began arriving in Glengarry County at the end of the eighteenth century and who made up about 90 percent of the original settlers.

The same phrase, with 'Scotch' replaced with 'Scots,' can be heard in Glasgow or Dundee. Most residents of modern Scotland, with only a vague idea that the Gaelic element once played an important part in the history of the country, imply something else. Today the Gaelic-speaking population of Scotland represents about two percent of the total, the vast majority of the people identifying with the non-

KENNETH J. McKENNA was born in 1931 in Montreal of an Irish-Canadian father and a Scottish-born mother. His wife of forty years comes from a similar background. Their eldest daughter Sìne is fluent in Scots-Gaelic. Ken McKenna writes a weekly column called 'Highland Paths' in *The Glengarry News* of Alexandria, Ontario, in which he chronicles Highland Scots traditions in Canada as well as 200 years of Gaelic influence in Glengarry.

Gaelic, or Lowland, group. There are many, of course, who would claim that they are Highlanders, but in the modern sense of having a Gaelic name or ancestry, having served in a Highland regiment, or having forebears who once lived in the Highlands. But to the eighteenth century Gael, (and to many even today), the Gaelic language is the basic essential. Without it, one is simply a 'Gall,' a foreigner or a stranger. In Gaelic, there is no word for 'Highlander' or 'Lowlander.' If you were not a Gael, you were an alien, whether Lowland, English or Martian.

When the Scottish Court, 800 years ago, ceased to function in Gaelic, the clans looked inward and seldom became involved in matters beyond their territories, except to form allegiances from time to time with those who shared their interests. The concept of nationalism was vague until the middle ages, most identifying more with language, region, or blood ties than with a nation. The Gaels of Scotland often had more in common with the Gaels of Ireland than with the Galls of Scotland. They shared the same language, virtually identical for a thousand years, and there was constant coming and going between the two countries. It was easier for a Hebridean or a resident of the Western Highlands to sail across to Ireland than to travel to the Scottish capital in the Lowlands, home to Scots who spoke a language derived from many of the same sources as English and having a culture and a mind-set quite different from, and often opposed to, that of the Highland Gael.[1]

The people of the 1802 Lochaber emigration were Gaelic-speakers. Some may have had a passing knowledge of the Lowland tongue, but only if they had lived among Lowland people. Archibald 'Murlaggan' McMillan, who had lived for many years in London, spoke and wrote excellent English and later, when he lived in Montreal, became fluent in French.

The chiefs and clan gentlemen, usually better educated, had a foot in both camps.[2] Their hearts, however, were still Highland and clannish. The North West Company thrived on such clannishness. The first place many Highlanders headed for after arriving in Montreal was the home of Simon MacTavish, or after his death, the home of Roderick and Henry MacKenzie, or indeed, for the home of any Highlander already established there. Their common language of Gaelic was their visiting card.

The Lochaber Emigration of 1802 can be described as a certain number of people leaving a certain area at a certain time and sailing across the ocean to Canada. We know the place of origin of these people, we know their names, the names of the ships that carried them and how many there were of them. We know some details about the organization of the emigration and some of the reasons behind it. But all this information might apply to any similar departure of emigrants from the British Isles. Fleshing out these dry bones of history, though hazardous, must be attempted if the historian is to breathe life into the story.

Lochaber means 'the confluence loch,' because many rivers and streams emptied into it, though there is no actual loch of that name today. Lochaber is an area of some 1,200 square miles in the Scottish High-

lands that extends in the east to Badenoch, in the north to Glengarry (although that glen is sometimes considered part of Lochaber), in the west to the 'rough bounds' of the MacDonald of Clanranald country (the historic spot where Bonnie Prince Charlie and his Jacobite supporters raised the Royal Standard in 1745 – Glenfinnan in Moidart marks the eastern limits of Clanranald territory and the western limits of Lochaber), and in the south to the districts of Morven and Mamore. The Rev. Somerled MacMillan, Lochaber historian and genealogist of Clan MacMillan, always claimed that Upper Loch Linnhe was anciently known as Loch Aber. Whatever the case may be, the name eventually came to be identified with the whole region. It includes the highest mountain in Britain, Ben Nevis, and dozens of other peaks of over 3,000 feet. It includes placenames brought to Glengarry in Canada by the early settlers: Lochiel, Fassifern, Glen Nevis, Laggan and Glen Roy. Many, if not most, of the Highland immigrants to Glengarry came from Lochaber.

The predominant name in Lochaber 200 years ago was Cameron (if Glengarry is excluded) and under Cameron of Lochiel, the clan chief, were the many septs or lesser clans who followed the Cameron banner, including the MacSorlies of Glen Nevis and the cadet (senior) branch of the MacMartins of Letterfinlay after whom Martintown in the Canadian Glengarry is named. Other adherents of the Camerons were the MacMillans, the MacPhees, the Kennedies, the MacMasters, the MacGillonies and some MacLachlans and MacKenzies, although the latter name was associated more with Kintail in the northwest and the ancestral home of the MacLachlans was on Loch Fyne farther south.[3]

To the east of the great Glen which divides Lochaber was the territory of the MacDonalds of Keppoch in Glen Roy who acknowledged no superior, not even the titular holders of their land, the MacIntoshes. For many generations the Keppoch MacDonalds held their land 'by the sword,' and their claim was seldom challenged. This contempt for 'paper laws' was shared by most in the Highlands. The Lochaber people had the reputation of being particularly adept at flouting the laws of the country which they considered contrary to their interests. The ancient custom of cattle lifting, once an accepted practice, lingered on in Lochaber long after it had been eradicated elsewhere, much to the annoyance of the more law-abiding citizenry.

Other names associated with Lochaber, although their clan lands may have been elsewhere, were some Campbells, Stewarts, MacArthurs and even some Burkes, Boyles, and O'Handleys who had come to the area generations earlier through marriage or in the service of the great Montrose and his Irish general, Alasdair MacDonald of Antrim, who led the Loyalist troops to victory over the Earl of Argyll and the Covenanters at the Battle of Inverlochy in 1642. If Glengarry is included in the Lochaber area, the MacDonells and their clansmen, the MacDougalls, Gillises, MacGillises and MacLellans must be included, and the predominant name would then be MacDonald or MacDonell.[4]

As was traditional in the days of clan feuds, a name was often changed if it was unpopular at the time. It was unwise to bear a clan name in MacDonell country at certain times that might arouse suspicion or animosity, such as Campbell, unless the bona fides to the particular bearer of the name had been approved and accepted, such as in the case of the Campbells of Lochnell, staunch Jacobites and allies of the Clanranald MacDonalds. And not all the Lochaber emigrants were natives of that specific area. In fact, the majority seem to have come from other districts as far apart as Strathglass, Skye, Kintail and the 'sma Isles' of the Inner Hebrides. However, the organizers and original subscribers of the 1802 emigration were from Lochaber, and hence that is how the emigrants were described.

The early Celts left few written records and even seemed to disdain those who relied on the written word. As the Romans found when they first met the Gauls, writing was forbidden among certain of the tribes. It was as if they felt that only the weak-minded had to resort to the written word. To the Celt, anything worth knowing could and should be memorized. The Latin authors were particularly impressed with the schooling of the Celtic poets, although their lack of interest in writing baffled them. It is still difficult for modern scholars, inheritors of the Greek and Roman civilizations, to fully comprehend. Even that great Englishman, Samuel Johnson, who dragged his aged bones to the Highlands in 1773, decided that, although he revered the antiquity of the Gaelic Scots, they had no claim to a true culture because he believed that they had no written records, although some exist in ancient epics and church documents, but not in the ordered Latin fashion acceptable to Johnson whose brilliant eighteenth-century mind could not understand an oral tradition. The possibility that such a tradition, governed by strict rules which made it essential not to deviate by as much as a word from accepted wisdom, might be even more accurate than the written word, did not impress him. He had the common perception of the scholars of his day that only the written word could be accurate. That the victor inevitably writes the history and the vanquished are unsung did not seem to enter his thinking. But he kept a remarkably open mind to all he saw and heard on his memorable trip, even though his magnificent rationality made it difficult. Two hundred years later the Poet Laureate John Masefield, in the introduction to his epic poem 'Cuchulainn,' said that as his life was drawing to a close, he had come to the conclusion that the only authentic folk tradition of the British Isles was Celtic. Such a statement would have been received with disbelief in the eighteenth century by all except those of the Gaelic culture.

But the long road to oblivion was coming to an end for the Highland Scots, even as Johnson visited them. By the end of the eighteenth century many Highland Scots had given up hope. Culloden may have been only a minor engagement in the annals of British warfare, but it was the end of the Gaelic way of life that had endured for over a thousand years. It was not only a way of life but a way of thinking that was inherited from the Gaels of Ireland and from the pre-Christian Celts of mainland Europe. It was largely unintelligible to the other inhabitants of Britain, particularly after the Norman invasion brought the feudal system to full flower. Tribalism and communal land use as the basis of society was gradually replaced by land ownership and the wealth that flowed from it. No longer would men follow a nobleman into battle solely because they were related by blood – except in the Highlands of Scotland.

The romantic myth of the Scottish Highlander as a brawny, tartan-covered hero strutting through history with his loyal clansmen singing by his side and battling the English invader of his mountain Eden is simply that – a myth. At best, as in the Scott novels, it is a distorted picture. At its worst, as exemplified in the immensely popular music-hall entertainer Harry Lauder, the picture is an obscene mockery. An eighteenth-century Highlander from Lochaber probably would not recognize himself in the Scott novels, and would probably kill the stage Scotchman and enter a plea of justifiable homicide.

Ignorance of the way of life of the people of the Highlands was not confined to the English. Scottish Lowlanders often knew more about India or Africa. The very words Highlander and Lowlander are misleading. Edward Dwelly, the compiler of the monumental Gaelic dictionary of 1901, claims that 'The term Gàidheal (Gael) is frequently erroneously translated 'Highlander,' which is only a political Sasunnach (English) word invented to keep Gaels asunder and consequently comparatively helpless.' It was essential to the builders of an English-speaking empire that the two branches – Irish and Scottish – of the Gaelic world be divided for their numbers and fighting abilities, when combined, would have posed a serious threat to the hegemony of the British Isles. After the reign of the last Gaelic-speaking King of the Scots in the eleventh century, a policy of anglicization, implied or explicit, reduced the Gaelic-speaking areas until, by the eighteenth century, only those in the clan territories of the Western Highlands and Islands had Gaelic as their mother tongue and often knew no other.

The clan chiefs and the tacksmen traditionally sent their sons to the continent for higher education after studying at Aberdeen, St. Andrew's, Edinburgh or Glasgow. Paris, Rome, and the Scots College at Vallodolid in Spain were the choices of those studying for the priesthood. Medicine and the Law were the chosen professions of many and those not destined for a university degree often went into the army. The Protestants preferred Leyden in Holland or Geneva. The sons of Jacobite families, through choice or necessity, often spent their military careers in the service of foreign armies, fighting 'for every cause but their own.' In the two hundred years before 1800, over 400,000 Irish and Scottish names are listed in the military records of the French ministry of the army. Most are Irish, but thousands are Scots names. If Gaelic was the recruit's native tongue, he was often identified as 'Irlandais.'

Some of the Scots who left their native land for service in mainland Europe stayed there, as did the ferryman from South Uist who sailed Bonnie Prince Charlie to safety. He settled in France, married, and was the father of the man who become Napoleon's Maréchal MacDonald, Duke of Tarentum. When Sir Walter Scott was orchestrating the visit of George IV to Edinburgh in 1822, the great French marshall was an honoured guest. After the staged festivities, MacDonald insisted on visiting his father's birthplace at Howmore in South Uist, much to the consternation of his hosts who did not want the famous man to see the condition that the Highland people had been reduced to since Culloden. But he persevered, saw the ruins of his father's house, and filled a small vial with the earth and ashes of the hearth. When he died shortly afterward, and was given the largest funeral in French history, he was buried with the earth of the Hebrides next to his heart.

The association with France, begun in the days of Joan of Arc, lasted for centuries and only died out after the French Revolution. The 'Auld Alliance' against England produced Scotsmen who sometimes were more fluent in French than in English.

The social system of the Highland Gael was highly structured. All authority came from above, from God to the monarch to the clan chief and thence to the other members of the clan. This was typical of most societies, but the clan system was distinct in many ways. Justice was administered directly by the chief, the law courts often being too remote and hazardous of access. The chiefs had powers of pit and gallows (imprisonment or execution), and sometimes of fire and sword.[5] Although the system was rigidly hierarchal, there were certain elements in it of democracy, although that word would have been unknown to most Gaels and those who did understand it would have recoiled from it with horror, the older generations still remembering Cromwell, and the later generations associating the word with the American and French revolutions. But democracy there was nonetheless. A bad chief could be deposed and a new one elected and clan councils were held regularly. It was customary for a chief to put his first-born son into fosterage with another clan family until he reached maturity, thus becoming familiar with the everyday life of the ordinary people before he succeeded to the leadership of the clan.

Although the system was slowly changing by the eighteenth century, any changes were often fiercely resented and as fiercely opposed. The end of the Stuart dynasty in 1689, the imposition of a foreign Hanoverian monarchy and the abrogation of the heritable jurisdictions were the final straws. And to the Highlanders, many of whom were either Catholics or Scottish Episcopalians (not connected in any way with the Church of England), the coming of the state religion of Presbyterianism was a further cause of unrest.[6] Although the Loch Arkaig MacMillans and their Cameron clansmen were largely Presbyterian by the seventeenth century, they were surrounded by Catholic MacDonalds. The bloody reprisals after Culloden spared neither Catholic nor Protestant. A Highland name, no matter how remotely connected with the Jacobite cause, was sufficient for terrible retribution. Sometimes just a Highland name alone was enough for the government to presume guilt. The peace of Great Britain would never again be threatened by 'a race of half-naked savages, speaking a barbarous and unintelligible tongue,' as the Highlanders were often described by their enemies in the eighteenth century. The pacification of the Highlands would continue until the glens were emptied and the Gael reduced to a caricature.

The people of Loch Archaigside in Lochaber shared the common feeling of alienation and hopelessness. As Jacobites they had fought under the banner of the Camerons, not always willingly. Donald Cameron, the noble clan chief who was one of the first to throw in his lot with Bonnie Prince Charlie and who has come down to us in history as 'the gentle Lochiel,' was not so gentle when it came to forcing his clansmen into the Jacobite army. Enthusiasm for enlisting in the Lochiel regiment was encouraged by the threat that those averse to following their chief to the field would have their homes burned and their families evicted. There was nothing unusual in this behaviour by Highland chiefs. It was one of the darker sides of the clan system. It was not unique to the Highlands, but perhaps could be considered more heartless than the customs of other societies because the Gael really felt that his chief was the head of his family and more or less closely related to him.

Fifty years after Culloden, conditions in the Highlands had deteriorated to the point that emigration was becoming not just possible, but for many Highlanders the only possibility. Samuel Johnson was shocked at the craze for emigration that had seized the populace in the Highlands. On the Isle of Skye he and his biographer James Boswell witnessed a dance, newly invented, called 'America.' As the frenzied reel went on, the dancers left the floor one by one until no one remained. The symbolism was all too sadly accurate.

Unlike other parts of the British Isles where individual or at the most family emigration was the norm, entire communities in the Highlands were leaving, often taking every memory, every tradition, every song of their particular area with them. As Ted Cowan also points out in chapter 2, many of the landlords were concerned as the emigration fervour increased. They were losing a labour force, cheaper in many ways than actual slavery, because they did not have to feed, clothe or shelter the people. And the raising of regiments, now made respectable by the exploits of Highlanders in the far-flung outposts of Empire, was becoming increasingly important. 'Where there are no babes in arms, there will be no armed men,' says the Gaelic proverb. A serious attempt was made to write into law a fiat limiting emigration, but the craze continued.[7] The haters of the Gael, and there were many, rejoiced. The pacification of the Highlands, begun by military force, was entering its final, most brutal and most successful stage. If the Highlanders could not all be destroyed 'root and branch,' as the wording had it in the official orders for the Massacre of Glencoe one hundred years earlier, then a Pax Romana was the final solution. In Roman times the Caledonian leader Calgachus said it best: 'Where these people come, they create a desert; they call it a peace.'

Of course, no such policy was ever officially promulgated, but it is not difficult to discern the attitude of the non-Gael in the public and private records of the period. Even that great supporter of the Highlander as soldier, General James Wolfe, ended a private letter to a friend, extolling the virtues of the Highlander, with the chilling words 'small matter if they fall.' Before Sir Walter Scott created a romantic and largely bogus picture of the Highlander, Wolfe's feelings were shared by many. The Highland Scot was often considered little better than his Gaelic cousins in Ireland, and that was low enough. The English and later the British policy of dividing the Gaels of Ireland from the Gaels of Scotland was a great and continuing success. The result of such skilful manipulations, often aided and abetted by the Gaels themselves, secured the ascendency of English and the end of the Gaelic world. But salvation was always possible and readily available to the tattered remnants of that world. All that they had to do was become more like the English, and many did just that. Bedecked in once-forbidden tartan, playing the once-forbidden great warpipe of the Gael, they filled the ranks of the British army. In a reversal of its previous roll as persecutor of the Gael, the army had become the repository of some of the most obvious Highland traditions during the years when any distinctiveness was outlawed in civilian life. If the wearing of Highland dress and the playing of the pipes had not been permitted in the army, these outward signs of distinction may well have perished. But often the appearance of 'scottishness' was only that as far as the Gael was concerned. The ancient ways were long buried with the clans at Culloden.

Ironically it was the British army that perpetuated the use of the bagpipe, which along with the harp (clarsach) was the principal musical instrument of the Highland Gael. Pipers in Highland Regiments were not 'on strength' (officially recognized) in the army until well into the nineteenth century, but individual pipers were sponsored by regimental colonels who outfitted them, often in the commanding officer's own tartan. Pipe bands as we now know them came later.

With the glowing reports of the successes of the Highland regiments on active service in the Napoleonic wars and in India, their reputation was secure. The wild Highland warrior, fiercely fighting for his remote homeland and often for causes hardly understood by him, had become the orderly, disciplined, English-led British soldier. The chiefs were replaced by strangers who often spoke no Gaelic. And if the old threats by the chiefs of home burnings were no more, the impressing of men into the armed forces was a brutal reality. Officially sanctioned press gangs could seize men without warning to bring a regiment or a ship's company up to strength. The practice was most effective in the navy, of course, because escape at sea was more difficult than on land. Emigrant ships were boarded at sea and able-bodied men taken off to disappear forever, leaving families destitute.

Discipline in the British army was a new experience for the Highlander. Although he may have served his chief unwillingly at times and under threat of reprisal, the old forms of punishment were more psychological than physical. As cowardice was considered the unforgivable sin to the Gael, the warning that any sign of it would result in public disgrace was generally enough to ensure good behaviour. And since each company was derived from one particular glen or village, the knowledge that any fall from grace would be reported back home was more fearful than charging into battle. When the customary and revolting method of discipline in the British army, the lash, was attempted with Highlanders, the result was often useless. The pride of the Highland soldier was such that the imposition of any degrading type of punishment resulted in a destruction of self-esteem and such humiliation of spirit that even if the miscreant did not kill himself or desert, he was rendered useless as a soldier. Outsiders made fun of what they considered the ridiculous and overweening haughtiness of the Gael, to whom forelock-tugging and toadying were anathema. Respect was paid to social differences regardless of wealth. The rich man was due honour only as far as his accomplishments or bloodline deserved it. The fact that he had accumulated gold could even be considered a liability. This characteristic did not go unnoticed in France. The sight of a ragged Highlander bearing himself like an aristocrat inspired the phrase 'Fier comme un écossais' – 'Proud as a Scot.' Burns, who had a great love for the Highlander, was moved in frustration to exclaim, when visiting the Campbell stronghold of Inverary, 'There's naething here but Highland pride, and Highland scab and hunger…'. Although economic considerations were the chief causes of emigration for the Lochaber people (rents were increasing two to fivefold), the erosion

of their distinctive way of life, the reduction of their chief to a common and avaricious landlord, the arrival of great flocks of sheep and their Lowland shepherds and the devaluation of the clan, all tended to the destruction of their Highland pride. The 'gentlemen of the clan,' the tacksmen, foresaw what would eventually happen. They felt that they must leave before it was too late. Their foresight was uncannily correct. After the Napoleonic Wars when men were no longer needed to save Britain, the clearance of the Highland Scot began in earnest. But the Lochaber people were long gone. And none of their clan now remains on Loch Archaigside.

There were Highlanders, of course, who for one reason or another did not emigrate. Perhaps they could not bear to leave their native hearth and the graves of their ancestors. Perhaps they could not afford the passage, or were able to afford the increases in rent. Or perhaps they had a kindly landlord (there were a few) who still felt that kinship was important. Those who stayed were able to accommodate themselves to the new order somehow, and their descendants live there still. But many who did not actually leave Scotland were forced to move to the towns and cities where their language, their customs and their pride were swallowed up in the 'dark satanic mills' that were beginning to blight cities such as Glasgow and Dundee. After a generation or so, all that they retained were their Highland names. But the Lochaber emigrants and others like them may have been the lucky ones. Their hardiness, their honest pride and the fact that they could actually own their own land far from rack-renting landlords produced a people who helped to build a new country. And their language, their music and their children came with them.

So the people of a place like Loch Arkaig, no longer secure in their remoteness after the new roads of the 1700s were built, with a chief for whom they would have once given their lives reduced to nothing but a landlord, looked to the future with dread and trepidation. They had never been carefree, simple peasants dancing around a Maypole. They were the last remnants of a once-mighty race that had swept across Europe long before the coming of Christ. The Celtic world had begun its long decline before recorded history and the Gaelic offshoot of that world was well on the way to extinction by the fourteenth century. But old ways take a long time to fade. One of the chief characteristics of the Gael was a fierce love of home. When they had ceased wandering, fighting ancient Greeks and Romans and anyone else who came in their way, the Gaels put down roots. No matter how poor the land and hard the life, the Highlands of Scotland had become, to those who settled there, the land of heart's desire.

No one leaves a homeland and the dust of their ancestors on a whim. What made the Disarming Act of 1746 particularly terrifying to the Gael were the words embodied in it, inspired by a deep understanding of the Highland mind: the penalties for wearing the Highland garb and playing the pipes included the words 'If I break any of the provisions of this Act, may I die in a foreign land among strangers and be buried far from the graves of my ancestors.' The thought of such a fate was almost too much to bear for the Highlanders after Culloden. It was still a terrible thought to them fifty years later.

The Loch Arkaig lands are not on the ocean. Most of the people there had never gone to sea or even seen a large ship. The terrors of an Atlantic crossing were yet to be experienced.

An emigrant ship in 1800 was often a coffin ship. Passengers usually had to supply their own food and water, but it was often of poor quality and often ran out before the voyage was over or turned fetid and poisonous. Sanitation was nonexistent. Men, women, and children were crammed together with no privacy in the dark, dank hold, trying to maintain a modicum of decency amid the excrement, vomit, and rats. The hatches were battened down during bad weather, which often meant most of the time. If they were lucky, passengers could get some fresh air on deck on

a clear day, if they had a kind captain. The crew usually preferred to have them below deck out of the way. The spectre of typhus, smallpox and cholera hung over them all. And the ships were often nothing but unsafe hulks. Without any controls or inspections, any ship, no matter how unseaworthy, could be chartered for emigrants. Lifeboats were inadequate, if they existed at all, and there was no life-saving equipment. If a ship went down out of sight of land, death was a certainty. As the seas were so cold, even the rare person who could swim could and did drown, sometimes within a few yards of the shore. Their heavy woollen clothing and leather boots pulled the strongest swimmer down within seconds. Among fishermen and sailors it was generally felt that the inability to swim was an advantage. Death came sooner and with less suffering.

That the Lochaber emigrants suffered few of these horrors was due entirely to the foresight and humanity of Archibald 'Murlaggan' McMillan. He arranged special conditions for the safe passage of his people. He did not overload the three ships which he had chartered – the *Friends*, the *Jane*, and the *Helen*. He ordered special air ducts installed to conduct fresh air to passengers in the hold. He successfully sued the shipowners when they attempted to cheat the passengers on their arrival in Montreal. Although often frustrated by the attitudes of some of his people, he defended and supported them to the end of his life.

Getting to Glengarry was hard enough, but when they arrived at their allotments they found the land covered with a primeval forest. Luckily the Loch Arkaig area had been partially forested and the people were accustomed to wood cutting and logging, unlike many other immigrants from the treeless West Highlands and Islands, who had never used an axe. As Ted Cowan also notes in his chapter, the Lochaber settlers took readily to the lumber trade and were able to generate some income from the forest as they cleared the small plots that would eventually supply them with crops.

The fact that entire communities left together,

leaving whole glens deserted, made Highland emigration different from emigration from other parts of the British Isles. These communities remained together in places like Cape Breton and Glengarry, keeping alive the language, the music, and the traditions of their particular areas in the Highlands. When incomers moved in to re-populate the empty glens, they brought other ways with them. Even if they were Gaelic-speaking Highlanders, they may have had customs and traditions somewhat different from the original inhabitants, whose way of life went with them over the ocean. If the incomers were Lowland shepherds, and there were many of them after huge flocks of sheep were introduced into the Highlands, an alien tongue as well as an alien culture replaced the ancient ways.

Among the Loch Arkaig emigrants brought to Canada by Allan McMillan 'Glenpean' and his cousin Archibald 'Murlaggan' was a most remarkable woman. She was Harriet (Kennedy) MacMillan, a

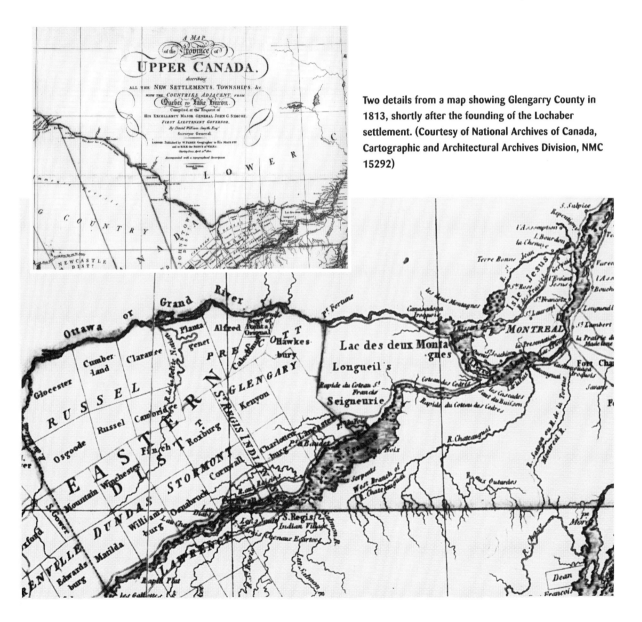

Two details from a map showing Glengarry County in 1813, shortly after the founding of the Lochaber settlement. (Courtesy of National Archives of Canada, Cartographic and Architectural Archives Division, NMC 15292)

widow with fourteen children. One son, John (later to be known as Roman John) could not leave with the family until his army service was over (he had been 'pressed'), but joined them a year later. After the usual rigours of an Atlantic crossing, they struggled for miles through the bogs and forest of Glengarry, carrying their few worldly possessions on their backs. They eventually found a clearing in the woods and built a log house. Harriet and her children cleared the forest, bit by bit, and some of their descendants still live in the area. Eight generations later Harriet's shawl which she brought from Scotland is treasured in the family of Hugh Allan MacMillan, who still plays the Gaelic airs of the Highlands on the violin in his home in Lochiel Township.

In the two centuries since Harriet MacMillan and her children left their native glen, her progeny have spread across North America. Many achieved prominence in the church, in business and in the daily life of their communities. They were not unique. After the initial hardships of life in the new land, the Highland settlers thrived in the rich soil of their adopted country. For generations in Glengarry they lived almost exclusively in a Gaelic-speaking community not unlike their ancestral land. If the early settlers spoke another language it was as often French as English.

In Glengarry in Canada these 'different' people were not different at all. In this hospitable land, they were the majority. They could live their traditional lives for untold generations, and with two distinct advantages over those who were left behind. Their chiefs, reduced to impotent landlords, stayed in Scotland. Most importantly, the new arrivals could own their own land. In the fertile land of Canada, they put down new roots. The first generations sang the sad Gaelic songs of exile and longing for their lost country. Succeeding generations sang the same songs but to a faster rhythm. The 'children of tempest' contributed to the making of a new land. This love song could represent a Highland woman lamenting the loss of her lover. It might also represent Scotland singing of her lost children.

Hi eile ho gu
My love has gone across the sea.

My love has gone on the boat;
Safely may he come home.

My love left a year ago
And my reason left me this week past.

The red doe and her fawn
Will my beloved bring home,

And the green-headed wild duck
That comes from the banks of Loch Arkaig.

My love left a year ago
And my reason left me this week past.[8]

## NOTES

1. The clan system was effectively destroyed in most of Ireland after the Anglo-Norman occupation which began in the 12th century. Ireland was a fertile agricultural land and easily accessible to the invader. Only in remote and mountainous districts did the Gaelic ways live on, constantly under attack and harassment. Tartans, for example, never evolved as a distinctive garb in Ireland as they might have if the Gaelic culture had not been undermined. But in the Scottish Highlands, remote, difficult of access and unattractive for farming, the Gaelic Scots lived virtually undisturbed – until 1746.

2. Clan is the Gaelic word for children. The 'gentlemen of the clan' were closely related to the chief, usually, but not always, the 'tacksmen.' A tack was a parcel of land, sometimes of several thousand acres, that was held on a lease from the chief and further leased out in smaller lots by the tacksman. The tacksman, in the case of the larger clans, was the middleman between the chief and the other members of the clan. It was his responsibility to pass on some of his rental income, generally in the form of produce, to his chief. More importantly, the tacksman ensured that the clansmen under his control rallied to the chief's banner in time of war. Service to the chief was considered part of the rent owed, and the tacksmen became the officers in a clan regiment The gentlemen of the clan could usually read and write and speak English, and often French as well, which made them especially important when they came with their clansmen to places like Glengarry in

Canada. Greenfield, Abercalder, Leek, Cullachie, Inch, Scotus, Sandaig, Croulin, Lundie and Muniall, among others, were all MacDonald (or MacDonell) tacksmen. The names are still recognized in Glengarry after 200 years. Murlaggan and Glenpean were the two MacMillan tacksmen who organized the 1802 emigration. In the early days of settlement they acted as a buffer between the French and English, and served as members of the government. They made it possible for Glengarry to exist as a cohesive Highland community for many generations. They and the clergy were the mortar that held the dispersed Highland people together.

3. Not all clan names were connected. MacLachlan, 'the son of the man from Norway,' may have had no affinity with the Strath Lachlan clan on Loch Fyne, and may have had a different progenitor in Lochaber. This independent identification is particularly common in names referring to a trade. Not all MacIntyres, 'the son of the carpenter,' for instance, had a common ancestor. Carpenters lived throughout the country, and the name was associated with many clans. The same applies to MacGowan, 'the son of the (black)smith.' Sometimes, if he lived on the Highland-Lowland border, a man might be known as MacGowan on one side and Smith on the other. To further complicate matters, in an area where almost all last names were the same, nicknames were a necessity, and eventually became family names. Some names, although obviously Highland, were known quite differently in Gaelic, such as Munro, which is Rothach (pronounced Rhow-hahk) in Gaelic. Although most names in the pre-Culloden era were closely associated with clan lands, this was not always the case. The name MacKenzie, for example, would be associated with Ross-shire and Kintail in Wester Ross, where that powerful clan held sway, but there were several reasons why that name might also appear in other areas. The MacKenzies of Lochaber might have been completely unconnected with the same name in the north – the name means Son of Kenneth, and may have referred to a different progenitor – or the name may have been brought to Lochaber through marriage or because an ancestor may have been forced to seek refuge and protection in other clan lands. Often the name of the dominant clan was adopted as in the case of the Irish Burkes of Brae Lochaber who became MacDonalds. The O'Handleys of Glen Roy, on the other

hand, kept their name and brought it with them to Cape Breton.

4. MacDonéll is the favoured spelling in certain areas, possibly to distinguish the Glengarry clan from Clanranald. A problem with Highland names and the identification of origins and family connections is that they are properly spelled in the Gaelic language only; all other spellings are just approximations, corresponding more or less to the sound of the name in English. MacIntosh, for example, is spelled in over thirty different ways in English, but only the Gaelic is historically correct – Mac an toisich, the son of the leader, at least in the nominative case. (The case changes in Gaelic are another story, and one more suited to the Gaelic scholar.) The problem is that once the Gaelic spelling is replaced, members of the same family often spell the name differently, leading to genealogical confusion. And to complicate matters all the more, chiefs and sub-chiefs were not known by their lands, as in English, but by their patronymics. Most Gaelic-speakers, hearing the name Mac 'ic Alsadair, would know that it identified the chief of the MacDonells of Glengarry; indeed, it was the only proper way to address the chief, and his own clansmen would have been able to give the 'sloinntearachd' or pedigree of their chief back many generations to the progenitor of the name. Such an ability was natural to a people who had, for the most part, no written language until the eighteenth century. As the feudal system of land ownership gradually replaced the clan system and the value of blood ties became less important than profit, the Gaelic terms of identification also began to disappear, adding to the alienation of the Highland people and the difficulties they experienced in leaving one world for another. Among the larger and more powerful clans such as the MacDonalds, the Campbells, the MacLeods and the MacKenzies many of the sub-chiefs were also known by patronymics, as was MacDonald of Glenaladale and Glenfinnan, who led his clan to Prince Edward Island (Isle St. Jean) in 1772, the year before the much-publicized ship 'Hector' reached Pictou, Nova Scotia. The Glenaladale chieftain, a cadet of MacDonald of Clanranald, was properly known as *Mac Iain Òig*, the Son of Young John. His grandson, although destined for the priesthood, chose to peddle tobacco instead, founded The Macdonald Tobacco Company and died Sir William Christopher Macdonald in Montreal, one of Canada's wealthiest men, the greatest

benefactor of McGill University and of many other institutions. It is doubtful if he would have ever been addressed as *Mac Iain Òig*, or if he would have even known what it meant. So Highland names in Gaelic mean more than simple forms of identification. Much of the history of the Gael is embodied in names and patronymics. What, for instance, does the name Dewar mean to an English-speaker other than a brand of Scotch? But to one familiar with the language and oral tradition of the Gael the name meant a keeper of a holy relic, in particular the keeper of the crozier of St. Fillan. This sacred staff was the responsibility for centuries of the Dewars of Perth and was carried by the bishop who presided at the coronation of the Scottish sovereign. Names such as Beaton (Bethune) and Munro are associated in the Gaelic mind with medicine, as Morrison is identified with the ancient law interpreters of the Lordship of the Isles, when Clan Donald ruled a sea kingdom separate from mainland Scotland. Not all Gaelic speakers would be aware, of course, of every aspect of their culture. Some just spoke the language and took no interest in any other part of their heritage. But a surprising number can still be found who have kept the oral tradition alive, as any traveller can discover in Gaelic-speaking areas once the shyness and reserve of the Highlander is overcome.

5. The Heritable Jurisdictions meant that the government ceded to the Highland chiefs the administration of justice in the areas under their control and was often the cause of serious complaints. They were abolished in the 18th century. The loss of these absolute powers was bitterly resented by many of the chiefs and was one of the grievances that led to the Jacobite uprising of 1745. In an interview with the Duke of Argyll, the Chief of Clan Campbell, in Inverary Castle in 1964, the author asked why the Campbells were so disdained by many other clans. 'It's quite simple,' he said. 'We often had letters of fire and sword delegated to us as the most powerful clan in Argyll and when we exercised these powers against other clans we were naturally resented.' Not the complete answer, but a good one nonetheless.

6. The Reformation came late, if at all, to the more remote areas of the Highlands. The imposition of the state religion of Presbyterianism in 1690 was opposed not only by the Roman Catholics but by Scottish Episcopalians. The MacDonalds and their followers in Glengarry, Knoydart, Moidart, Morar, Arisaig, Glen Roy (Keppoch)

and South Uist remained stubbornly papist, as well as the MacNeill Isle of Barra and several of the Inner Hebrides. The haughty Chisholms of Strathglass near Inverness maintained the 'Olde Religion' and insisted that only three persons in the world were entitled to use the definite article 'the' – the Pope, the King and the Chisholm (the clan chief). A large area known in seventeenth-century documents as 'ane nest of papistes' was the Enzie in the eastern Highlands of Banffshire, bordering on Aberdeenshire, protected by the powerful Catholic Gordons – the same family that produced the mad Lord George Gordon of the anti-Cathloic Gordon Riots, which were the cause of Archibald McMillan's leaving his employment in London and returning to Lochaber in 1780. Braemar, Balmoral and Glenlivet in the same area had, and still have, a large Catholic population. The majority of the Jacobite forces at Culloden were Catholic or Scottish Episcopal. For the most part, the Presbyterians were on the other side. A census commissioned in 1755 (National Library, Edinburgh, MS 89) shows only a few hundred Catholics listed in all the Lowlands, but over 15,000 in the Highlands. The penal code, enacted to destroy Catholicism, was effective in part, but in many cases only succeeded in driving it underground, or, as with the MacDonalds of Glenaladale and Glenfinnan, to Canada. Incredibly, the original name suggested for the Glengarry Fencibles of 1794, which came to Canada en masse in 1804, was the Roman Catholic Regiment (see chapter 6, document one).

7. There is a false notion that the Gael is nomadic by nature. The opposite is closer to the truth. Unless forced out by factors beyond their control, the members of a Highland community seldom travelled more than a few miles from their birthplaces in their entire lives. Only the chiefs, the sub-chiefs and perhaps some of the tacksmen had the opportunity, the wherewithal, or the inclination to travel away from their homes. Even if the people lived near the sea and fished to augment their meagre incomes, they disliked sailing beyond sight of land. Unlike the Norse who controlled the Western Isles and adjacent mainland for centuries, the Gael was not a sea-adventurer. The oceans were fraught with dangers, real and imagined. Monsters, water horses, seals that embodied the souls of the dead and whirlpools that could swallow up a boat and its crew abounded. Although not evil, *tir-nan-og*, the land of the ever-young, lay somewhere to the west and, like the

Christian heaven would sooner be achieved at the end of one's life and at an advanced age. The long list of superstitions, beliefs, incantations and spells had endured a thousand years in spite of Christianity. No matter how often the old ways were denounced, sometimes only a veneer of varying thickness concealed the Celtic soul. A very real but remote danger was capture at sea by Barbary pirates, who ranged as far north as Orkney. Corsairs out of Salle on the coast of Morocco reputedly kidnapped thousands of Christians. It was only in the early 1900s that these raids ended. The incredible story of the Scots girl who was captured at sea and became the concubine of the Sultan Mohammed in the latter part of the eighteenth century and the story of the Moroccan pirates is told in 'The Empress From Muthill' by A.C. McKerracher in *The Scots Magazine*, July 1983, 349. Any reference to the horrible fate of men (and women in particular) taken by pirates was suppressed in the eighteenth and nineteenth centuries as 'indelicate,' but the dangers would have been well known nevertheless.

8. As recited by Calum Iain MacLeod to the author in Cape Breton, 1960.

# PART III

# GLENGARRY AFFAIRS

# CHAPTER 5

# DOCUMENTS AND LETTERS RELATING TO THE LOCHABER EMIGRANTS OF 1802

PREPARED BY IAN MacMILLAN

### 1. LETTERS FROM ARCHIBALD 'MURLAGGAN' McMILLAN

These letters, selected from Archibald 'Murlaggan' McMillan's letterbook, 1803-29,[1] illustrate his continuing concern for his fellow Highlanders. In this letter to his first cousin, Lt. Col. Alexander McMillan, he is anxious to steer business from half-pay officers to John Munro, a merchant in Quebec City, and Archibald's agent and contact person there.

Montreal, 18 June 1808

My Dear Cousin,

Having perceived an advertisement in the Quebec Gazette purporting that the Gentlemen on Half Pay & military allowances on the establishment of the British American forces are by a late regulation to rise their pay in Quebec after the 25th of December last & that it would be necessary for them to appoint an agent there, I beg leave to recommend to you one who I am sure will acquit himself to your satisfaction as he is well known for integrity & a thorough knowledge of business. I mean Mr John Munro merchant there. I should fain hope Highlanders will give him preference as he is himself a true one, & ever ready to serve his countrymen. I have experienced the greatest friendship from him ever since my arrival in the province. I need not add that it would be highly gratifying if you would use your influence in his behalf with the Gentlemen half pay of your acquaintance.... I have no news from the old country or the West Indies since I saw you.

Your cousin.

Yours sincerely,

AMcM

IAN MacMILLAN lives in Leeds County, Eastern Ontario, in a restored stone schoolhouse. Since childhood, he has heard tales about the MacMillans. Ian has studied history at the University of Guelph, where one of his professors was E.J. Cowan. After graduating from Guelph, Ian completed an MA in history at Sir Wilfrid Laurier University. He also has talents as a cabinet maker and carpenter; and he has been employed in museums and other historical fields including as collection manager with the Ontario Heritage Foundation, based at Fulford House, Brockville, Ontario.

In this second letter, Archibald advises John Munro that their Highland kinsmen in the United States (the 'Union') are concerned about a possible war (later known as the War of 1812), and having to fight their own people in Canada. Who were these kinsmen who predicted the War of 1812? Clearly Archibald wanted to help by contacting James McGill of Montreal to lobby the government to settle them on undeveloped crown land, called 'waste lands.'

> Montreal, 16 Oct 1809
> My Dear Sir,
> There was a friend of mine in town lately who resides in a Scotch or rather a highland settlement in Vermont state... he informs me that not only that settlement but all the Highland settlements in the Union of which there are many are awakened to a sense of loyalty & patriotism on the prospect of a war with their native countrymen to avoid which many of them expressed of a wish to move to Canada should government give them encouragement. I recommended this to Mr McGill here who made it known to government.... I have submitted some propositions to Mr McGill here on the subject of letting part of the Waste Lands of the Crown with some of our loyal patriotic countrymen now settled in different parts of the Union who are roused in consequence of the prospect of war with their friends.... I hope Mr McGill will have government pay heed.
> Adieu,
> AMcM

The following letter, dated 16 October 1829, from Archibald McMillan to John McMillan, son of Allan 'Glenpean,' concerns the old North West Company, whose affairs were being settled eight years after its merger with the Hudson's Bay Company. John's brother James, referred to in the letter, had been a wintering partner with the North West Company, and in 1821, James became a trader with the Hudson's Bay Company. In 1827, James founded Fort Langley near the mouth of the Fraser River (see chapter 9). In

Campbell's *History of St. Gabriel Street Church, Montreal* (published 1887), Archibald is listed as a North West Company trader and merchant. There is no record of his going west as a trader, but he did invest in the company, which shows his close contact with North West Company partners, nearly all fellow Highlanders.

> Montreal, 19 Feb 1829
> John McMillan Esq.
> My reason for writing you at present is that I think it would be proper that as early as a communication could be made to your brother James it should be intimated to him that in consequence of some favourable circumstances in the affairs of the late North West Co they will be enabled to pay all their creditors in full and lest he might be among the number[,] the precaution of an early intimation is the more necessary ... others may have been kept in the dark from sinister motives thereby obtaining from 5 to 6 shillings on the pound the property of individuals in that company.
> Affectionate compliments to you my dear John
> AMcM

## 2. LETTERS FROM LT. COL. ALEXANDER McMILLAN (BROTHER OF ALLAN 'GLENPEAN' McMILLAN)

These two letters, written to Major General Shaw, who was in charge of the militia, show some of the Alexander's concerns at the start of the War of 1812 — shortages of weapons and men being away in the lumber trade. The white pine timber trade in the Ottawa valley was just commencing, and as Ted Cowan points out in his chapter, the skills which some of them brought from Lochaber would have stood them in good stead.

> Lancaster, 2 April 1812
> In consequence of the Rev'd Mr. McDonell's representing to me that it was his Honor the president's wish that the 1st Reg. of Glengarry Militia should be divided into 2 Regts I took the earliest

opportunity of doing so … it will ease some of the men who are much scattered in this county from coming a distance of 20 miles to a General Meeting, the reason of their being so much divided in this part of the province is owing to the Loyalists possessing several concessions in different townships without being inhabited. I am sorry to report to his Honor the President that three fourths of the young men of this county are at present abroad in the lumber line all over the province & at Quebec & will I am afraid remain so for four or five months to come. I sincerely wish some means could be devised to oblidge them to return home & to remain in the county at least for a certain time, otherwise in case of a ballot we should have very few men fit for service.

Lancaster, 27 May 1812
Respecting the flank companies ordered to be created: The near approach of the General Elec-tion which is to take place on monday next induces me to defer convening the Regt under my command until the fourth of June, in hopes that his honor will consider the inconvenience that would occur to the people spread over so large a space of country as they are, by being assembled so often in so short a period, a suffcient justification for the delay. He is ordering arms for all the flank co'y … but the bad state of the roads at present, and the great distance of my place of residence from the water side render it impossible to have those arrangements completed with as much expedition as I would wish. Capt. Wm Corbet and John R. Campbell are recommended for charge of Flank Co'y. Capt Corbet is a young man of education and I believe very active.[2]

### NOTES

1. NA, RG 91, B1, Letterbooks of Lt. Col. Alexander McMillan, Vol. II.

2. NA, Letterbooks of Alexander McMillan, Vol. II.

# CHAPTER 6

# DOCUMENTS AND LETTERS RELATING TO THE LOCHABER EMIGRANTS OF 1802

## PREPARED BY KENNETH J. McKENNA

*A*rchibald 'Murlaggan' McMillan left much information about his life, mostly in a large number of letters. His cousin Allan 'Glenpean' McMillan, with whom he organized the emigration of 1802, left no records. Most of the following letters were written by Archibald McMillan, who was born in 1762 on what is often described as Murlaggan 'farm' near Loch Arkaig, in the district of Lochaber.[1] McMillan's letters reveal a remarkable man. Although Gaelic was his mother tongue, his years in London had perfected his English. There is hardly a trace of the Gaelic idiom in his writings. His English is smooth, unaffected and pointed. His letters reveal a man straddling two centuries in calendar time but far longer in emotional time.

He was born sixteen years after the Battle of Culloden, when his clansmen had charged the British bayonets with pikes, battle-axes and scythes. From the lips of the survivors, he had heard tales of valour and tragedy, and of the horrors inflicted on the Highlanders after the battle, of rape, slaughter and the burnings of homes. Government policy in the years after Culloden was aimed at the destruction of the clan system and the replacement of an ancient way of life with an alien culture. Among the thousands who suffered were the Lochaber residents. Records listing the losses endured by the Highland people can be found in the Scottish Record Office, Edinburgh. A typical entry reads as follows:

> FASSIEFERN: Acc.t of What Catle etc Were taken from the lands of ffessifern [the spelling varies] by a party Sent by Lord George Sackvill from the head of Locharkaig June 7th and by Colonel Cornwallis June 8th 1746; 132 cowes – 37 horses – 382 Sheep and goats – to the amount of three hundred and eighty-four pounds, 14 shillings, 6 1/3 pence.

Attached is a statement which reads in part:

> Compear'd John Cameron of ffessifern Who Being Solemnly Sworn and Interogate Anent the loss he sustain'd by the troops Carrying off his Catle in the month of June Seventeen Hundred and forty six years Depones that the above Number of Cowes, horses and Sheep Worth at the

Long Sault Rapids, Ottawa River, near the home of Archibald 'Murlaggan' McMillan. (Courtesy of George MacMillan, Chief of Clan MacMillan, Finlaystone, Langbank, Scotland)

lowest Computation the prices above – And that he rebuilt New Houses – of Corpach and Achnacarrie after the same were Destroyed by the Kings troops who Also Carried Away the fforesaid Catle, and that, after Showing them A protection from Alexander Campbell, Lieut.-Governour of Fort William And Capt. Caroline Frederic Scott – then Captain Commandant of that Garrissone – And also a letter from Sir Everard Fawkener at Desire of His Royal Highness The Duke of Cumberland. A Coppie of Both is hereto prefix'd, And the Above He Declares to be truth As he shall answer to God.

The declaration was signed by John Cameron, Patrik Campbell, Lach. Campbell. The written guarantees of safety signed by Caroline Scott, the Lowland of-ficer who despised the Highlanders, and the protection of 'Butcher' Cumberland, whose name is still reviled in Scotland, were ignored with impunity.

Archibald was born during a time of great change. Unlike many of his contemporaries, he adapted to the new order. Brought up among a people who had been Christian for a thousand years and, in the case of his clan, Presbyterian for generations, he would nonetheless have been aware of the strange beliefs and superstitions which still filled the Celtic mind no matter how vigorously the ministers raged against them. While many of fellow-Gaels were still living (or attempting to live) as their forebears had for millennia, settling differences and feuds by the sword, Archibald was evincing a nonviolent nature and the social conscience of a nineteenth-century liberal. Although a

Map showing Templeton, Buckingham and Lochaber Townships, surveyed for Archibald McMillan's proposed settlement of 1802 on the Lower Canadian (Quebec) side of the Grand (Ottawa) River where his dreams of living like a laird were never realized. (Courtesy of National Archives of Canada, Cartographic and Architectural Archives Division, NMC 104146)

staunch Presbyterian, he was so horrified by the anti-Catholic Gordon riots of 1780 in London that he left his employment in that city forever and returned to his native Lochaber. Once back in the Highlands he soon realized that the social and economic conditions there had become intolerable. As the leading tacksman of Loch Arkaig he determined to organize the emigration of 1802 to Canada.

The McMillan letters show that at one time he entertained the hope of living as a laird in the new world, collecting rents from a grateful tenantry and directing their lives in the traditional Highland way. The settlement in the new country would be a mirror-image of life in Scotland, without the injustices. The dream came to naught. In the freedom of the Canadian wilds and with legal titles to land ownership, the old ways were unworkable. Archibald soon adapted.

While Highland leaders of an earlier day may have settled disputes violently, Archibald abhorred physical violence and even legal entanglements. He was often frustrated in his various business excursions but never seems to have lost his equilibrium even when involved in bitter altercations with Governor Lord Dalhousie, who sided against McMillan in favour of the Wright brothers, Philemon and Ruggles, the American adventurers on the Ottawa. Dalhousie was a Presbyterian Lowlander and may have had the typical Lowland prejudice against the Highlander.

By the time of the War of 1812, the principle of joining the colours was well established in Canada. Volunteer battalions were raised in every settled area to serve in the defence of the country. Archibald was commissioned a major in the Argenteuil Militia, composed mostly of Lochaber immigrants, and, although this aspect of his life is poorly documented, we know that he conducted raids in the Highland tradition around Ogdensburg N.Y., his men 'going as infantry and returning as cavalry.' Not all early settlers (or potential settlers) in Glengarry, however, were as loyal to the British Crown. After the Revolution, while most of the Highlanders and Palatine Germans of the Mohawk Valley settlement followed Sir John Johnson to Canada, some stayed behind. In Glengarry, during the War of 1812, contrary to fondly-held beliefs, there were instances of desertion to the Americans. Some were doubtless inspired by greed and the belief that they would be better off in the United States, but some may still have harboured a distaste for the Crown which their Jacobite forebears had fought against at Culloden.[2] After the War of 1812, McMillan persevered when the Lochaber settlement suffered years of near-famine and was forced to petition the Government for relief. One of McMillan's admirable qualities was a respect for different religious beliefs. In his correspondence with Denis-Benjamin Papineau, he pleaded for the erection of a Catholic church on his land in the Grenville area on the Quebec side of the Ottawa. Although his motives were not entirely altruistic – he believed that the presence of a priest would help to control the bad behaviour of some of the more recent arrivals in the area – his plea shows generosity of spirit. The church was eventually built on land that he donated.

Archibald seems to have been in regular communication with the priest of St. Raphael's in Glengarry, Father Alexander MacDonell,[3] the man who embodied the characteristics of a true Highland chief and was the de facto leader of the Glengarry people. Archibald McMillan was cut from the same honest Highland broadcloth as his contemporary, the first Presbyterian minister of Upper Canada, the Reverend John Bethune,[4] who became the close friend of the priest of St. Raphael's. The two men worked together in amity for the benefit of their Highland people.

Although a seemingly dull and stolid character unlike some of his more flamboyant and swashbuckling fellow Highlanders, Archibald's quiet perseverance and sensitivity are revealed through his letters. In spite of the many setbacks of his life, he never succumbed to Celtic gloom, nor did he turn to the panacea of the bottle.

McMillan was a sensitive and intelligent Highland gentleman and his death in 1832 was particularly poignant. He died of cholera during one of the early epidemics in Montreal possibly caused by the arrival of victims of the potato famine in Ireland. One of his sons followed him to the grave within days from the same affliction.

### SELECTION OF DOCUMENTS, MOSTLY LETTERS TO AND FROM ARCHIBALD McMILLAN

1. Letter from Archibald McMillan to Duncan Cameron, Montreal, 30 September 1803:

> All those who have accompanied me here have got Government lands near Cornwall [Stormont & Glengarry Counties]. Glenpean [his cousin Allan McMillan] & family are amply provided for in land & every family of the rest have 200 acres – I am not certain yet if I can get lands on account of my having settled here in Lower Canada as it appears to be incumbent on every settler to live upon the lands. If this condition cannot be departed from I must give up hope of

becoming a Laird. I must content myself with the condition of a humble citizen here of which I believe I would have no reason to repent if I had the advantage of having established a correspondence in Britain before I left it – had I done this I could carry on business on a more extended scale. I however have no cause to complain; last winter and most of the spring while the season lasted I had as much business as I could conduct. I never spoke more Gaelic any winter in Lochaber [Scotland] than I did last winter. The Highlanders pouring down every day in most astonishing numbers as besides the emigration they increase beyond calculation so that I believe this land will contain more Highlanders[5] than the old country notwithstanding the measures which I hear are pursuing by our Government at home to prevent emigration.

I Believe I wrote you last year of my intention of going home to carry more of my countrymen along with me, the war [the Peninsular War] having broke out prevented my carrying that intention into effect… Arch'd McMillan.

Within a year of the arrival of the Lochaber people Archibald's problems, which plagued him to his death in 1832, were beginning. He saw that he would not be able to have his homogenous Highland settlement established with himself as laird. He realized that his trading business in Montreal would be limited because of his lack of connections in Britain. His life was to become a series of problems and failures. He never went back to Scotland.

2. Letter to Archibald McMillan from John Munro, McMillan's loyal agent in Quebec City, and a fellow-Highlander:

Quebec, 29th August, 1804
My dear Sir,
This will be handed you by Mr. Felix Gawler a young man who has served Mr. Jones in the capacity of a Clerk these four or five years, but is now solicitous to get into some good berth in

Montreal. I beg leave to recommend him to your civilities, and if you can introduce him to any of your friends, who may have it in their power to forward his views, it will be conferring a favor on Mr. Jones and me.

I had the misfortune my dear friend, to lose my dear sweet Babe[6] on the day after I last wrote you – Good God! what lovely children I have been deprived of – indeed my lot is peculiarly hard, and my poor little wife at this last stroke is much affected in her health and otherwise – but tis our duty to own and acknowledge the divine dispensation just and submit with fortitude and resignation, however difficult the task. My beloved dear infant after suffering much by teething had not strength to withstand the fatal hooping cough. Yet though we regret her being taken from us, what a great consolation it is to know and be assured that she is happy with her departed little brothers and their kindred angels, in the Regions of immortal bliss – adieu my dear Sir and believe me always
Sincerely yours,
John Munro

Arch'd McMillan, Esq.
Montreal

3. Letter to the Reverend Fr. Alexander MacDonell from Archibald McMillan in Montreal, 4th June 1805:

Dear Sir,
The surveyor is to provide some time this week to survey the lands on the Grand River and I have sent notice to make this public in Lancaster and Glengarry, that such as entertain doubts of the quality of the lands may satisfy themselves as to the truth or falsehood of the prevailing report. At the same time, requesting of those who are in arrears of fees, to come forward on or before 1st of September. I have no doubt but that they continue. Otherwise, that others who are daily applying, would be substituted in their place still too wavering in their resolves, but as it is neces-

sary that they should now act a decided part I have every confidence that they will endeavour them to direct them to proceed so as the least to embarrass me and themselves. With best respects to you and your brother and family.

I am, dear Sir,

Yours most sincerely,

Arch'd McMillan

Archibald's convoluted phrasing betrayed his hurt feelings, if not his fury, over the behaviour of some of his people, who were questioning the suitability of the lots on the Grand, or Ottawa, River,[7] and refusing to pay the fees needed to hold the land. He had led them out of their bondage, carried them safely over the ocean, selected lands on the banks of a great river for them and attended to all the many details that such a massive undertaking entailed. If the necessary expenses were not paid, the land would be forfeited and his dream of a new Lochaber gone forever.

His settlers, however, were not enamoured with the prospect of an unbroken virgin forest, bordering the east shore of the Ottawa River, with years of backbreaking toil ahead to prepare the soil for planting and, what was worse to the gregarious Gael, isolation from any kind of a community. They preferred Glengarry, where they could live in Gaelic among their own people who could teach survival skills. Even if the newcomer had to work as a day-labourer, it was more appealing than disappearing into the wilderness. Some settlers did stay on the east shore of the Ottawa and their descendants live there still. But many moved across the river into Glengarry and west to Finch Township, in Stormont County. There is hardly a founding family in Glengarry today that does not have the blood of the Lochaber people in its veins.

In the last decade of the twentieth century, when most North Americans are either non-religious or irreligious and even the faithful are inclined towards ecumenism, the fact that a Presbyterian would conduct a correspondence with a Catholic priest, the subject being criticism of the behaviour of other Presbyterians, may not seem too earth-shattering. But to a man of the eighteenth or nineteenth century, it is truly remarkable. Apart from the obvious, that Father MacDonell was an accepted leader of the Glengarry settlement and Archibald needed his support, there was also the old Highland respect of one 'gentleman to the clan' for another. Each would have known the other's genealogy in detail, and their mutual respect would have overcome any doctrinal differences. (See remarks on 'Letter to Denis-Benjamin Papineau').

4. Letter from Archibald McMillan to Ewen Cameron of Fassiefern, October 20th, 1805:

Our countrymen have a great aversion to going on new land. They are afraid to encounter fresh difficulties and they live among their friends [in Glengarry] formerly settled in the country, who encourage them as they find them useful in clearing their land, without considering that they are losing time for a bare subsistence. This disposition among them has kept them back from entering on the lands provided for them in the Upper and Lower Province by Glenpean and myself and to this disposition among them together with the influence of the gentlemen residing in the Scotch settlement of Upper Canada who wish all those who arrive to settle in some shape or other near them; as the more population the more will their lands become valuable. This disposition among them, I say, and these reasons, together with the credulity of the new settlers have been the means of embarrassing me very much as I am obliged to pay the fees of office and survey myself; few of them coming forward to fulfill their obligations though they partly dragged me into the business. But having gone so far I must endeavour to go through with it and as soon as I get those who are not inclinable to come forward, to relinquish it. I am not afraid that I will find much difficulty in getting plenty of settlers for it who know it to be more valuable than any now to be obtained in the upper Province on account of its contiguity to market, as being situated on the banks of the

Grand or Ottawa River through which the trade to the North-West is carried on, and their Company [North West Company] will always give the settlers the Montreal prices for their produce at their doors, for their flour, pork, butter, etc. There are farmers now there of 3 years standing who sell 60 & 100 fat hogs of their own raising, and that same river is stocked with the greatest quantity and abundance of fish, and the woods full of deer, by which some choose to live an idle roving life subsist their families without labouring the ground or raising cattle. Though this mode of life is to be condemned, the advantages alluded to, together with its being confessedly the best grazing land in this part of America is found beneficial to the settlers. The Scotch Settlement in Upper Canada [Glengarry] being an old settler country the fish and game have largely abandoned it and there is a distance of about 18 miles and before they bring their wheat and other produce down here in winter the expense of it nearly eats it up.

Archibald's dream of a cohesive Highland community in Canada was never realized. Once his clansmen found that they could settle almost anywhere they wished and get clear title to the land, they no longer felt limited to the acreage allocated to them. Some were satisfied, but many chose to take up land among their fellow-Highlanders who had settled earlier in the Greater Glengarry and Stormont area, even if it meant working as hired hands. Some did not pay the fees attached to their land, perhaps from penury or because they felt that if Archibald had chosen their plots without consulting them, he could pay the charges involved. This added substantially to Archibald's expenses because he obviously did not want the land forfeited, but although he had some capital, it was limited, and his disappointment and bitterness shows. Ever the optimist, he hoped that the advantages of settling on the Ottawa river instead of in the centre of roadless Glengarry would be obvious. His statement that in the 'old settler country' the fish

and game had mostly disappeared is nonsense. The oldest part of the area, the 'front' on the St. Lawrence, had only been settled for some fifteen years and the back of the county was still largely unpopulated. After upwards of 200 years of cultivation, Glengarry still abounds in deer, moose, partridge, and small game. Some of his Lochaber McMillans even left Glengarry in 1804 and were the first to settle in Finch Township and in Stormont County to the west, far from either the St. Lawrence or the Ottawa.

5. Letter from Archibald McMillan to Ewen Cameron of Fassiefern, 1805, excerpt, closing sentence:

> We cannot help looking to our native spot with sympathy and feelings which cannot be described, yet I have no hesitation in saying that considering the arrangements that daily take place and the total extinction of the tyes twixt Chief and clan, we are surely better off to be out of the reach of such unnatural tyranny.

The Gaelic word *cianalas* can only be partially translated as 'homesickness.' To the Highlander it means far more. It represents the Celtic melancholy, sorrow, and sadness for a past that will never return. When Archibald writes about 'feelings which cannot be described,' he is expressing the *cianalas* that haunted the exile and that only time would heal. After 200 years and many generations those feelings, romanticized as they may have become, still lie deep in the psyche of the dispersed children of the Scottish Highlands. No matter how time and circumstances have intervened, a word, a song, or a picture are enough to bring on a flood of nostalgia for a place and a way of life that may never have existed except in imagination.

It has been the fashion since the time of the romanticizing of the Highland chiefs by writers such as Sir Walter Scott to portray them in a largely false light. Any references to abuse by the chiefs and the plight of the dispossessed Highland people were suppressed, or denigrated as the actions of a few agitators.

In spite of the published accounts of witnesses such as Donald MacLeod in his *Gloomy Memories of Strathnaver*, it is only in recent years that the truth about the betrayal of the Highlanders has been revealed by writers such as John Prebble. Archibald called it 'tyranny' in 1805, and he was right. Perhaps Archibald's later problems with Lord Dalhousie may have been due, in part, to the voicing of such anti-establishment sentiments.

6. Petition for Relief – Threat of Famine in 1817:

To His Excellency Francis Gore, Esquire, Lieutenant Governor of the Province of Upper Canada, etc, etc,.

THE MEMORIAL OF THE INHABITANTS OF THE COUNTY OF GLENGARRY IN THE EASTERN DiSTRICT OF THE PROVINCE OF UPPER CANADA – MOST HUMBLY SHEWETH:

That your Excellency's well-known kindness and attention to the wants of the unfortunate within your Government emboldens your Memorialists to intrude upon your notice. That it is with the most painful feelings your Memorialists find themselves under the sad necessity of imploring the assistance of Government to relieve them from their present distress and from the horrible prospect of approaching starvation. That no less than five hundred and fifty families within the County are sufferers from the total failure of the crops, the greater part of whom have not at this moment provisions sufficient for the support of their families for one week. That the scarcity occasioned by the scantiness of the crops in this Country in the year 1816, caused your Memorialists to pay out what little money they had for provisions for their families last summer. That your Memorialists were in hopes that the last harvest would have afforded them abundance of every species of grain and vegetables for their families besides a considerable surplus for market; but in this, as in many other occurrences in life, were doomed to meet with fatal disappointment, the early frosts which have unfortunately destroyed the crops in many other parts of the Province – having entirely ruined the crops of every kind in the backparts of this County – That your Memorialists will consider it as a mark of kind regard and particular favour should your Excellency be enabled to afford them that assistance which their wants so loudly call for, and will be happy to give any security to Government that they will return the amount of any assistance that may be afforded to them, when it may be the will of the almighty to grant more propitious seasons – your Memorialists therefore most humbly and earnestly pray that your Excellency will be graciously pleased to afford them such aid as may be in your Excellency's power and as in duty bound your Memorialists will ever pray.

The petition was dated at Glengarry, Upper Canada, 15 February 1817 and was signed by Alex McLeod, Allan McPhee, Alex McDonell, John McMillan, Donald McMillan, John McDonell, Ewen Kennedy, Donald Kennedy, Arch. McDonell, Roderick McDonell, Angus McDonell, John McInnes, John McDougall, Ranald McDonell, Archibald McInnes, Angus McGillivray, Norman McLeod, Archibald McGillivray, Murdock McLeod, Alex. McLennan for themselves and on behalf of others. (They all signed with an x.) Relief was evidently provided for 1816, 'the year of no summer,' when there was frost in every month. Relief was also provided the following year.[8]

The popular conception of the Highland emigrations to Canada, shared even by the modern descendants of the early settlers, often is that they left Scotland merely to better themselves, and after some strenuous exertion clearing the land, lived happily evermore. Among those who consider material success as proof of righteousness and divine approval, the word 'honest' qualifies 'poverty,' and 'frugality' is preferred to 'starvation.' But in 1817 these people had no money and no food, after fifteen years of toil. They had just

suffered through 1816, the year with no summer. That
their Highland pride allowed them to admit that they
had only enough food for one week is sufficient proof
that they were desperate. That their plea was heeded
by the authorities, which may not have been the case
if they had still been in Scotland, strengthened their
fierce loyalty to this country.

7. Letter from Archibald McMillan to His Son Alexander:

> Grenville, 31st January, 1823
> My Dear Alex'r,
> I received your favor intimating that John
> [another son] is for the present in Mr. Gordon's
> employ at which I an much pleased and trust in
> God that he May conduct himself with propriety.
> I inclose here two documents the one a draft of
> £25. by Alex'r Dewar on Alex'r Forbes and the
> other an account for damages promised to be
> paid by John Finlay to Allan Cameron in re…
> [handwriting unclear] for £48. On these things I
> have advanced money to Ewen [another son] and
> would need to be reimbursed as soon as possible.
> Will you write to Mr. Finlay and indorse Ewen's
> name on the back he being not here at present.
> You will also lose no time communicating with
> Forbes who I understand went to Quebec for
> money if he is not returned. He is a quirky body.
> The best time to apply to him is on his arrival.
> If you recover part of all these sums let the
> amount be at my disposal with liberty of draw on
> you. I think I have written something to you in a
> former letter relative to land matters of which
> you have not taken notice, by the way I believe it
> was in my last. Duncan's [another son] leg is still
> bad. I fear it is something much more serious
> than a sprain. there is some fear of its breaking
> out an becoming a running sore which may ulti-
> mately affect the limb.
> I am, My dear Alex'r,
> Your most affectionate Father,
> Arch'd McMillan.

> P.S. Could you not see Mr. Finlay on this occa-
> sion and express to him my surprise at my claim
> not having been taken notice of which I had rea-
> son to believe would be among the first as I be-
> came a sufferer years before the others and from
> the deportment of Mr Finlay himself towards me
> who seemed desirious [sic] to find his aid in or-
> der to do away any ill impression that Govern-
> ment might have imbibed against me and who
> professed that in making out his estimates he was
> not to be influenced by Government or any un-
> der them, but solely to be guided by observations
> made on the spot and by his own discretion. In
> these circumstances I am surprised at not hearing
> from him.

Archibald's problems take up most of his extensive
correspondence. His son Ewen was a great disappointment to him; his son Alexander died in 1832 of
cholera, three days after his father.

8. Letter from Alexander McMillan to his father Archibald:

> Montreal, 15th June 1824.
> Dear Papa,
> Respecting Wright's cause the Court has granted
> a delay until the 1st Sept. next to file papers and
> plead, during that time full time will be left to
> write both to Mr. Munro and Mr. Bouchette to
> endeavour to get a certified copy of the list. If it
> can't be got; by examining Mr. Bouchette and
> Mr. Munro its authenticity may be established
> and the questions I will myself draw out so that
> no ingenuity of Mr. Bouchettes can avail him, if
> he really knows the papers, this examination of
> course takes place after or during October, in fact
> I am fully aware of the importance of your cause
> and will neglect nothing that can benefit you.
> William Cameron I will write to on the subject of
> his conversation with Wright, if I knew where he
> was I should have done so before now, it is said he
> is on his way to Quebec. Be perfectly easy re-
> specting Cameron's case, the papers are lost and
> without them you know Grant can do nothing

although he seemed to threaten the Prothonotaries [clerks charged with the records of the Court] with an action of damages for the loss – without this, the business would certainly have come on again, but I should think without more success than heretofore. I understand that Archy is confined by illness to the house, had you better not speak to some Doctor as his malady is of that nature, that it would require being attended to in time, I think that he ought to take some mercury during two or three weeks. I send enclosed my measure for the boots that you promised, if Mamma could send a yard & quarter of the black cloth it would save me the expense of a finer pair of pantaloons during the present dusty weather.
I remain Dear Sir,
Your dutiful Son,
A. McMillan.
Montreal 15th June 1824.

Alexander's letter is concerned with the ongoing problems with Philemon and Ruggles Wright. The 'lost' papers raise some interesting questions, but there is no reason to believe that Alexander or any other of Archibald's agents were responsible. The mention of mercury as a medication is a reminder that it was once considered beneficial.

8. Letter to Denis-Benjamin Papineau, younger brother of Louis-Joseph, regarding the erection of a Catholic Church in Grenville, Lower Canada (Québec):

Grenville, le 12 février 1828.
Cher monsieur Papineau,
Votre honorée lettre du 31 dernier m'est arrivée pendant mon absence, à Montréal. A mon retour je me suis empressé de faire part de son contenu à la population catholique de Grenville et de Chatham, ayant convoqué une assemblé dimanche dernier, chez M. Edwin Prinddham, d'ici. Je les ai trouvés unanimes à désirer se joindre à leurs frères de la Petite Nation pour supporter un pasteur. Je puis dire avec confiance qu'ils payeront annuellement vingt à trente louis, et aussi beaucoup [sic] dans un avenir très prochain, à cause

du développement très rapide de la colonie lequel sera encore accéléré par l'érection de culte divin.

Il y a environ 28 familles catholiques à Grenville, et environ 14 familles à Chatham et à Lachute, ce qui formera deux cents âmes, en comptant cinq âmes en moyenne par famille. Ajoutez à cela que ceux qui sont employés aux travaux du canal sont pour la plupart catholiques.

L'endroit le plus central, ici pour y dire la messe serait ce qu'on nomme aujourd'hui le 'Camping Ground,' sur le premier rang, près du canal militaire, lequel terrain appartient à la couronne. Si le gouvernement s'y refuse, alors, comme je suis le propriétaire des terres de chaque côté et au-dessus ou en arrière du dit terrain, je donnerai bien volontiers l'emplacement voulu avec le privilège de l'employer de la même façon pour y construire une chapelle.

Je prends la liberté de suggérer une mesure pour arriver à une conclusion pratique: qu'il soit notifié par écrit qu'un prêtre dûment assigné par l'évêque remplira les fonctions du culte ici, à un jour désigné à cet effet. Il y a une maison d'école érigée, cette année, qui pourra répondre au but puisqu'il y a déjà des bancs, un poêle et autres commodités.

Je termine avec l'assurance de mon empressement à coopérer à l'œuvre que vous entreprenez, de mettre fin à ce manque de christianisme qui caractérise les endroits où nous vivons. Des crimes et des forfaits de tous les genres y sont commis presque journellement, ce qui est dû en grande partie aux travaux publics qui s'y font, particulièrement les travaux du canal. La venue du prêtre s'y fait donc grandement sentir. Puisse-t-on le comprendre!
Votre très obéissant serviteur,
Archie McMillan.

(Translation)
Grenville, 12 Feb 1828
Dear Mr. Papineau,
Your much appreciated letter of the 31st of last month arrived during my absence in Montreal. On my return I quickly made the contents of your letter known to the Catholic population of

Grenville and Chatham, during a meeting held last Sunday at Mr. Edwin Pridham's home here. I found them unanimous in their desire to join their brethren of the 'Petite Nation' in supporting a pastor. I can say with confidence that they will pay annually twenty to thirty louis, and much more in the very near future due to the rapid development of the colony which will increase with the erection of a place of worship.

There are about twenty-eight Catholic families in Grenville and about fourteen in Chatham and Lachute, making up about 200 souls, if we count an average of five souls per family. Add to that those who are employed on the canal works, who are mostly Catholic.

The most central place for mass to be said is at what is called 'the camping ground' on the first line near the military canal, which land is owned by the crown. If the government does not allow it, then, as I am the owner on both sides of the land and above and below the crown lands, I will gladly donate the site needed, with the honour of having it used for the erecting of a chapel.

I take the liberty to suggest a way of arriving at a practical solution: That it be announced in writing that a priest, duly assigned by the Bishop will take up his duties to the congregation as of a certain date. There is a schoolhouse, built this year, which would suit as it has benches, a stove and other amenities.

I close with the assurance of my readiness to cooperate with you in the effort to put an end to the lack of Christian worship that characterizes the area in which we live. Crimes and outrages of all types are committed almost daily, for the most part caused by the public works in the area, particularly because of the work on the canal. The presence of a priest will be greatly appreciated. You know what I mean!
Your most obedient servant,
Arch'd McMillan
Grenville, 12th February, 1828

Although Archibald McMillan was a loyal Presbyterian, his letter shows a familiarity with the proper Catholic terms. Whether it is entirely the work of Archibald himself or was written with the help of a Catholic friend, he signed it and the land for the church was indeed donated by him. That one of his purposes was to abate the unruly behaviour of the Catholics in the area by having a priestly authority installed is undeniable, but that he should write the letter at all is extraordinary. The Reformation came late to the Highlands and never to many of the neighbouring MacDonald lands, but by the eighteenth century the Cameron country of Lochaber was almost solidly Presbyterian. The so-called 'Gentle Lochiel' of the Jacobite Rising, although supportive of the Catholic House of Stuart, was intolerant when it came to the Catholics on his own territory. He forbade his brother, a Catholic priest, to preach anywhere on his lands. The Penal Code, applied with various degrees of severity over the centuries, but applied with particular harshness after any risings that could be considered Catholic-inspired, resulted in the Catholic church going underground. The Code applied to all dissenting religions including the Scottish Episcopal Church (unconnected with the Church of England) but the Catholics were singled out for special attention because they were perceived as being not only wrong in their beliefs but as posing a very real threat to the security of the nation. In Archibald's day, no Catholic could hold a commission in the army, be elected to public office, own property worth more than ten pounds, or worship in public. By the end of the eighteenth century, there were only a few Catholics left in the Lowlands of Scotland, and those mainly aristocratic families who defied the law. In the Highlands, however, it was quite different.

The religious wars which swept the Lowlands in the seventeenth century led by fanatical Covenanters such as Richard Cameron (a Lowlander in spite of his name) seldom extended to the Highlands, except for the exploits of the Royalists Bonnie Dundee and his cousin Montrose, who carried the war against the Covenanters into the Highlands more by accident than design. The battles of Killiekrankie and Inver-

MacMillan Emigration Plaque Unveiling, 5 August 1962, at Williamstown, Glengarry County. Left to right: General Sir Gordon MacMillan (Chief of Clan MacMillan); Harriet MacKinnon (then president of the Glengarry Historical Society); the Rev. Somerled MacMillan (Clan MacMillan bard and historian); Jack Barker (great-great-grandson of Archibald 'Murlaggan' McMillan, the Rev. D.B. MacDougald; W.H. Cranston (then chair of Ontario's Historic Sites Board); Lorne MacMillan, grandson of Archibald 'Murlaggan' McMillan; Fernand Guindon (then MPP, Glengarry); and the Rev. Kenneth MacMillan. (Courtesy of Archives of Ontario, Photograph Collection)

lochy were as much clan struggles for supremacy as they were for religion. The Highland Gael, although doctrinaire and unyielding in matters of faith and ferocious in battle, lived in comparative peace and harmony with his neighbours, regardless of differences of religion. There is no record of clan battles having been fought on purely religious grounds. And many families, such as that of Cameron of Lochiel, had members who professed the 'Old Religion,' in spite of obvious difficulties. Some families produced both Presbyterian Ministers and Catholic priests, but the heated exchanges and condemnations that this pro-

duced stopped short of bloodshed. 'Kinship will withstand the rocks' says the Gaelic proverb, and it was never more true than in the religious differences of the people of the Highlands.

9. Letter from Archibald McMillan to his son John:

> Montreal, 10th May 1831
> My dear John,
> You cannot forget that at parting I requested and promised writing from Prescot and also on your arrival at York. Your Mother and I have been uneasy and disappointed at your long silence espe-

cially on account of so many accidents happening in the early part of the season on the [writing unclear]. We have removed from our old residence and have made an exchange more satisfactory to the corner of the Hay Market on the boundary of the little creek facing the Mountain. The house is in every respect more eligible than the last and what makes the remove still more desirable is that it is for 1/3 of the rent viz. £20. It is true that Alex'r has to pay £15. for an office in Notre Dame Street next door to Herrin & Rascoe.

I have heard from Grenville lately, they are all well. Duncan is still with Mr. McGill, on what terms is not yet decided not having spoken to him on the subject. Mr. Hamilton is here just now from Stanstead, he writes in your favor to some friends of his in York, the Hon. Thomas Dun and the Hon. William Allen. I fondly hope that ere now you are occupying the situation assigned to you and that you are pleased with it and giving satisfaction in discharging the duty of it. In this hope and confident expectation I give you a Father's blessing recommending it to you daily and nightly to implore the guidance of protection of your Heavenly Creator. Your mother and brothers join me in love and most affectionate regards and cordial good wishes for your prosperity and happiness,
Ever my dear John
Your fond Father,
Arch'd McMillan.

P.S. There was a gentleman called here for you on 1st of this month name I think Jas. Comet. Thomina [Archibald's daughter] is allowed to go today with Mr. Hamilton to Stanstead on a short visit to Margaret [another daughter].

Ever the optimist, Archibald made moving to cheaper quarters sound like an improvement. Perhaps it was, but in the thirty years that he laboured, until his death in 1832, he never seemed to have achieved material success. The Wrights had finally been victo-rious in 1827, and Archibald subsequently admitted to 'an indolence' brought on by a life of disappointment. Yet his faith remained strong, and he showed a tender regard for his family to the end of his long and honourable life.

## NOTES

1. The term 'farm' is misleading when applied to most of the Scottish Highlands. To a Canadian, a farm is generally understood to mean a piece of clearly defined land, mostly arable, and capable of being worked with horses or tractors. The original land grants in the Glengarry area were of one or two hundred acres. Today a successful dairy operation needs many hundreds of acres. A Highland farm bears little resemblance to that concept. When a Highlander leased a tack of land from a chief or laird, it generally consisted of hundreds or even thousands of rough, rocky, mountainous acres suitable only for grazing, with small patches of arable land scattered throughout the lower reaches. These patches, usually of only a few acres or less, were seldom large enough to be cultivated by horses. The most suitable and practical implement for turning up the soil in the stony fields was the *cas-chrom*, a sort of foot plough peculiar to the Highlands, which could turn over more ground in a day than four men with spades. Arable land was used for growing barley or oats, and potatoes, after they were introduced in the eighteenth century. The term croft better describes the Highland farm: a few acres of tillable land, many acres of grazing land, sometimes with access to water for fishing. Although it is difficult for a modern visitor to the Highlands to believe that the largely deserted glens could ever support humans, the people who lived there, although never prosperous, managed to survive and sing songs of praise and devotion to their native hills and valleys.

2. After 1746 it was not entirely clear that the 'Jacobite Menace' was eradicated for all time. Highland chiefs in exile continued for many years to plot against the Government and plan for another uprising. British Spies kept tabs on expatriate Jacobites in Paris and Rome and enlisted the help of Highlanders such as MacDonell of Barrisdale and The Young Glengarry, 'Pickle the Spy,' to inform on the activities of their fellow-countrymen. The Young Glengarry ended up in a Paris gutter with a knife in his heart.

George III may have lost America but he and his son George IV followed the advice of those who knew the Highlanders best and refrained from overreacting when reports of cabals and intrigues among the exiles reached them. They knew that the Highland Scot was at heart a Royalist and, once he realized that another rising would never occur, would eventually transfer his allegiance to the new Royal Family, and that is what happened. The vast majority of the Highland people became the most loyal of subjects, the atrocities of 1745 fading with time and with the realization that the Crown was behaving with benevolence. There were those, of course, who never lost the dream of a return of the Stuarts. Agents from the court in exile went back and forth from France for years after 1746, collecting monies from Scots for the support of the exiles. Allan Breck Stewart, the probable assassin of Campbell of Glenure, featured in Robert Louis Stevenson's *Kidnapped*, was one of the better-known Jacobite agents. For many years after Culloden, the Government was wary of forming regiments from the Jacobite areas of the Highlands, such as Lochaber and the Clan Donald lands, preferring to place its trust in staunch anti-Jacobite battalions like the Black Watch. But after the successes of Wolfe and his Highlanders in the New World in 1758 and 1759, and the increasing need for soldiers to fight Britain's colonial wars in the far-flung outposts of Empire, Jacobite antecedents were ignored. The Highlands were a gerontocracy; every able-bodied male between the ages of 12 and 70 was considered fit for soldiering. After the reprisals of 1746, poverty was so widespread that even the pittance earned in army service was often the only cash the Highlanders ever saw. Once the oath of allegiance was taken, few Highlanders would break it.

3. At the time of the letter (1805) Fr. Alexander MacDonell was parish priest of St Raphael's, the oldest Catholic parish in Upper Canada. He had arrived in Canada a few years before with the disbanded soldiers of the Glengarry Fencibles and their families. This regiment, which in 1794 he had been instrumental in raising was the first Catholic regiment in the British Army since the Protestant Reformation. Although the titular colonel of the regiment was MacDonell of Glengarry, Fr. MacDonell as chaplain was the de facto commandant, showing a genius for organization and diplomacy that later, in Canada, gained for him the reputation of greatness and generosity.

Later, as Bishop of Kingston, his see extended from the Quebec border to the Great Lakes. He was the most respected and influential person in the early years of the Glengarry settlement in Canada and it was largely due to him that the loyalty of the Highlanders to the British Crown was assured. He was revered by Catholics and non-Catholics alike, and his close friendship with the first Presbyterian minister of Upper Canada, John Bethune, testifies to a spirit of kindness and generosity so often characteristic of Highland Scots. Fr. MacDonell served for some years as a missionary to the Catholics of Lochaber before coming to Canada and was well-known and respected among the people there. The fact that he was descended from some of the early Glengarry chiefs and that his mother was Presbyterian and also a well-connected Cameron from Lochaber gave him further legitimacy as a leader.

4. The first Presbyterian minister in Upper Canada, Bethune came to Glengarry in 1787. He lived in Williamstown from 1805 until his death in 1815. His house is still preserved there. Born on the Isle of Skye, he first went to North Carolina to minister to the Highland immigrants there, but was forced to leave at the time of the American Revolution and went to Montreal, where he founded the St Gabriel Street Presbyterian church. Upon hearing that the Highland Scots in Glengarry were without a minister, he left Montreal and settled with his family in that Gaelic-speaking community, where he lived for the rest of his long and adventuresome life. He and his wife had a large family, the members of which spread throughout North America and many of whom became famous in their own rights. The hero of Red China, Dr. Norman Bethune, was a descendant. The founder of many Presbyterian churches in Ontario, John Bethune was sometimes assisted in his ministry by his friend, the Catholic Bishop Alexander MacDonell, who often boasted that he knew 'all the Presbyterian prayers,' and proved it by attending at the bedsides of members of Bethune's congregation when the minister was unavailable.

5. Highland names in Glengarry County, Ontario, according to the census of 1852: MacDonald and MacDonell, 3,228; MacMillan, 545; MacDougall and MacDougald, 541; MacRae, 456; MacLeod, 437; Grant, 415; Cameron, 399; MacGillis, 349; Kennedy, 333; MacLennan, 322; Campbell, 304; MacIntosh, 262; MacGillivray, 243; MacKinnon, 242; MacPherson, 195;

Fraser, 176; MacPhee, 157; MacIntyre 140; Ross, 139; Chisholm, 133; Morrison, 99; MacCormick, 83; MacMartin, 72; Mackay, 72; MacLauchlan, 68; Cattanach, 50.

6. It is difficult for those born after the middle of this century to realize that until fairly recently, children (and adults) often died from diseases that have been largely forgotten.

7. In French, the river was called 'le Grand.'

8. National Archives of Canada, Civil Secretary's Correspondence, Upper Canada, Upper Canada Sundries, January-March 1817, RG 5, A1, vol. 31, 14233-912.

# PART IV

# CARIBBEAN CONNECTIONS

# CHAPTER 7

# FAMILY AND ETHNIC BONDS BETWEEN WEST INDIANS AND CANADIANS

## STANLEY R. BARRETT

The anthropologist arrives in a distant land, pulls out a notebook, and begins to question local inhabitants about their culture. 'Just a minute,' one of them interjects, thumbs through a scholarly book, and then launches into a discourse about the social organization of his people. The stunned anthropologist soon realizes that what is being offered is not the 'native's' viewpoint, but instead an analysis and interpretation

STANLEY BARRETT was born in Orangeville, Ontario. He was awarded a BA by Acadia University in 1963, an MA by the University of Toronto in 1968, and a PhD by the University of Sussex in England in 1971. From 1963 to 1965 he taught secondary school in Nigeria under the auspices of CUSO. Since 1971, he has taught social anthropology at the University of Guelph. He has done research on a West African utopia, the radical right in Canada, class and ethnicity in rural Ontario, and vendetta and feud in Corsica. He has published numerous scholarly articles and five books. His most recent books are Is *God a Racist? The Right Wing in Canada*, and *Paradise: Class, Commuters and Ethnicity in Rural Ontario*, both published by the University of Toronto Press. His current research involves a study of gender and violence in Corsica.

provided by the previous generation's anthropologist. A variation on this little joke is to have the researcher arrive in a village far away, eager to renew acquaintances with her or his favourite informant from an earlier visit, only to discover that the informant has emigrated to the United States or Canada, and now lives in a state or province next door.

The world has changed. Today people read and populations migrate. Hitherto geographically separated ethnic groups find themselves thrown together in new settings, competing for scarce resources. In a study of population movements, this phenomenon is termed 'postmodern,' and the story of the MacMillans is surely postmodern. Between 1792 and 1802, five brothers emigrated from Scotland. Alexander, Allan, and John Roy MacMillan ended up in Glengarry County, Ontario. Archibald and Ranald (as well as Allan's son Alexander) settled in the West Indies.[1] Almost two centuries later, not only do we find the progeny of the three Scotsmen who went to the West Indies alive and well, assimilated through marriage, but also some of these same progeny living here in Canada.

In the pages that follow, I shall provide a snapshot of West Indian history, and then take a brief look at two families which trace their roots back to the five brothers who left Scotland so long ago. One of these families is from the West Indies, the other from Canada. Due as much to accident as design, but reflecting global population movements that are becoming more commonplace by the decade, they find themselves neighbours in Ontario. What makes these two families special is that they have discovered each other, and thus have begun to close the family lines that separated 200 years previously.

The history of the West Indies is the history of colonialism, slavery, indentured labour and plantations. Following the first siting of the West Indies by the Spanish, various European nations rushed in to establish colonies. The first casualties were the Arawak and Carib, the indigenous peoples of the region. As sugar plantations sprang up, a shortage of labour led to slavery, beginning in 1505. The slave population grew to 1.7 million. On the island of St Kitts, there were 1,234 Europeans and 1,436 African slaves in 1678, and 1,612 versus 15,667 in 1834, when slavery in the British West Indies came to an end.[2]

The end of slavery led to a crisis on the plantations. Although apparently an attempt was made to manipulate the newly-freed slaves by introducing an 'apprenticeship' system that would retain plantation control over them, this ruse was not successful, and the colonial governments, at the desperate urging of the planters, began to recruit workers from around the globe. Early on, it was the Portuguese islands of the Azores and Madeira that provided the needed labour power, on the theory that 'white immigrants might supply a middle class for the West Indies and set an example of industry to the Negroes.'[3] Eventually immigrants were attracted from Spain, Mexico, Indonesia, China and especially India. As indentured labourers, they committed themselves from three to five years, working five and one-half or six days per week. They were obligated to live on the planter's estate.

From the outset, the owners and managers of the plantations were Europeans, and the workers African slaves. Their interests were contradictory, with the first wanting cheap labour and the second freedom. Elites everywhere in history seem to have complained about the lack of initiative and dependability of their slaves (or servants), which can be interpreted to mean that protest, in this case a sort of work to rule, has always been alive. Yet in the West Indies, as elsewhere, there existed a much more dramatic form of resistance: escape. Despite the determined opposition of the planters, aided by militias to which they belonged and by colonial miliary personnel, the slaves did indeed escape, and in sufficient numbers to earn them a special name – the Maroons. Apparently even today Maroon villages can be found in the hills of Jamaica. Some descendants of Maroons en route by ship to Sierra Leone, part of an ambitious repatriation program organized by black leaders in the New World, actually settled in Nova Scotia.

The European population included planters and plantation overseers, soldiers and missionaries, as well as 'small whites,' many of them Portuguese and Chinese, who freed themselves from indentured labour and established modest shops and other businesses.

Even in the days of slavery, the African-origin people did not form a homogeneous entity. Skilled mechanics, masons, carpenters, tailors and domestics enjoyed higher rank than those who worked in the fields. Maroons, and 'coloured freedmen,' the progeny of liaisons between Europeans and Africans and other ethnic groups formed another rank. When the three Scots MacMillans arrived in Trinidad and Grenada about 1800 as plantation overseers, slavery still existed, and it is probable that they themselves had slaves. Overseers had to contend with runaway slaves, as well as cholera and malaria. In 1801, a cousin of the MacMillan brothers railed at the 'cussed country' the Scotsmen had adopted as their new home.[4] For slaves and indentured labourers, conditions must have verged on the intolerable.

One of the ironies of the post-Second World War era has been a sort of reverse immigration. From 1951 to 1961, some 250,000 Caribbean people emigrated to Britain. Between 1950 and 1972, about 100,000 West Indians migrated to Canada, and twice that number to USA. 'Mixed-blood' people, whose progenitors represent two or more ethnic groups, tend not only to be middle class, but also to emigrate permanently from the Caribbean to First World nations. Richardson also suggests that the lighter the skin colour, the more probable one will be accepted in the new country. Lower-class people migrate as well, but the pattern is different. First, they more often than not are seasonal workers, returning to the islands when the crops have been harvested. In addition, it is the poorer people – mostly men – who are inclined to migrate in search of work from island to island within the Caribbean, which partly explains the prevalence of the matrifocal family – mother and children, with the father absent. That such internal population movement now exists is itself significant, because it was severely restricted during the era of European control. At that time, residents of each island were taught to be hostile towards residents of other Caribbean islands.[5]

For a couple of generations, the MacMillans of the Caribbean kept in touch with their brothers and cousins in Glengarry Country, Ontario. Although the link was broken sometime in the middle of the last century, in recent years it has been partially mended, thanks largely to Hugh MacMillan. Always curious about his family background, and aware that some of his ancestors had migrated to the Caribbean, he was determined to find out more. In 1962 he arranged to publish a letter of inquiry about the descendants of his Scottish ancestors in newspapers in Jamaica and Trinidad, informing people of a MacMillan clan reunion in Cornwall, Ontario, later that year. Quite a number of people responded. 'I am happy to inform you that I am of the McMillan descendants,' one woman wrote. 'I was told that my grandfather was the son of one of the three Scotch brothers who came out to the West Indies sometime around 1800 or thereabouts…. My grandfather died before I was born, but his wife – my grandmother, who died around 1936 or 1937 – told her grandchildren they are of a Scotch descent, and at the time of her marriage she was the envy of the village, being the daughter of a slave and married to the son of a Scotch man.'

MacMillans began springing up in Trinidad and Tobago. One letter asked Dear Canadian Cousins to send financial assistance after a devastating hurricane; another writer expressed the hope that Hugh MacMillan would assist his two children to get into a medical school in Canada. A third writer ended her letter by telling Hugh MacMillan, 'You can also let me know how much you will be able to pay me for doing this for you.' Apparently some writers assumed that there was a wealthy MacMillan estate to divide.

Since there never was a pot of gold to divvy up, it is hardly surprising that a quarter of a century later the contacts between the West Indian and Canadian descendants of the five brothers who originally emigrated from Scotland have pretty much faded away. There is one great exception.

Dr. Henry Courtenay Clarke, who was born in Trinidad in 1925, traces his roots back to Alexander MacMillan, who had settled in the West Indies in the early 1800s, and whose father had emigrated to Canada from Scotland a few years earlier. From 1947 to 1952 he studied medicine at Howard University in Washington, DC. During this same period he added an Master of Science (MS) in biochemistry, awarded by Georgetown University, to the Bachelor of Science (BSc) that he had already earned at Howard. He also studied French and Spanish at the Catholic University of America while taking his medical degree. Later he completed the course work for a PhD degree in biochemistry, and throughout his working life he has not only practised medicine, but has also published more than 20 scholarly articles.

After graduating in medicine in 1952, Dr. Clarke

Dr. Henry Courtney Clarke on right, with daughter Natalie and wife Linda. (Hugh P. MacMillan Collection, Guelph, Ontario)

have one foot in each of these worlds? The secret apparently was his physical appearance, which reflected the several ethnic strands of his forbearers.

Dr. Clarke's family roots include Scots, English, French, Spanish, Portuguese, Dutch, Jewish and East Indian (both Hindu and Muslim), Carib, and African. In the Caribbean, he claims, the ideal physical appearance is a 'golden brown' or 'high brown' skin colour, and fine, silky or 'blow' hair. Blue eyes are undesirable. According to Dr. Clarke, 'if you're too light, it means you're a foreigner ... an outsider.' His own appearance fits this ideal model, and it is his appearance that has made it possible throughout his life to readily adapt to whatever racial or ethnic group with which he has associated.

Dr. Clarke was quite forthright about the social class basis of West Indian society. His own upbringing had been one of high status and privilege. Yet he was adamant that racism had not been part of his childhood experience, in spite of his comment that Trinidadians practise 'selective cross breeding' in order to produce ideal offspring with an appealing

was a resident at Reddy Memorial Hospital in Montreal for two years, at the end of which he returned to Trinidad to set up his own practice. In 1962, he learned about Hugh MacMillan's letter of inquiry about descendants of the three Scotsmen who had settled in the West Indies. Although aware that he himself was one of the descendants, he ignored MacMillan's letter. In 1971 he returned briefly to the United States, where he was an instructor in Obstetrics and Gynaecology at State University of New York and the Roswell Park Memorial Cancer Research Institute. In 1974 he returned to Canada, where he continues to practice medicine today in Windsor, Ontario, after brief stopovers in Toronto and Sault Ste Marie. On a whim he contacted Hugh Macmillan.

Dr. Clarke reminisced about what it had been like to attend simultaneously Howard University with its predominantly black student body, and Georgetown University, which he described as an extremely racist white school. At one point in the day he would be with white students, listening to them joke about the African Americans who had been shot in nearby parks and streets the night before. What was ironical, he said, was that 'I was the guy who removed the pellets at the Negro hospital.' How was it possible for him to

(Left) Joseph Nakhid (ca. 1828-1908), grandfather of Dr. Henry Clarke. An East Indian Hindu Priest, he married a granddaughter of Alexander McMillan, son of Allan 'Glenpean' McMillan. Sometime later, Joseph converted to Roman Catholicism. Upon the death of his first wife, he married her younger sister, fourteen-year-old Mary McMillan (right) (ca. 1854-1938), grandmother of Dr. Clarke. (Courtesy of Dr. Henry C. Clarke, Windsor, Ontario)

Margaret McMillan, great-great-great-granddaughter of Allan 'Glenpean' McMillan, which makes her a distant cousin of Dr. Clarke. Born in Trinidad, she now resides in Montreal, Quebec. (Hugh P. MacMillan Collection, Guelph, Ontario)

'golden brown' complexion. A West Indian woman whose own ethnic roots are English, French, African and Amerindian claimed that many families, including her own, 'spent generations marrying lighter skin people to get ever lighter skin people.' She was raised in Guyana where people of Indian origin compose about 60 percent of the population.[6] 'I grew up to be very prejudiced against East Indians,' she claimed. The East Indians who became indentured labourers after slavery was abolished, according to this woman, were pariahs, looked down upon by higher caste East Indians who later settled in the Caribbean. These pariahs were much more likely to remain in the West Indies than other indentured people when their contracts had expired. 'Politics in Guyana,' she commented, 'is organized on a racial basis.' The Civil War in Guyana in 1964, she insisted, had been a racial war between African and East Indian origin people.

Similar opinions were expressed by a man raised in Jamaica, now residing in Canada. His ethnic roots are African, Indian and Chinese. 'My aunt, she used to call me three nation,' he claimed, adding that people in Jamaica still use the highly derogatory term 'coolie boy' or 'coolie man' to refer to East Indians. He also recalled a violent incident in Jamaica when numerous Chinese-owned shops were damaged after the word spread that a man of Chinese origin had kicked a black woman.

Nevertheless, these two individuals agreed with

Dr. Clarke that one's ethnicity plays little part in one's life chances in the West Indies. As the woman observed, 'Here in Canada, it's between white and black. There it's different shades.' The impression they conveyed is that racial matters are immensely more complex and subtle in the Caribbean in comparison to Canada, a direct result of the multi-ethnic society, and subsequent inter-marriage, generated by colonial interests. They also emphasized the wide variation in terms of social class and ethnic relations that prevailed from one island to another. The only thing that unites West Indians, they joked, is their internationally-renowned cricket team.

Dr. Clarke, it must be said, has faced his share of problems in Canada. When he moved to Windsor, Ontario, he was denied professional privileges at one hospital, apparently because of negative letters of reference from other Canadian hospitals with which he had been previously associated. A hospital appeals board in 1985 found the allegations against him false, and the hospital in question was ordered to grant him the normal privileges enjoyed by a general practitioner. While Dr. Clarke does not completely rule out the possibility that racism played a part in this matter, in his opinion the more probable explanation concerns his pioneering techniques and invention of instruments for the specialized procedure known as laparoscopy. Envy, and possible financial gain, he thinks, rather than racism, are what motivated his colleagues to cast doubts on his competence.

Dr. Clarke has two children. Henry, a charming and personable young man, was born in Trinidad. His mother, who now lives in Florida, is Chinese in origin. Henry was raised by his father's mother, but eventually moved to Canada to live with his father. Having completed a BSc degree in biochemistry at the University of Windsor, he now plans to follow his father's footsteps into medicine, hoping to study in Trinidad. Like his father, Henry stressed his adaptability to a wide range of ethnic groups. At the University of Windsor, where he had been on the Student Council, he belonged to the Chinese, Indian, Carib-

Henry Clarke, biochemistry student, Windsor, Ontario, son of Dr. Henry Clarke, and great-great-great-great-grandson of Allan 'Glenpean' McMillan, Trinidad. (Hugh P. MacMillan Collection, Guelph, Ontario)

mosque, has been quite 'shocking.' She also has found North Americans aloof and unfriendly. The only reason for leaving Trinidad, she thought, was financial, and in view of the life she has led in North America, she has serious reservations about whether it is worth it. No doubt her attitudes reflect a nostalgia for life in the Caribbean (she stressed how much she misses the food back home), plus her youth, but at least one thing has given her pleasure in Canada. Freya, like her brother Henry, expressed great satisfaction in getting to know her Scottish-origin relatives, the mutual descendants of the pioneering emigrants.

bean and Jewish Student Associations. Given his Chinese mother, and the varied ethnic roots of his father, he often is queried about his own mixed ethnicity. Rather than getting upset, he thinks the topic is 'a good icebreaker.' Henry regards himself as part Chinese and part Trinidadian, and of course Canadian. Since his public school days, he has been aware of his Scots ancestors, which he claims is also 'a good conversation piece.'

Henry's half sister Freya was born in Trinidad in 1969. She describes her ethnic background as 'Hindu, Catholic and West Indian.' Her mother is a Catholic. Freya grew up in the home of her grandmother, a Hindu, and attended a Hindu school. In 1990 she came to Canada to live with her father. Unlike her brother, this attractive and engaging young woman's time in Canada has not been entirely pleasant. She loved living in the countryside in Trinidad with her grandmother, and only reluctantly, at the insistence of her mother, did she agree to join her father, although she was appreciative of the efforts he had made to support her at the University of Windsor.

Perhaps it was merely the clash of wills between the generations, but whatever the reason, she took a temporary leave of absence from university, moved to Detroit, and found a job. That experience has been an eye-opener for her. Racism, she insisted, is nonexistent in Trinidad. What she has experienced in North America, especially Detroit, where she attends a

Like Dr. Clarke, Hugh MacMillan, the man who had the letter of inquiry published in two West Indian newspapers, traces his roots back to one of the five brothers (John Roy) who emigrated from Scotland around 1800. Born in 1924, the son of a Presbyterian minister, Dr. MacMillan was raised in various manses in eastern Ontario and western Quebec, with the summers spent in Glengarry County. Archivist *extraordinaire*, he has also been a soldier, sailor, writer, farmer, salesman, circus hand, publicist, and agent for a hypnotist. And along the way he has been honoured with a Doctor of Letters degree by Laurentian University. His ethnic roots, compared to Dr. Clarke's, are homogeneous: Scots on his father's side, Irish on his mother's. Apparently the typical pattern in Glengarry County was for Scot to marry Scot, or at least someone from Britain. The one exception concerns James MacMillan, the son of Allan and the brother of Alexander. Allan's offspring were an adventurous pair. Alexander ended up in the West Indies, while James joined the North-West Company in 1802 as a clerk, and the Hudson's Bay Company in 1821. He lived with several Aboriginal woman, the 'country wives' of Heather Devine's article in chapter 9. James was the progenitor of a line of Metis which thrives to this day.

Hugh MacMillan has an insatiable interest in family history, which began as a teenager, partly sparked by his paternal grandmother. 'I think it is a healthy thing,' he argues. 'It may make us better people.

Because we know where we came from. Good and bad. It provides a psychological anchor in a mixed-up world.' That may well be the case, but not everyone, it must be said, including members of his immediate family, shares his enthusiasm. 'I've been criticised as having an obsessive interest in this stuff.' Sometimes he and his wife, whose ethnic roots are English and Irish, joke that if they ever divorced, it will be because his unswerving pursuit of the MacMillan story has driven her around the bend; and one of his sons regards his father's passion for family history as somewhat elitist. One might well question his consuming concern with his Scots ancestors on his father's side, and the relative neglect of his Irish ancestors on his mother's side. I suppose the ready answer may simply be that since there never is enough time to do everything, the greater amount of accessible documentation on the Scots line made it an obvious choice. Also nudging him in that direction may have been his childhood experiences in the Scottish environment of Glengarry County, plus possibly an unconscious assumption (a common bias) that male-centred history carries more weight.

Reacting to the criticisms that sometimes have been levelled at him, Hugh MacMillan declares, 'I think I'd be just as interested in my family history if I was Pakistani.' There is no reason to doubt his words. He has been the driving force behind the efforts to establish contact with West Indies and Métis cousins.[7]

Hugh MacMillan's son Neale was born in 1959. He has an undergraduate degree in journalism, and an MA in political economy. He has lived and studied in Mexico and Spain, and is fluent in Spanish and French. Once a member of the New Democratic Party (NDP), at university he was involved in anti-Apartheid groups. Idealistic, with a social conscience, and an urge to solve social problems, especially those involving the environment and Aboriginal issues, he currently is employed by the International Development Research Centre (IDRC) in Ottawa. At age 11, he accompanied his family on a trip to Scotland.

More recently, he has travelled on his own to England, but perhaps significantly did not include Scotland in the itinerary. He describes himself as Anglo-Celtic, reflecting the ethnic biography of each of his parents. Although wary of state-organized multiculturalism, he strongly supports the concept of a multicultural society free from political manipulation. He does not share his father's passion for family history. He expressed concern, indeed, about possible 'pride in ethnicity,' adding 'Sometimes I react against my father, in the sense you can refer to Scots as a race.' In Neale's opinion, it is much more enriching to focus on ethnic groups beyond those in one's own family tree.

Neale points out that one of his Scots relatives was somewhat intolerant of other ethnic groups. Neale's father was considerably more caustic about some of his Scottish Canadian relatives, one of whom apparently was an outright racist who vowed that 'no MacMillan would ever marry a black.'

Since childhood, Neale had been aware of the Metis connection in his family history. As a teenager, he realized his family tree also included West Indians. From his point of view, it may well have been tiresome to grow up in a family in which the daily topic at the dinner table was the intriguing lives of his Scots ancestors. Yet in the end he regarded the contacts with his West Indian and Metis relatives as a valuable gift from his father. He hopes that these contacts will increase, since they 'give you a better sense of solidarity with different groups.'

The attitudes expressed by Neale were similar to those revealed by his older brother Ian, who holds BA and MA degrees in history.[8] Currently employed as the collections manager at Fulford House in Brockville, Ontario, Ian too was active in the NDP and concerned about environmental issues. In a sense, his interests in Scottish history seem simultaneously closer and more distant to his father's than are those of his brother. He commented on the influence of spending his first seven years in Glengarry County, which unavoidably made him conscious of being

Scottish. He too had accompanied his family to Scotland when he was a teenager, and in fact he returned there on his own when he was twenty-three years old. He also expresses admiration towards migrants of Scottish origin, whom he thought were much more adaptable to their new environments than were the English, and less ethnocentric. Ian also has conducted his own research on Scottish people, although his interests, as he pointed out, are more in labour history than in family trees. What worries him about people like his father who dwell on ethnic roots is that their interests can grow into 'bourgeois nationalism.' In the end, however, he too echoes the views of his brother, and of the children of Dr Clarke, all of whom expressed pleasure that their generation had been brought together.

Several years ago an American businessman met the president of Haiti. 'What percentage of your people are white?' asked the businessman. 'About 99 percent,' came the answer. The stunned businessman blurted out, 'How in the world do you define white?' The president countered, 'In America, how do you define black?' The businessman's answer was 'Anyone with black blood.' The bemused president beamed and replied, 'That, of course, is precisely how we define white.'

This apocryphal tale serves to remind us that there are no pure races, in the biological sense, anywhere in this world. Homo sapiens has been around too long, and population movements and inter-marriage have been too extensive, to produce any other outcome. As a result of colonialism, and the labour needs of the plantations, the degree of ethnic heterogeneity may be particularly pronounced in the Caribbean, although with each passing decade Canada moves closer to its model. I do not mean to suggest that ethnic relations, even in a heterogeneous society, are always (or even usually) harmonious. However, it is human consciousness, the striving for power, and the part played by ethnocentrism, scapegoating and xenophobia – not our genetic makeup – that divides us. Then, too, there is the matter of social class. Any attempt to understand ethnic relations in today's world cannot ignore the class factor. The Brazilian expression 'money whitens' is apparently true for the Caribbean. In other words, the very conception of race is shaped by the cultural idiom.

Human beings are adaptable creatures. Take a child of British origin from Canada and raise her in a family in Italy or Japan, and the child becomes culturally Italian or Japanese. One could go further: dress most of us up in the clothing worn by people in other cultures, and our own ethnic identity would disappear. This scenario is especially appropriate to the Caribbean. While it is true that African descendants constitute the largest single ethnic base there, it is an error to assume, as so many Canadians seem to do, that all West Indians look the same.

The story of the emigration of the three Scotsmen to the West Indies, the subsequent assimilation of their offspring into a multi-ethnic society, and the bringing together of the Clarkes and the MacMillans strikes me as wonderfully positive. The Clarkes, by moving to Canada, have kept the connection between Canada and the West Indies alive. Perhaps the next step will be up to this generation of the Canadian branch of the MacMillan clan – following in the footsteps of their ancestors, and making lives for themselves in the sunny Caribbean.

### NOTES

1. Before emigrating to the West Indies, Ranald and Allan lived briefly in Canada. Archibald may have done so as well, but this is not clear from available documents.

2. Bonham C. Richardson, *Caribbean Migrants*, (Knoxville: The University of Tennessee Press, 1983), 63.

3. K.O. Laurence, *Immigration into the West Indies in the 19th Century* (Kingston, Jamaica: Caribbean Universities Press, 1971), 9.

4. Private Archives of Hugh P. MacMillan, Letter, Captain Dugald Cameron of the Grenada Loyal Black Rangers to his father in Scotland, 1801.

5. Richardson, *Caribbean Migrants*, 49.

6. Interview with Canadian of West Indian origin who wishes to remain anonymous, December 1993.

7. I interviewed three members of the Clarke family, three members of Hugh MacMillan's family, and two people unconnected to the MacMillan clan who were born and raised in the West Indies, but now live in Canada.

8. A cultural preference for golden brown may well have existed in the Caribbean when Dr Clarke was a young man, but the black is beautiful movement in the 1960s and 1970s probably rendered it obsolete.

9. Although Guyana is located on the continent of South America, she stated that West Indians consider it to be part of the Caribbean.

10. Such open-mindedness cannot be taken for granted as I learned first hand in one of my other research projects, involving in part interviewing people in rural Ontario whose progenitors included African Canadians (See Stanley Barrett, *Paradise: Class, Commuters and Ethnicity in Rural Ontario* (Toronto: University of Toronto Press, 1994). As a result of several generations of inter-marriage, the physical appearance of the current generation was European. There was considerable opposition in the region to investigations into family history, and denial of one's black ancestors was the rule rather than the exception.

11. The interview with Ian MacMillan was conducted by telephone, and thus lacks the quality and depth of the other interviews.

12. The use of the term 'ethnic' here is intentional. To regard Africa as one homogenous 'race' is quite ridiculous. In Nigeria alone, there are about 250 distinct ethnic groups, speaking separate languages, and over 800 major dialects.

# PART V

# WESTERN CONNECTIONS

# CHAPTER 8

# WESTWARD
# FROM
# GLENGARRY

HUGH P. MacMILLAN

*I*n order to understand the motivations of Highland emigrants coming to Canada, it is essential to consider the social, political, and economic structure of Highland Scottish society of the late eighteenth century. Marianne McLean's *The People Of Glengarry* shows that Highlanders viewed land as a communal resource held in trust by the chief on behalf of the

HUGH P. MacMILLAN, U.E., antiquarian and writer was born in 1924 at Fitzroy Harbour, Ontario, the oldest son of Rev. John A. MacMillan and Dulcie Pearson. He claims being brought up in a Presbyterian manse is a mixed blessing. He has been at various times a soldier, sailor, farmer, salesman, publicist, and even a promoter for a circus and a hypnotist. Throughout all, he maintained an active interest in family history. Later, he became field officer with the Archives of Ontario. In 1984 he was granted an honorary Doctor of Letters degree from Laurentian University, Sudbury, Ontario, for his pioneering work in the acquisition of manuscript and pictorial material by means of investigative genealogical research, field trips, lectures and publicity. He now resides at Guelph, Ontario with his wife Muriel and remains active as a collector, dealer, appraiser, and lecturer in the field of family history and antiquities.

clan, which had access to land in return for rent. Highland agriculture was successful in maintaining a balance between the needs of the community and available physical resources. After the Jacobite defeat in 1746, Highland society came increasingly under the control of the '… capitalistic, oligarchic Kingdom of Great Britain.' Highland elites soon adopted the profit motive and rents were to be paid in currency rather than in personal service or produce in kind. The introduction of capital-intensive sheep farming resulted in eviction of tenants. Highlanders had to choose between migrating to the Lowlands or overseas. Marianne McLean suggests that those emigrating were not rejecting social change but were refusing the meagre offering that social and economic change left them in escalating rents or a future as landless labourers.

The 2,300 inhabitants of the Lochiel estate were not spared. Between 1788 and 1804, rents increased more than eightfold on Locharkaigside.[1] In 1803, Archibald McMillan expressed his horror to his friend, Allan Cameron:

Lochiel's lands are in the Papers to be let at Whitsuntide first, nothing but spurring and hauling, and I am afraid, the tenantry have no chance. What think you of £2,000 being offered for Glendessary, Glenkingy, Moncuach as report goes, and I believe that the highest bidder for rent, whether Moffat or Lochaber, will be preferred.

The following year, Cameron wrote that 'great are the changes that have taken place along both sides of Lock Arkaig, every single tenant is to be dispossessed.'[2] This was a time of major social disruption for the tenants of Lochiel and for Highlanders in general, and over 3,000 of them left for America in 1802. Emigration to British North American and to the United States offered an alternative whereby their community could remain relatively intact and where its members did not necessarily have to sell their labour.

Duncan Ban McMillan (1783-1861), son of John Ban McMillan (1729-1820) and Christian McCalman (1743-1807), was among those dispossessed from their traditional land holdings. Like many other Highlanders seeking employment, Duncan at age eighteen or nineteen ventured south to Glasgow, a 'dignified and impressive city.'[3] Although Highlanders were sometimes described as 'a pastoral, a fishing, or an agricultural people not suited to work in factories or to weaving,'[4] Duncan himself worked as a weaver.[5] In the late eighteenth century the handloom weaving industry remained almost entirely domestic, with weavers working in their homes or in an adjacent loom shed. When Duncan joined the trade, it was in a period of rapid expansion. The number of Scottish cotton weavers increased from 8,000 to 50,000 between 1792 and 1803, a period known as the 'golden age' of hand-loom weaving, when real income was relatively high. Unlike factory work, domestic weaving did not require any major organizational or institutional changes for weavers and their families. Working a handloom was far removed from the tyranny of factory hours and discipline, and relatively little capital was needed to enter the trade.

The majority of weavers appear to have belonged to weavers' societies and nearly all villages in Scotland had one. The Paisley and Glasgow societies were at the heart of the movement. Besides providing benefits to members and their families upon unemployment, sickness, or death, weavers' societies had three goals: to maintain trade standards by insisting on a seven-year apprenticeship; to stop all forms of embezzlement in the industry; and to have magistrates fix reasonable wage rates for weavers in the cotton trade. An attempt to implement the last objective led to the Scottish handloom weavers' strike of 1812, after legal judgements in favour of the weavers did not bring improved wages. The strike was lost, and the weavers began returning to work in January 1813. Whether he participated or not, Duncan could not help but have been affected by the strike.

As was true in Duncan's case, weaving was often combined with other occupations, the most common of which was agriculture, taken up when weaving work was unavailable due to cyclical market slumps. A downturn in the weaving trade at the end of the Napoleonic Wars may have persuaded Duncan to return to his family. His opportunity to emigrate came in the early months of 1815 through a program devised by Lord Bathurst, the Secretary for War and the Colonies. The first public notice of the emigration program appeared in Edinburgh and Glasgow newspapers in late February of 1815 under the heading 'Liberal Encouragement to Settlers.' The encouragement was indeed liberal: each applicant received transportation to the colony, free grants of 100 acres of land for each head of a family and for sons on coming of age, rations for eight months or until establishment; axes, ploughs, and other implements at prime cost; and a minister and school teacher on government salary. In return, applicants had to supply testimonials to their 'general good character' obtainable from 'Justices of the Peace, Clergymen or Elders of the Parish, or other respectable persons,'[6] as well as a deposit of £16, to be returned two years later when the emigrant was settled. Duncan was eager to emigrate to Canada, for he was the first to register for the program.

Vessels carrying the emigrants left the Clydeside city of Greenock on 11 July 1815, and the arrival of the vessels in Quebec City was announced in the *Montreal Herald* on 9 September 1815. At about the same time, Lord Bathurst was informed by the Lieutenant Governor of Ontario that 'the lands in the vicinity of Glengarry in

> the Eastern District, I wish to reserve for the new settlers from Scotland. They will be more comfortable, and will prosper more rapidly, under the friendly assistance and Local Knowledge of their countrymen, than if dispersed over more distant parts of the country, and the Eastern District when fully located will be a powerful support to the Province in either Peace or War.'[7]

The number of prospective emigrants from the Highlands had exceeded expectations of government officials and more than half of the 699 participants settled in Glengarry County. During the winter of 1815-16, the settlers stayed in the communities of Lancaster, Cornwall, Brockville, and Kingston along the lower St. Lawrence.

Since Duncan had relatives in Finch township, he probably proceeded there in the fall of 1815, where he was located on the south half of lot 23 in the 3rd concession. By then, Finch was one of the last settled townships in the area, because of its distance from the Ottawa and St. Lawrence Rivers. While surrounding townships had grown to several hundred people, only fifteen settlers were assessed in Finch, including McMillans and Camerons who had been brought to Finch in the previous decade by Allan 'Glenpean' McMillan. Walking through the primeval forest of Finch Township, Duncan Ban McMillan would have discovered only 182 acres of cleared arable pasture and meadow. The township's livestock consisted of forty-seven horses, fifty-one milking cows, and five 'young horned cattle.' Finch could not boast of any substantial homes, store houses, shops, or saw mills. From

this inauspicious beginning, it would appear that Finch developed relatively quickly. In 1820, Agnes McKinnon petitioned the government for the deed to her property, a request normally granted only after the land had been improved. In the petition she stated that her late husband had been a Sergeant in the 1st Battalion of the Royal Scot's and that on his discharge at Quebec he was located by Lieutenant Angus McDonell in Finch township. Her husband had improved the land 'to the extent of ten acres, & Built a House and Barn, that since his decease Petitioner has Built a Saw Mill and a Grist Mill, and improved thirty Acres more of the said half Lot, on which her sons continue to improve.'[8] The 1829 map of Finch shows that nearly all land had been settled or allocated.

Soon after Duncan arrived in Ontario he married Mary McMillan, between late 1815 and early 1817. Mary was born in 1794 at Achnacarry, the place name given to Cameron of Lochiel's home at the eastern end of Loch Arkaig. Her parents, Angus McMillan of Callich, Loch Arkaig, and Margaret McMaster of Corriebeg, Loch Eil, had emigrated to Canada in 1802, in the party of Allan Glenpean McMillan, and settled on Lot 20 in the 1st concession of Finch.[9] Duncan and Mary's first child, Daniel, was born in 1817. During his first few years in Canada, Duncan would have been occupied clearing and preparing his farmland to grow crops. It is difficult to determine whether he did any weaving. In the United Kingdom weavers were counted among the unemployed. Yet in 1819, Hugh McEwan, a resident of Glengarry, wrote to his brother:

> If you come out you will bring your reads [for weaving]. Bring also temples and shuttles. All iron work is very dear here; so you had better bring with you whatever your loom requires. Endeavour to furnish yourself well with body clothes, especially wearing clothes. Woollen cloth is high in price here as for linen, it is little used for it stands up no time in this place.[10]

Although there may have been a short-term demand for some woven goods, in Glengarry and Stormont the weaving loom was known as the 'four posts of poverty' by the late 1820s.[11]

Once his farm was established, Duncan became active in the religious, social, and political life of the community. He served as a Treasurer and Elder in the late 1830s of the founding committee of St. Luke's Presbyterian Church located on the south west corner of lot 19, concession 2, land donated by Cole McMillan in 1836. Land for the 'McMillan Cemetery' was donated by Ann McMillan on lot 19, concession 1.[12] McMillans dominated membership of the congregation, and many of Duncan and Mary's children were no doubt married at St. Luke's, including Daniel (to Isabella Sutherland); Mary (to Allan Morrison), Angus D.B. (to Margery McMillan); and Margaret (to Joseph R. Sutherland).

Duncan also participated on the local education board, as a School Commissioner for Finch township. In this capacity he and the residents of Finch petitioned the Warden and Municipal Council of the Eastern District about an education act passed in 1841. Before 1841, funding for schools was provided from general provincial revenues. The new education act placed the onus for school taxes on the local community. On 1 August 1842, Duncan sent a petition on behalf of the residents of Finch, asking the government not to 'force upon them the new Law, for Establishing Schools among them

> by Taxation, as they are not as yet able to bear such, being in a great measure a new Settlement, therefore would humbly request to remain under the old Law for Establishing Schools, which we earnestly pray should Continue, As to hire our own teachers and pay them according to the arrangements we have already made with some of them or may hereafter make, which is generally by paying the greatest part of their Salaries in produce which is of great advantage to us, as we are far from Markets to make money out of our produce, and your petitioners would further

humbly and respectfully Solicit through your Honourable Council, a Continuation of the Government Allowance of School money, as we have had heretofore, and your Petitioners will ever pray....[13]

The petition makes it clear that the Highland residents of Finch were still accustomed to the barter economy which they had known in Scotland and wished to pay salaries for teachers 'in produce [,] which is of great advantage to us.' The concerns of the residents of Finch and of many other communities led to the withdrawal of the education act eighteen months after its introduction.

In order to reach the local church and school, residents of Finch required passable roads. Maintaining this service was the principal duty of Duncan as the Superintendent of 'Pathmasters,' local officials responsible for the maintenance of roads. They were nominated and elected by taxpayers on the first Monday in March of each year, in townships with not less than thirty householders. Duncan, along with the town clerk, John Cockburn, and several other office holders petitioned the Eastern District Council about the condition of Finch Township's roads, complaining that they had 'difficulty in admonishing the trespasser to remove the obstruction [perhaps a tree? a shanty?]. Your Petitioners therefore trust your Honorable council will pass some act expressly compelling the trespassers under fine and Penalties to remove these obstructions after some certain number of Days notice and your Petitioners as in Duty Bound will ever Pray.'[14]

Inverness County, Scotland, from which the McMillans had emigrated, was the largest and best wooded county of Great Britain, containing 163,000 acres of wood.[15] In nineteenth century Canada, exports of timber surpassed fur, and after farming, the timber trade became the most important economic activity in the settled regions of Canada during Duncan's lifetime. The Scots were drawn to the trade, and according to historian Arthur Lower, they filled most of the important positions in the trade. 'Apart from their role as entrepreneurs and merchants,' Lower notes, 'the Scots held specialized positions in the industry. Scottish Canadians from Glengarry County and the St. Lawrence Front were the teamsters in the camps and, along with Scots direct from Scotland, the mechanics in the mills. About 1847 over two thousand teams, it was said, used to go every year from Glengarry and the Front to the camps above Bytown (today's Ottawa).'[16]

Soon after the area was settled, Duncan B. McMillan's father-in-law, Angus McMillan, owned a small sawmill on lot 14 of the 3rd concession of Finch.[17] Built at a cost of between one and two thousand dollars, Angus McMillan's mill supplied lumber for local consumption, for instance for the building of St. Luke's Presbyterian Church in 1840. By 1851, however, the mill appears to have been abandoned. John Cockburn, the town clerk responsible for taking the census that year, stated that 'there is one old Saw Mill on the Payne River in the 3rd Concession but is almost good for nothing belonging to the aforesaid Alex. B. McMillan.' The mill was probably in disuse for a number of reasons: it was upstream from the main timber supply, and it had become outdated. The timber trade throughout Eastern Canada was depressed from 1846 to 1849 owing to a lack of demand and overproduction. Increasingly, finished products produced at sawmills became the norm. The mill appears, however, on the 1862 map of the United Counties.

About 1850, Duncan B. and Mary McMillan's second eldest son, John, left for Wisconsin. During the mid-nineteenth century it was common for Canadians to migrate to the midwestern and northern United States where agricultural land was available. By the 1850s most arable agricultural land in southern Ontario had been occupied. Glengarry's population doubled from 8,500 in 1832, to 17,596 in 1852. The United States was a frontier for Canadians, just as Ontario had been a frontier for Americans earlier in the century. In 1852, shortly after John McMillan arrived in Wisconsin, he was joined by his younger brother, Alexander, with whom John formed a partnership. Their company, the Black River Logging Company, had its headquarters at La Crosse, and it took the first log raft down the Mississippi to St. Louis in 1853. It was a good time to invest in the timber trade since American demand increased 200 percent in five years and Chicago had become the greatest lumber market in the world.[18]

Like Minnesota, Wisconsin had a highly concentrated supply of high quality pine which could be harvested for the large midwestern and Chicago markets. In 1859 John and Alexander were joined by their younger brother Duncan D. McMillan, who had been working at lumbering in Canada West,[19] an era chronicled in Ralph Connor's *The Man from Glengarry*. Duncan worked with his brothers in the lumber trade of Wisconsin until 1861, when he began to study law at the La Crosse Law offices of yet another brother, Ewan Hugh McMillan.

Meanwhile in Ontario, Duncan Ban McMillan died at his farm in Finch township on 10 August 1861 at the age of 77. The first bequest in Duncan's will was that his soul be given 'to him who gave it in the certain hope of a glorious resurrection.' The farm was inherited by Angus Duncan Ban McMillan, Duncan B.'s son, born in 1829, probably because he was the only son who had stayed at home. Besides, Daniel, his eldest brother, already had a farm in Finch township.

With the farm came many responsibilities. Angus had to 'maintain and support his unmarried sister [Catherine] till … married or otherwise provided for.' If she married, the will stipulated that 'she shall have two cows and one heifer and also Bed and Bedding the same to be given when convenient.' Livestock was still an important form of wealth. No actual currency changed hands in Duncan's will. In addition, Angus had to care for Duncan B.'s 'Dear Sister [Sarah (1766-1863) emigrated to Canada 1823] who [was] in the ninety fifth year of her age [and provide for her] the use of the Room in which she now reside[d] during her life with Comfortable Bed and Bedding and all other necessaries....'

Although Duncan's wife Mary had 'the use of all my stock of cattle and personal property.... After her decease my will is that the same shall belong to my son Angus McMillan his heirs and assigns for ever.' If Angus D.B. had no heirs upon his death, the farm was to be inherited by his brother Duncan D., provided that he return from Wisconsin within six months. Were he not to do so, the property would be left to Daniel's son George. In other words the property would revert to the eldest son of the eldest son.[20]

Duncan Ban McMillan had accomplished a great deal during his life in Stormont County. He was active in the religious and social life of the community, in establishing St. Luke's Presbyterian Church, and a School, and thereby helped to solidify the social foundations of the County. He was materially better off than he likely would have been had he remained in Scotland. Unlike most Scottish farmers, he owned his own farm and during the last decade of his life built one of the few stone houses in Finch township for himself and his family.

Duncan D. McMillan had been in the United States for just two years when he became involved in the Civil War by accepting 'a clerkship in the Quartermaster's Department, at Memphis, Tenn., under Col. A.R. Eddy, a position he held during portions of 1863 and 1864.'[21] On his return to Wisconsin, Duncan bought an interest in his brothers' lumber business. Together, they formed the Black River Improvement Company (BRIC) to which the Wisconsin Legislature granted an exclusive franchise for logging and transportation on one of the states's major rivers. BRIC was to keep the river clear of obstacles causing log jams, as well as to build timber chutes around major obstacles. In return, it was given the privilege of collecting tolls from other companies using the Black River. 'It has been fully demonstrated by the experience of ten years,' explained a Wisconsin Legislative Committee, upon granting the franchise, 'that individual effort would do but little for the improve-

ment of the navigation of the river, and hence the necessity of some organized corporate effort became apparent, both to the loggers and manufacturers of lumber on the river.'[22]

BRIC had just been formed when John McMillan, the first brother to follow the timber trade from Ontario to Wisconsin, died in 1865. The company then passed into the sole ownership of Alexander and Duncan. In 1866 Duncan D. married Mary J. McCrea, daughter of Stephen McCrea and Elizabeth Johnston, of Huntington County Quebec.[23] The social ties of 'greater Glengarry' were still intact even though Duncan had been in the United States for seven years. Duncan D. and Mary settled in La Crosse where Duncan continued his business activities.

Daniel McMillan, Duncan's eldest brother, came to La Crosse in 1867 from Finch with his wife Isabella Sutherland and their ten children. Daniel had been engaged in farming and lumbering in Ontario. George McMillan, Daniel's eldest son, had moved to Wisconsin in 1863 and studied civil engineering in the office of Bliss and Sill until his appointment as Superintendent of the La Crosse Gas Works owned by his uncles, Duncan D. and Alexander. The purpose of Daniel's visit to Wisconsin may have been to visit his son and brothers, or it may have been to become engaged in the business activities of his brothers. In 1868, while in Wisconsin, Daniel died at the age of fifty-one. Daniel's wife gave birth to their youngest son, Daniel, while in the United States. She then returned to Stormont County, Ontario with her eleven children.

Agriculture, religion and local education allowed Duncan Ban McMillan and fellow Lochaber emigrants in Finch township to maintain familiar lifestyles. The emigration of Duncan's sons to Wisconsin demonstrated that they were able to adapt to changing economic circumstances. Chain migration brought Duncan Ban to Finch to be among fellow Highlanders. So too Alexander, Duncan D. and Ewan

Hugh followed their elder brother John to Wisconsin where they became leading citizens of La Crosse. Although only a few of these people became millionaires, the movement and success of McMillans westward from Ontario to the American midwest is typical of many Glengarry families.[24]

## NOTES

1. Marianne McLean, *The People of Glengarry*, (Montreal and Kingston: McGill-Queen's University Press 1991), 74.

2. Cameron's letters quoted in Somerled MacMillan's *Bygone Lochaber*, (Glasgow: K. & R. Davidson 1971), 81 and 182.

3. Robert and William Chambers, *The Gazetteer of Scotland* (Edinburgh 1832), 468.

4. Norman Murray, *The Scottish Handloom Weavers 1790-1850: A Social History*, (Edinburgh: John Donald Publishers Ltd. 1978), 31.

5. National Archives of Canada (NA), MG 11, CO 385, Vol. 2, John Campbell's registry book for the emigration of 1815.

6. *Glasgow Herald*, 27 February 1815, 3.

7. Royce McGillivray, and Ewen Ross, *A History of Glengarry*, (Belleville: Mika 1979), 38.

8. Archives of Ontario (AO), *Township papers*, Finch Township, 0286.

9. The place of origin is confirmed by Finch Township Land Records; see also S. McMillan, *Bygone Lochaber*, 81.

10. Glengarry Historical Society, *Glengarry Life*, (Cornwall: GHS 1986), 13.

11. McGillivray and Ross, *A History of Glengarry*, 44.

12. AO, MU 537 #7 (Transcript of ledger book of founding committee of St. Luke's Presbyterian Church).

13. AO, Ms 40, reel 3, School petitions.

14. AO, MS 40, reel 2, Road Petitions.

15. The Rev. John Grant's *Old Statistical Account of Abernathy and Kincardine*, written in 1794, contains detailed information on the timber trade in the Highlands and references to saw mills and rafting timber. On the Spey River, west of Loch Arkaig, 'the quantity of spars, deals [planks of a minimum size], logs, masts and ship-timber, which they send to Garmouth or Speymouth yearly, is immense, every stage of the manufactory, brings money to the country; generally once a year they send down Spey a loose float, as they call it, of about 12,000 pieces of timber of various kinds; whence they send it to England, or sell it round the coast' (130-5).

16. A.R.M. Lower, *Great Britain's Woodyard: British North America and the Timber Trade 1763-1867*, (Montreal: McGill-Queen's University Press 1973), 187. Lower also notes that 'a list of the names of the great lumber families of Canada would almost sound like a roll-call of the Scottish clans – Frasers, MacLarens, Gilmours, Gillies, McLaughlins et al. Most of the founders of these families or firms began at the bottom.'

17. This property had one of the mill sites originally owned by Allan Glenpean McMillan. At one time, he or his sons owned all potential mill sites in the township.

18. *Charlton's Annual Review of the Market for Timber* (Quebec: [Publisher Unknown] 1855); and the Cornwall *Freeholder*, Obituary of Alexander McMillan, 1901.

19. *History of Northern Wisconsin*, (Chicago: Western Historical Company 1881), 476. There were other early McMillan settlers in Wisconsin, but their relationship to the McMillans from Finch Township is unknown. Details on these other McMillan settlers in Wisconsin can be found in the *Wisconsin Historical Collection*, Vol. IV, 383-92.

20. The Stormont County Land Record Office, Cornwall, Ontario, holds Duncan's will. Duncan's executors were his eldest son, Daniel, his son-in-law, Allan Morrison, and his brother-in-law, John McMillan Cnoc (Gaelic for 'hill').

21. *History of Northern Wisconsin*, 477.

22. James Willard Hurst, *Law and Economic Growth; the legal history of the lumber industry in Wisconsin, 1836-1915*, (Cambridge, Mass.: Harvard University Press 1964), 235.

23. *History of Northern Wisconsin*, 477.

24. McGillivray and Ross, *A History of Glengarry*, 451.

# CHAPTER 9

# THE INDIAN–METIS CONNECTION: JAMES McMILLAN AND HIS DESCENDANTS

HEATHER DEVINE

*A* very steady, plain blunt man, shrewd & sensible of correct conduct and good character, but who has gone through a vast deal of severe duty and is fit for any Service requiring physical strength firmness of mind and good management provided he has no occasion to meddle with Pen & Ink in the use of which he is deficient his Education having been neglected. An excellent Trader, speaks several Indian languages and is very regular and Economical in all his arrangements; a good practical Man, better adapted for the executive than the Legislative departments of the business. His plain blunt manner however cannot conceal a vast deal of little highland pride,

HEATHER DEVINE is an independent cultural heritage consultant in Edmonton. She holds an advanced degree in secondary education (Educational Media) and is currently a doctoral student in history at the University of Alberta. She has published and presented numerous articles on curriculum development in archaeology, Native history, and heritage interpretation. Her current research and publication interests include Métis and fur trade ethnohistory, cultural resource management, and archival studies.

and his prejudices are exceedingly strong, but upon the whole he is among the most respectable of his class and a generally useful Man.[1]

James McMillan was thus described by his old friend, Governor George Simpson. The year was 1832, and McMillan had spent about thirty years in the fur trade.

Who was this man, this plain, blunt man of great physical strength, who spoke several languages yet, according to Simpson, at least, was unskilled with pen and ink? This respectful man who was proud and prejudiced? Born in Scotland about 1783, James McMillan was nineteen when he emigrated to Glengarry, Upper Canada, in 1802. James' father, Allan McMillan of Glenpean, Loch Arkaig, Scotland, and Allan's cousin Archibald McMillan, had chartered three brigs, the *Friends*, the *Helen*, and the *Jane*, to carry relatives and members of forty-seven other families to Glengarry in 1802. On board was James. In Glengarry, he and fellow passengers joined relatives and friends who had moved from New York State to Glengarry after the American Revolution.[2]

Soon James McMillan became a clerk with the North West Company, the commercial enterprise formed in Montreal in the 1770s with the amalgamation of several small companies operated by fur traders and merchants, mostly Scottish. For many Highland expatriates like James, participation in the fur trade provided an arduous but lucrative avenue for social and economic improvement. The opportunity to accumulate considerable wealth in a comparatively short time appealed to young Highlanders dispossessed by the Clearances and other economic changes in Scotland. Also the fur trade offered adventure and freedom from the strictures of settlement life. During the late 1700s and early 1800s, many men from Glengarry found employment as clerks and labourers in the North West Company.

Like many other fur traders, James contracted unions with native women *à la façon du pays* (according to the custom of the country) shortly after arriving in the interior. In addition to providing companionship to lonely traders, marriage to a native woman reinforced trading alliances with local native bands, thus ensuring a steady supply of furs and provisions. A novice trader learned aboriginal social etiquette from his kinsmen and wilderness skills from his native father-in-law.[3] Aboriginal women's knowledge of local culture and languages enabled them to function as interpreters and brokers between Euro-Canadian traders and Indian groups. These women were also excellent guides, for they were familiar with waterways and landscape. In addition, they gathered berries, edible root vegetables, wild rice, sap, and medicinal plants; they hunted small animals and birds; they caught fish, and prepared pemmican; and they manufactured canoes, processed hides, strung snowshoes, sewed moccasins and other clothing.[4]

During James McMillan's tenure in the fur trade, he contracted three successive 'country' marriages, first to Josette Beleisle, daughter of a Canadien *engagé* (contract labourer) and Josephte, a native woman. At the time, McMillan was a clerk in the Fort des Prairies Department, his first posting (ca. 1804-1808). The

Department covered a wide area, roughly what is now central Alberta.[5]

In 1808, James McMillan was transferred to the North West Company's Columbia Department, a vast and disputed area of the Pacific Northwest including present-day southern British Columbia and the states of Oregon and Washington. In March of that year, McMillan made the first of many trips across the mountains from Fort Augustus (near today's Edmonton) to Kootenay House, located on the Columbia River on the western slopes of the Rocky Mountains, returning to Fort Augustus with a load of furs. Later that year, he made a second trip to the mountains to deliver horses to David Thompson, a colleague in the Columbia Department. The two men met at Kootenay Plains, on the eastern slopes of the Rockies, near Rocky Mountain House, Alberta. There they wintered and traded with the Kootenay Indians. In the spring of 1809, McMillan was once again in the Saskatchewan region, returning to the Kootenay area later that year.[6] This pattern of migration between the Columbia River region and posts of the eastern slopes of the Rockies and on the North Saskatchewan River continued in subsequent years. During this time, McMillan was also situated at Spokane House near the Lower Columbia River and at Saleesh House,[7] at Clark's Forks in Montana.

Perhaps because he was more permanently situated in the Columbia region, James McMillan dissolved the union between himself and Josette Beleisle through a process known as 'turning off,'[8] whereby a trader transferred responsibility for the welfare of his wife and children to another trader in exchange for some form of financial settlement, usually an annuity to provide financial support for the family left behind. This custom was practised when a trader left the interior to accept responsibilities elsewhere.[9]

Soon after his transfer in 1808, McMillan took a second country wife, Marie Letendre, daughter of Jean-Baptiste Letendre, a Canadien *engagé,* and an Indian woman.

By 1821 James McMillan's distinguished service in

the North West Company had earned him the rank of Chief Trader of the Columbia District in the restructured Hudson's Bay Company, formed by the amalgamation of the North West and Hudson's Bay companies in 1821. James was now in charge of the vast Columbia District. About the same time, McMillan 'turned off' his second wife. Perhaps new responsibilities required him to establish alliances with tribal groups in the Oregon region of the Pacific Northwest where American fur traders, under the command of John Jacob Astor, competed fiercely, often violently, with British-Canadian traders, especially after 1821. James McMillan contracted a third country union with Kilakotah (Marguerite), daughter of the Clatsop sub-chief Coboway of the Chinook tribe and a relative of Chief Concomly. Kilakotah had been married to a clerk in Astor's Pacific Fur Company.[10]

In 1822-23 McMillan was granted furlough to attend to family business in Glengarry.[11] Upon his return he accompanied George Simpson, Governor of the Hudson's Bay Company, on a long journey from York Factory on Hudson Bay to Fort George on the Columbia. Later, McMillan led a party exploring the lower Fraser River area. After returning from that region with Simpson in 1825, he was given the responsibility for Fort Assiniboine, on the Athabaska River, about 160 kilometres north west of Fort Edmonton. That same autumn, he supervised a survey of the trail

**Kilakotah (Marguerite), a daughter of the Clatsop sub-chief Coboway of the Chinook tribe, and third country wife (ca. 1821-1829) of James McMillan. (Courtesy of Harriet Duncan Munnick, West Linn, Oregon)**

from Jasper House in the Rockies to the head of the Fraser River west of Jasper. Highly impressed, the Committee of the Hudson's Bay Company informed Governor Simpson that 'such spirited conduct is entitled to our warmest commendations, and we trust that the example of Mr. McMillan will be followed by every Gentleman in the service.'[12] By 1827 McMillan had been appointed to the position of Chief Factor in the Columbia Department, and that same year he established Fort Langley on the Fraser River.

By 1828, however, years of privations, injuries and stress had taken their toll. On 21 January 1828, he wrote to his friend, John MacLeod, at Kamloops: 'I do not know when I will be allowed to quit this side of the mountains but to be plain with you my good sir I am tired of it. I would willingly be quit of it.'[13] McMillan's exhaustion had already been noted by Governor Simpson, who decided to transfer him out of the Columbia Department in order that he might 'enjoy a little repose in some one or other of the peaceful retreats of Ruperts Land.'[14] In the spring of 1829, McMillan left the Columbia Department. At Fort Garry, he was joined by Governor Simpson in his journey eastward to Upper Canada.[15] Accompanied by Simpson, McMillan went on furlough to Scotland in 1829-30, returning with a Scottish bride, Eleanor McKinley, and an infant daughter. McKinley was the sister of newly-appointed Hudson's Bay Company clerk (later Chief Trader) Archibald McKinley.[16] The couple settled in Red River, where McMillan managed the Experimental Station at Red River, not an entirely successful tenure. In 1834, he was transferred to the Lake of Two Mountains District in the Montreal Department. He was granted furlough once again in 1837, and lived with his brother John at Pointe Fortune on the Ottawa River.

James McMillan retired from service on 1 June 1839 and by 1841, he was living in Scotland with his Scottish wife and their large family. During the 1840s and 50s McMillan was proprietor of Alexandria House on the outskirts of Perth.[17] He was mentioned frequently in the correspondence of other fur traders travelling

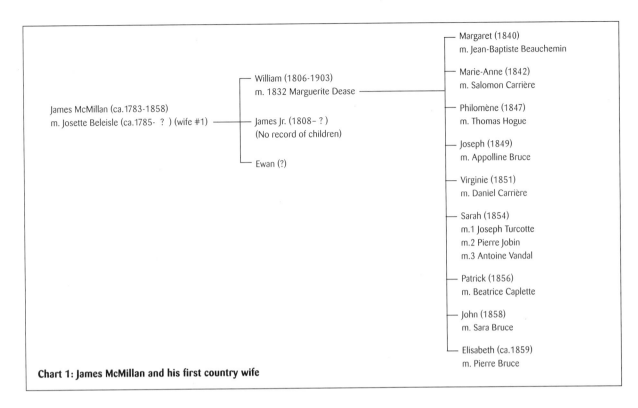

**Chart 1: James McMillan and his first country wife**

through, or resident in, Scotland. In 1847 Robert Cowie paid the McMillan family a visit, noting that 'the house is very good with 17 acres cost[ing] £1800 for which he has been offered £2300.' Cowie was less impressed by the McMillans' eight 'rather rough' children.[18]

James McMillan's Scottish business ventures were largely unsuccessful, and his final years were plagued by poverty and ill health. The considerable correspondence (ca. 1841-1869) between James McMillan, his family and the officers of the Hudson's Bay Company in London after the move to Scotland paints a poignant picture of increasingly desperate financial circumstances. James McMillan died at 15 Abbotsford Place, Glasgow, on 26 January 1858, at 75 years of age. In August of 1869, when Eleanor McMillan died, her daughters wrote to the Hudson's Bay Company one last time, requesting further financial assistance in order to bury their mother beside James in the Western Section of the Southern Necropolis cemetery, Glasgow.[19]

What became of James McMillan's three country wives and their numerous children? Fortunately for the historian, their biographies are closely intertwined with the prominent people and events of nineteenth-century Red River.

James McMillan's first country wife was Josette Beleisle (see genealogical chart #1). There were three children, William, born ca. 1806[20]; James Jr., born ca. 1808[21]; and Ewan, born shortly thereafter. Raised by his mother and her kin in the vicinity of Fort des Prairies (near today's Edmonton), he became an accomplished hunter like many of his Métis brethren. In 1825, Governor Simpson noted that William, at age eighteen was 'the boy of Mr. James MacMillan Chief Trader and [was] under no agreement with the company but never the less [would] … do anything the company require[d] of him,' and that 'he was born and brought up at the N.W. Co Fort.'[22] By 1826 William McMillan had become a contract employee of the Hudson's Bay Company, as a middleman on the York boats. He retired as a bowsman in 1835.[23]

William McMillan married Marguerite Dease[24] at

William McMillan (1806-1903), Métis son of James McMillan, with wife Margaret Dease (1813-1905). (Hugh P. MacMillan Collection, Guelph, Ontario)

St. Boniface in 1832, and settled in the parish of St. Charles. A prosperous farmer and storekeeper,[25] he imported fast horses from Kentucky for buffalo hunting.[26] The couple's nine children[27] were Margaret (born 12 January 1840[28]), Marie-Anne (18 January 1842[29]), Philomène (ca. 1847[30]), Joseph (4 December 1849[31]), Virginie (ca. 1851[32]), Sarah (5 March 1854[33]), Patrick 'Patrice' (18 May 1856[34]), John (ca. 1858[35]), and Elizabeth (ca. 1859[36]).

James McMillan and his second country wife, Marie Letendre, had four children (see genealogical chart #2). Eldest was Hélène (ca. 1811-ca. 1876).[37]2

She and husband Baptiste Boyer[38] had seven children: Emilie (ca. 1836)[39]; William (ca. 1840)[40]; Baptiste[41]; Clémence[42]; Félicité[43]; Hélène[44]; and Marguerite.[45]

The middle two children of James McMillan and Marie Letendre were Margaret (ca. 1813)[46]; and Angelique 'Nellie' (ca. 1815), who with husband John Warren Dease, Jr.,[47] produced two children: Ellen (ca. 1841)[48] and Michael (ca. 1848).[49] The fourth child of James McMillan and Marie Letendre was Allan, born

ca. 1816,[50] and there may have been a fifth child, Suzanne.[51]

Allan followed his father into the fur trade, entering the service of the Hudson's Bay Company in 1836 as an apprentice clerk. Soon he was assigned as an agent instructed to thwart the ambitions of 'General' James Dickson, allegedly a wealthy Englishman who had spent time travelling with a caravan of traders from New Orleans to Texas in 1834-35. The expedition was attacked by Mexican bandits and several members of the party were killed or wounded. Dickson managed to escape. Back in New Orleans, he vowed revenge. He secured funds in England, and by 1836 had arrived in Montreal intent upon raising an army of Indians and Métis to take California from the Mexicans by force. In Montreal he recruited several Métis sons of former Nor'Westers, including John George McKenzie, Charles McBean (McKenzie's stepbrother), John McLoughlin, Jr. and Alexander Roderick McLeod, Jr.[52]

Governor Simpson, however, feared that the volatile Dickson would stir up the Métis population and interfere with trade. Simpson set about to break up the expedition by writing letters to young McLoughlin and McLeod in September of 1836, offering

Métis group at Batoche, North West Territories, ca. 1878. Standing at left is Baptiste Boyer, son of Hélène (McMillan) Boyer, daughter of James, son of Allan McMillan. (Courtesy of Environment Canada, Parks Service, Batoche, Saskatchewan)

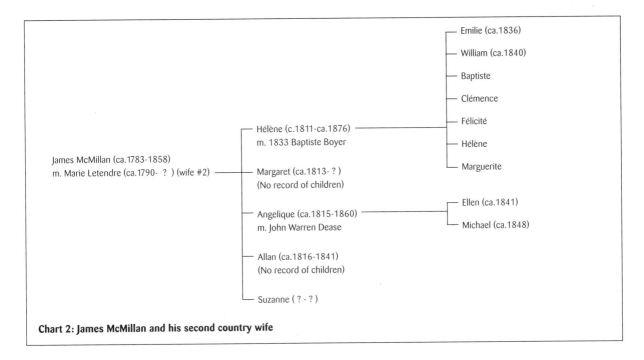

**Chart 2: James McMillan and his second country wife**

them employment in the Company's service if they would break their ties with Dickson.[53] Shortly thereafter, the Governor wrote to Chief Factor Alexander Christie, Governor of Assiniboia, informing him of his intention to employ young mixed-blood employees in the Company's service to dissuade their kinfolk from following Dickson. One of these young men was Allan McMillan, who was, thought Simpson, 'a fine, spirited, powerful, active young man and being related to the Batosh[54] family he will have a good deal of influence among the Saskatchewan Half Breeds who are the most troublesome people in the Settlet.'[55] Allan McMillan was given the responsibility of travelling westward from Lachine, Simpson's headquarters, to Red River with dispatches designed to guide senior officials in their dealings with Dickson. When McMillan reached Lake Superior in the late fall of 1836, the waterways were closed to navigation and he was forced to travel from there to Red River on snowshoes.[56]

By the spring of 1837 Dickson had abandoned his endeavours and left Red River, never to be seen again. Sickness and desertion had decimated his troop of

Métis followers, and the purported refusal of the Hudson's Bay Company to sell him supplies and provisions effectively prevented any long-distance campaigns.

Perhaps as a reward for his efforts, Allan McMillan was promoted from shopman to clerk at the Forks in the Red River Settlement, and by 1838 he had assumed the clerk's responsibilities at Fort Garry where he remained until 1841, when he was reported to have left the Company's service and retired to Upper Canada.[57]

By his third country wife, Kilakotah, James McMillan had one daughter, Victoire, born ca. 1821[58] (see genealogical chart # 3). She married three times, first to Joseph McLoughlin (ca. 1810-1848), son of Hudson's Bay Company Chief Factor John McLoughlin and Marguerite Wadin.[59] There were no children from this marriage. In 1850, Victoire married a second time, to Pierre LaCourse Jr. (1828-1861), son of Pierre LaCourse Sr., an *engagé* with the Pacific Fur Company at Astoria[60], and a Cree woman. Victoire and Pierre had six children: William (born ca. 1851, died without issue); Louis (born ca. 1852, died with-

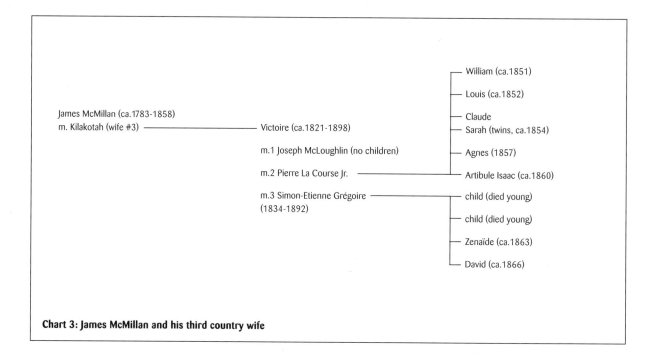

James McMillan (ca.1783-1858)
m. Kilakotah (wife #3) ———————————— Victoire (ca.1821-1898)

m.1 Joseph McLoughlin (no children)

m.2 Pierre La Course Jr.

m.3 Simon-Etienne Grégoire
(1834-1892)

William (ca.1851)

Louis (ca.1852)

Claude

Sarah (twins, ca.1854)

Agnes (1857)

Artibule Isaac (ca.1860)

child (died young)

child (died young)

Zenaïde (ca.1863)

David (ca.1866)

**Chart 3: James McMillan and his third country wife**

out issue); twins Sarah (born ca 1854, died without is-sue) and Claude, who married Malvina Bellique; Agnes (1857-1860); and Artibule Isaac (born ca. 1860, died without issue). In 1863 Victoire married a third time, to Simon-Etienne Grégoire (1834-1892), son of Etienne Grégoire, Jr. and a Saulteaux woman. The couple resided near St. Louis and had four children, two of whom died in infancy. The surviving children were Zenaïde (ca. 1863) who married a man by the surname of DuRette; and David (ca. 1866) who mar-ried Josephine Labonté[61].

Many of James McMillan's Métis descendants ex-perienced prosperity and assumed influential roles in nineteenth-century Red River. William, eldest son of James, enjoyed a relatively affluent life as a merchant and farmer in Red River even though after 1821 he spent his Hudson's Bay Company career as a boat-man. His lack of education impeded promotion.

Despite his minor status in the company, William McMillan and his family were prominent in Red River society. They enjoyed close kinship ties with other members of the ruling class whose status was determined in part by membership in the Council of

Assiniboia,[62] the governing body in Red River from 1835 until 1870, when jurisdiction over Rupert's Land passed from the Hudson's Bay Company to the gov-ernment of Canada. The Métis, who constituted the majority of Red River's people, demanded that the Hudson's Bay Company appoint members of their community to this governing body. These council-lors, representing a diverse population of farmers, hunters, and small businessmen, dealt with a variety of issues from road maintenance and business licens-ing to negotiations concerning Assiniboia's entry into Canadian Confederation in 1870. The fortunes of the McMillans, the Deases, the Brelands, and other Mc-Millan relatives are associated closely with the Coun-cil of Assiniboia.

It is thus not surprising, therefore, to find several of James McMillan's descendants inextricably tied to participants in the Red River resistance of 1869-70, and in the North-West rebellion of 1885. The Métis settlements at Red River and in the Saskatchewan River region were small communities, and most of the Métis farmers and businessmen were linked by marriage or friendship. Riel himself came from an af-

**Joseph McMillan (1848-1922) and wife Polly Bruce (1853-1922). Métis great-grandson of Allan 'Glenpean' McMillan, and son of William McMillan, Joseph spent most of his life in Winnipeg. (Courtesy of Orval McMillan, Toronto, Ontario)**

fluent Red River family, prominent in the social and political history of the community.

Today James McMillan's descendants live in communities throughout Western Canada, particularly in the Winnipeg area. Other McMillan kin related to the Red River branches of the family can be found in North Dakota and Ontario.

Not all James McMillan's Métis descendants identified with the social and political life of Red River, especially those who lived elsewhere. For instance, Victoire, McMillan's daughter by Kilakotah, was born and grew up in the Pacific Northwest. Separated from her siblings at Red River, she could not have developed a distinctive ethnic affiliation as a Métisse. Like

many mixed-race people resident in regions now part of the United States, Kilakotah's descendants did not have the opportunity to assume an aboriginal identity unless they became part of a reservation community. Their only viable option was assimilation.

This portrait of James McMillan, his achievements, his family, and his legacy elicits more questions than answers. How could a man leave behind so many children and begin a new life in Scotland? Today the values of a fur-trade society that promoted liaisons with native women, then encouraged and condoned the custom of abandoning country wives, seem alien. James McMillan, however, was responding to the rigorous demands of his profession. Furthermore, by marrying his country wives and daughters to responsible partners and by ensuring that his sons were offered opportunities in the fur trade, McMillan obeyed the customs of the country. He was indeed, as his friend James Hargrave contended, 'an honest, kind hearted, manly fellow, a character not often found among the every day walks of life, and still more rarely sown in this land.'[63]

## NOTES

1. 'The Character Book of George Simpson, 1832,' in Glyndwr Williams, ed., *Hudson's Bay Miscellany 1670-1870* (Winnipeg: Hudson's Bay Record Society 1975), 183-4. For an analysis of James McMillan's personality, see Private Archives of Hugh P. MacMillan (PAHPM), Guelph, Ontario, James McMillan File, 'Assessment of James McMillan's Handwriting' by Mrs. Hannah M. Smith, Graphologist, Vancouver, British Columbia.

2. The earliest settlers of Glengarry were the refugee tenants and militia soldiers of Sir John Johnson, the son and heir of Sir William Johnson, the former Northern Superintendent of the Indian Department in the colony of New York. Many of these individuals were Scottish Highlanders who had emigrated to North America as soldiers in the service of the British crown during the Seven Years' War. When this conflict ended, several chose to settle in the Mohawk Valley as tenants of Sir William Johnson, in the hopes that they, too, would eventually become proprietors of large tracts of land. While resident in the Mohawk

**Six McMillans in the 1990s: Left to Right: William, son of John Sr.; John Sr.; Anne, wife of John Sr.; John Jr., son of John Sr., Grenada descendants of Alexander McMillan who went to the Caribbean; Penny McMillan and her husband Orval McMillan, Toronto descendant of Alexander's brother, James McMillan and his country wife, Josette Beleisle. Photograph taken in living room of Hugh and Muriel MacMillan, Guelph, Ontario, 1992. (Hugh P. MacMillan Collection, Guelph, Ontario)**

Valley, some of these individuals worked for Johnson as employees in the Indian Department, or participated in the colonial fur trade of the Great Lakes region. Additional Scottish settlers from Lochaber migrated to the Johnson estates in 1773. After Johnson's death and the onset of the American Revolution shortly thereafter, the bulk of these tenants chose to migrate to British North America where they settled in Glengarry and adjacent counties. Sir William Johnson's former employees in the Indian Department, and the Scottish merchants participating in the Great Lakes fur trade, also migrated northward, to resume trading. For a summary of Sir William Johnson's patronage of the Lochaber Scots in New York State see Heather Devine, 'Roots in the Mohawk Valley: Sir William Johnson's Legacy in the North West Company,' in Jennifer S.H. Brown, William J. Eccles and Donald P. Heldman, eds.,

*The Fur Trade Revisited: Selected Papers of the Sixth North American Fur Trade Conference* (East Lansing, Michigan: Michigan State University Press 1994), 215-40.)

3. See Duncan Cameron, 'A Sketch of the Customs, Manners, Way of Living of the Natives in the Barren Country About Nipigon,' in L.R. Masson, *Les Bourgeois de la Compagnie du Nord-Ouest* (New York: Antiquarian Press Ltd. 1960), 251-2.

4. For a discussion of the economic and social contribution of native women to fur trade society, see Sylvia Van Kirk, *'Many Tender Ties': Women in Fur-Trade Society 1670-1870* (Winnipeg: Watson & Dwyer Publishing Ltd. 1983), 53-73.

5. In the early years of the trade the name Fort des Prairies was assigned to the most westerly fort in the trading area. When James McMillan began his career with the

North West Company (ca. 1804), the name Fort des Prairies referred to a series of forts along the North Saskatchewan River. Fort des Prairies later became Fort Augustus, then Edmonton House and finally, after 1821, Fort Edmonton, site of today's Edmonton.

6. See J.B. Tyrrell, ed., *David Thompson's Narrative. 1784-1812.* Publications of the Champlain Society, no. 40 (Toronto: Champlain Society 1962), 415-6.

7. Apparently McMillan accidentally discharged his gun while at Saleesh House, blowing off two fingers. See Elliott Coues, ed., *The Manuscript Journals of Alexander Henry and David Thompson 1799-1814*, Vol. II (Minneapolis: Ross & Haines, Inc. 1965), 674.

8. Josette Beleisle later entered into a union with Joseph Delorme. Their son Pierre became a Member of Parliament representing the constituency of Pointe Coupe-Ste. Adolphe, Manitoba. Apparently he was also a member of Louis Riel's Council. For a record of the union of Joseph Delorme and Josephte Bellisle ca. 1813, see 'Table I: Genealogies of Red River Households, 1818-1870,' in D.N. Sprague and R.P. Frye, eds., *The Genealogy of the First Metis Nation* (Winnipeg: Pemmican Publications 1983).

9. It is possible that 'turning off' enabled women to remain in their local region with their kinsmen, and was perceived as a kinder, gentler form of abandonment. Later, however, it was used by senior officers of the Hudson's Bay Company as a mechanism to rid themselves of unwanted native wives who could then be replaced by white women. See Van Kirk, *'Many Tender Ties'*, 50; see also Jennifer S.H. Brown, *Strangers in Blood: Fur Trade Company Families in Indian Country* (Vancouver: University of British Columbia Press 1980), 134-5.

10. Likely William or W. Matthews/Mathews, of New York, a clerk with the Pacific Fur Company, later engaged with the North West Company in January 1814. See Coues, ed., *The Manuscript Journals of Alexander Henry and David Thompson 1799-1814*, Vol. II, 788. Ellen, daughter of Matthews and Kilakotah, became the country wife of George Barnston, Chief Trader of the Hudson's Bay Company. See Van Kirk, 'Many Tender Ties', 136.

11. Apparently James MacMillan's father and uncle had died about this time. In addition to attending to matters concerning the estate, James took his daughter Margaret and his son Allan back to Glengarry in 1823 to be baptized at St. Andrews Presbyterian Church, where their

birthdates in the Northwest were recorded. See St. Andrews Church, Williamstown, Glengarry County, Ontario, 'Church Records Collection,' Vol. II, 279.

12. E.E. Rich, ed., *Simpson's 1828 Journey to the Columbia*, Vol. X (London: Hudson's Bay Record Society 1947), Appendix A, 137, Letter from Committee to Simpson, 23 February 1826.

13 *James McMillan, Miscellaneous Papers* (folio M 424), Letter from James McMillan to John Macleod, 21 January 1828.

14. Rich, ed., *Simpson's 1828 Journey to the Columbia*, Vol. X, 44.

15. PAHPM, 'Harriet Munnick Correspondence,' Letter from Munnick (West Linn, Oregon) to Hugh MacMillan, 10 February 1970. Before going on furlough, McMillan dissolved his union with Kilakotah, who married Louis Labonté Sr., with whom she had a daughter, Julienne (born ca. 1838), who married Narcisse Vivet and had several children.

16. Van Kirk, *'Many Tender Ties'*, 210; Brown, *Strangers in Blood*, 132; and PAHPM, 'Willard Ireland Correspondence,' letter from Ireland (Provincial Librarian and Archivist, PABC) to Hugh MacMillan, 5 January 1965. In June of 1840 Archibald McKinley married Sarah Julie Ogden, daughter of his *bourgeois*, Peter Skene Ogden. Apparently the couple had several children and lived out the remainder of their lives with their daughter, Sarah, at Savona, near Kamloops, B.C.

17. PAHPM, 'Connelly-McLaughlin Correspondence,' letter from Stephen Connelly (Archivist, District Libraries, Rose Terrace, Perthshire, Scotland) to Mrs. Morag MacLachlan, 20 August 1982.

18. PAHPM, 'Angus and Aenaes Cameron Papers,' letter from R. Cowie to Angus Cameron, 25 November 1847. Copy courtesy of Mrs. Elaine Mitchell.

19. 'Correspondence Concerning James McMillan, His Wife, and Family,' in *Clan Magazine*, 1967, 16-9, letter from Miss E.C. McMillan, Glasgow, to William G. Smith, Hudson's Bay Company, London, 19 August 1869.

20. There is some discrepancy over William McMillan's actual age. He is listed in the Red River Census of 1870 as age 62, which would place his date of birth ca. 1806. Also, Governor Simpson's journal entry of Wednesday, 21 September 1825, makes reference to William McMillan being 'a man going on 19 years' which would place his birthdate

1806-1807. See Hudson's Bay Company Archives (HBCA), B.60 a/23. However, his descendants' mass cards on the occasion of his 1903 funeral listed his age at death as being 103 years.

21. Glenbow Archives (GA), Calgary, Charles D. Denney Papers, James McMillan file (#491.000A), for the record of James McMillan Jr., born 1808. There is some confusion over details regarding the life of James McMillan Jr. In the 'McMillan Family File' at the St. Boniface Historical Society, a James McMillan Jr. is listed as having been born in 1813. According to data compiled from the Red River Census of Manitoba, James McMillan Jr. was buried on 13 May 1843 aged 30, at the Red River Settlement (burial recorded in the Burial Register of St. John's Anglican Church, Red River). For further information on the siblings of William McMillan, see also PAHPM, 'James McMillan File,' letter from Albert E. Dease (Walhalla, North Dakota) to Hugh MacMillan, 21 May 1966; and PAHPM, Ruth Swan, Research Report on William McMillan (Winnipeg: Ruth Swan Heritage Consulting 1992).

22. HBCA, B.60 a/23.

23. PAHPM, Ruth Swan, 'Research Report on William McMillan.'

24. Marguerite (born Rainy Lake, 26 May 1818) was daughter of John Warren Dease and Genevieve 'Jenny' Beignet. A member of a distinguished Irish-American fur trade family, Dease was son of Dr. John Dease and Anne Johnson, sister of Sir William Johnson, Northern Superintendent of the British Colonial Indian Department and one of the most influential men in colonial New York State. Dr. Dease had migrated from Ireland in 1771 to serve as personal physician to his uncle William. He later became an officer in the Indian Department. After the American Revolution he became part of the Indian Department in Canada. Many of his sons entered the fur trade and had distinguished careers. His son John Warren Dease, Marguerite's father, joined the North West Company ca. 1801, and was the *bourgeois* or chief trader at the fort at Rainy Lake from 1814-1821. After the coalition of the Hudson's Bay and North West Companies (1821), John Warren Dease became a Chief Trader with the new Hudson's Bay Company, responsible for Fort Alexander on Lake Winnipeg and later took charge of three forts on the Columbia River. He died in the Columbia region in 1829.

One of his sons, William Dease, became an important member of the Council of Assiniboia, which governed Red River from the 1830s to 1870. William Dease was married to the sister of another councillor, Maximilien Genthon. See Lionel Dorge, 'The Metis and Canadien Councillors of Assiniboia. Part III,' in *The Beaver*, Winter 1974, 56-8. There exists an extensive bibliography on the Johnsons and the Deases, but the sources used for the purposes of this paper have been extracted from the personal research records of R. Robert Mutrie of Ridgeway, Ontario, a historian, genealogist, and recognized authority on the Dease families of Ireland and America. Copies on file in PAHPM.

25. Provincial Archives of Manitoba (PAM), 'Red River Census, 1834,' where William McMillan is recorded as married and owning four horses and five mares. See also 'Red River Census of 1859,' where William McMillan is listed as owning two houses, two stables, one barn, seven horses, seven oxen, one bull, four cows, one calf, five pigs, one plough, one harrow, seven carts, one canoe, ten acres of cultivated land and a store full of merchandise.

26. Like his father, William had bad luck with firearms. Apparently while on a buffalo hunt, he surprised an Indian trying to steal one of his horses. The Indian attempted to shoot McMillan, who grabbed the barrel of the gun in his hand. The gun went off, burning the flesh off his hand and leaving it permanently withered. See PAHPM, 'James McMillan File,' Peter McMillan (Ashern, Manitoba), interview with Hugh MacMillan, 16 November 1968, re. his grandfather William McMillan and his great-grandfather James McMillan.

27. GA, Denney Papers, 'William McMillan File (#491.001); see also St. Boniface Historical Society, Winnipeg, 'James McMillan File.'

28. Margaret married Jean-Baptiste Beauchemin, son of Benjamin Beauchemin and Marie Parenteau. Jean-Baptiste was a prominent Métis of Red River who represented St. Charles in the Red River Convention of 1870, and served in the second Provisional Government of 1869-70. See George F.G. Stanley, Thomas Flanagan, and Claude Rocan, eds., *The Collected Diaries of Louis Riel*, Vol. V (Edmonton: University of Alberta Press, 1985), 219.

29. Marie-Anne married Salomon Carrière, son of Alexis Carrière and Suzanne Ducharme. Salomon's aunt, Angélique Carrière, was the wife of Louis Riel's uncle,

Benjamin Lagimodière. Salomon's cousin, Damase (born ca. 1851) was a member of Louis Riel's provisional Government of 1885. During the Northwest Rebellion, Damase was allegedly killed on the last day of fighting at Batoche when he was captured by Canadian soldiers and dragged behind a horse. See notes on the Carrière family in Stanley, et al., eds. *The Collected Diaries of Louis Riel*, Vol. V, 232-3. For addition information on the Carrière families, see also 'Table I: Genealogies of Red River Households, 1818-1870' and 'Table 4: Geographical Location and Children of Manitoba Families, 1870,' in Sprague and Frye, eds., *The Genealogy of the First Metis Nation*.

30. Philomène married Thomas Hogue, son of Amable Hogue and Marguerite Taylor, former country wife of Sir George Simpson, who 'turned off' Marguerite when he brought his new English wife, Frances, back to Red River after his 1830 furlough. Marguerite is reported to have lived out the rest of her life in increasing poverty after her marriage to Amable Hogue, a Company servant. See Van Kirk, *'Many Tender Ties'*, 184-8 and 281, fn. 25; see also Brown, *Strangers in Blood*, 125-6.

31. Joseph married Appolline 'Pauline' Bruce, daughter of Baptiste Bruce and Catherine Perrault. John Bruce, the brother of Baptiste Bruce (and Appoline's uncle) was a carpenter and avocational legal expert in St. Boniface. He was president of the Métis National Committee until replaced by Louis Riel, and subsequently served as Commissioner of Public Works in the Provisional Government of 1869-70. See Stanley, et al., eds. *The Collected Diaries of Louis Riel*, Vol. V, 229; see also Dorge, 'The Metis and Canadien Councillors of Assiniboia. Part III,' in *The Beaver*, Winter, 58; and George F.G. Stanley, *The Birth of Western Canada* (Toronto: University of Toronto Press, 1992) 69-71 and 86.

32. Virginie married Daniel Carrière, son of André Carrière and Marie-Anne Rivard. Daniel was Salomon Carrière's cousin (see note 29.

33. Sarah was thrice married, first to Joseph Turcotte, son of Vital Turcotte and Madeleine Caplette. Joseph's brother Norbert was a follower of Louis Riel. Norbert was connected by marriage to the Lépine family, ardent supporters of Riel in 1869-70 and 1885. Norbert Turcotte was married to Josephte Lépine, daughter of Maxime Lépine, who was a member of Riel's Provisional Government of 1885 and a leader of the Northwest Rebellion the same year. He was tried for treason and sentenced to seven years. His

brother Ambroise was Riel's military commander in 1869-70. Sarah's second husband was Pierre Jobin, son of Ambroise Jobin and Marguerite Mandeville. Pierre's brothers, Ambroise and Joseph, were both active in the Northwest Rebellion of 1885 and Ambroise was a member of Louis Riel's Provisional Government in 1885. He died from wounds sustained at the battle of Batoche. Sarah's third husband was Antoine Vandal, son of Antoine Vandal and Marguerite Berthelet. At least two members of the Vandal family (possibly cousins or nephews of Antoine) were tried for treason after the Northwest Rebellion. See Stanley, et al., eds., *The Collected Diaries of Louis Riel*, Vol. V, 275-6 and 353-4.

34. Patrick married Beatrice Caplette, possibly the daughter of Denis Caplette and Elizabeth Bremner, also residents of St. Charles parish.

35. John married Sara (Virginie) Bruce, daughter of Baptiste Bruce and Catherine Perrault. Although the William McMillan file (#491.001) in the Denny Papers (GA) do not explicitly identify the parents of Sara and Pierre Bruce, their parents can be determined by examining 'Table 4: Geographical Location and Children of Manitoba Families, 1870,' in Sprague and Frye, eds., *The Genealogy of the First Metis Nation* where the Bruce family resident at Lot 97 in St. Boniface have two children still living at home, Pierre aged 15 and Virginie aged 9. The head of this family, identified as #555, is Baptiste Bruce, married to Catherine Perrault.

36. Elizabeth married Pierre Bruce, brother of Sara, who was wife of Elizabeth's brother, John (see fn. 35).

37. Hélène died at St. Francis-Xavier, Red River.

38. Baptiste Boyer was son of Pierre Boyer and Josephte Leduc from Vaudreuil, Lower Canada (Quebec). The couple was married at St. Francis-Xavier, Red River. See PAHPM, letter from Diane P. Payment (Historian, Canadian Parks Service, Winnipeg) to Hugh MacMillan, 20 December 1989. Some of the genealogical notes on the Boyer descendants has been extracted from biographical information compiled by Ms. Payment for the *Dictionary of Canadian Biography*, Vol. XIII.

39. Emilie married George Fisher, son of George Fisher and Genevieve Courville (or Guatville) of Prairie du Chien, Wisconsin. The Fishers were an important trading family in the early west. George was a nephew of Hudson's Bay Company Chief Trader Henry Fisher; George was

thus a cousin to Betsey Fisher, wife of Louis Bousquet. See Art Fisher Private Archives, Regina, Saskatchewan, Fisher Family File, 'Pedigree Chart for George Fisher line.'

40. William married Julienne Bousquet daughter of Louis Bousquet and Betsey Fisher. Louis Bousquet was a protégé of Bishop Provencher from the age of four years old, when he was placed under his guardianship. He became a member of the St. Boniface Cathedral Choir, and taught at Provencher's school as a teacher before the Grey Nuns administration. He later became a petty magistrate, appointed by the Council of Assiniboia. Betsey Fisher was the daughter of Henry Fisher, Chief Trader of the Hudson's Bay Company and later a member of the Council of Assiniboia. See also Dorge, 'The Metis and Canadien Councillors of Assiniboia' Part I, *The Beaver*, (Summer 1974), 18; and Dorge, 'The Metis and Canadien Councillors of Assiniboia' Part II in *The Beaver*, (Autumn 1974), 39-45. William moved to Batoche in 1881, where he became a merchant. He did not support the Rebellion, and was arrested with Charles Nolin, who had successively married female relatives of both Louis Riel and Maxime Lépine, and who opposed Riel in 1869-70 and in 1885. See Stanley, et al., eds., *The Collected Diaries of Louis Riel*, Vol. V, 227-8 and 315-6.

41. Baptiste married Elizabeth Bousquet, daughter of Louis Bousquet and Betsey Fisher, and was therefore sister of Julienne Bousquet (see fn. 40).

42. Clémence married Baptiste Gervais at St.-Laurent, in what is now north-central Saskatchewan. 'Table I: Genealogies of Red River Households, 1818 – 1870,' in Sprague and Frye, eds., *The Genealogy of the First Metis Nation* indicates a marriage between Baptiste Gervais and Clemence Bouer [sic]. For additional information on the Boyer family see group chart prepared by Diane Payment for *DCB*, Vol. XIII (see note 38), which makes reference to Clémence's marriage to a Gervais at St-Laurent.

43. Félicité married Gilbert Breland, son of Alexander Breland and Emilie Wells. It is probable that Alexander is the brother of Pascal Breland, well-known Red River trader and member of the Council of Assiniboia.

44. Hélène married Charles Racette III, son of Charles Racette Jr. and an Indian woman. The patriarch of the Racette family was Charles Racette (born ca. 1766), an old trader who had been in the interior for over thirty years in 1817. In 1818, old Racette and his family were camped at the Grand Rapids of the Saskatchewan River when the witnessed the beating and abduction of Benjamin Frobisher, North West Company partner, by servants of the Hudson's Bay Company. Frobisher died while trying to escape. Racette was called back to Lower Canada to testify in the court case that followed. See Samuel H. Wilcocke, 'Narrative of Circumstances Attending the Death of the Late Benjamin Frobisher, Esq.,' in L.R. Masson, *Les Bourgeois de la Compagnie du Nord-Ouest*, Vol. II (New York: Antiquarian Press Ltd. 1960), 177-226.

45. Marguerite married Alexander Goulet, son of Jacques Goulet and Louise Versailles. Alexander was the cousin of Roger and Elzéar Goulet of St. Boniface. Roger was a surveyor, magistrate, and member of the Council of Assiniboia from 1866-69. After 1870 he worked for the Department of the Interior, and then served on the Half-Breed Scrip Commission of 1885. Elzéar was a mail carrier from Pembina to Fort Garry, and member of the court martial that sentenced Thomas Scott to death. Elzéar drowned in the Red River when fleeing from Canadian militia men. See Stanley, et al., eds., *The Collected Diaries of Louis Riel*, vol. V, 263-4; see also Dorge, 'The Metis and Canadien Councillors of Assiniboia. Part III,' in *Beaver*, Winter 1974, 56-8; see also information of the Goulet family from 'Table I: Genealogies of Red River Households, 1818 – 1870' and 'Table 4: Geographical Location and Children of Manitoba Families, 1870,' in Sprague and Frye, eds., *The Genealogy of the First Metis Nation*.

46. No record of issue. It is possible that Margaret McMillan and Angelique 'Nellie' McMillan are, in fact, the same person. It seems odd that Angelique would not have been baptised at Glengarry at the same time as her brother Allan and her sister Margaret, as they are so close in age. Therefore it is possible that Margaret is actually Angelique, given that no further records appear for this person. This individual should not be mistaken for Margaret McMillan, daughter of James McMillan and Eleanor McKinley, baptised 14 February 1833 at Red River.

47. John Warren Dease Jr. was the brother of Margaret Dease, the wife of Nellie McMillan's half-brother, William McMillan. See 'Dease Family Pedigree Charts' researched by Robert Mutrie; see also PAHPM, 'Albert E. Dease Correspondence,' letter from Dease (Walhalla, North Dakota) to Hugh McMillan, 28 October 1966 re. siblings of William McMillan. Angelique died in 1860 at Red River.

48. Ellen married Patrice Breland, son of Pascal Breland and Marie Grant. Patrice Breland was a successful farmer and trader. He was a road superintendent for the White Horse Plains District, St. Francis-Xavier Parish, Red River, and in 1851, he served as magistrate for the same district. He provided conditional support to Louis Riel in the troubles of 1869-70, was a member of the Council of Assiniboia, and also a member of the North-West Territories Council, 1878-79. He served one term as MLA for St. Francis-Xavier in the Manitoba legislature in 1879. Pascal's wife, Marie Grant, was the daughter of Cuthbert Grant, the Métis leader involved in the Battle of Seven Oaks in 1816, the founder of the settlement of Grantown, and Warden of the Plains 1828-49. He was later a member of the Council of Assiniboia, 1839-54. See Stanley, et al., eds., *The Collected Diaries of Louis Riel*, vol. V, 227-8 and 265; see also Dorge, 'The Metis and Canadien Councillors of Assiniboia. Parts I-III,' in *The Beaver*, Summer 1974, 13-5; Autumn 1974, 40-5; and Winter 1974, 53 and 58.

49. Ellen married Lucie Gladu, daughter of Charles Gladu and Madeleine Poitras. The Gladu family had close ties to both the Riel and Dease families. Pierre Gladu, son of Francois Gladu and husband of Nancy Dease, established a mill in partnership with Louis Riel's father. Pierre Gladu's son William married married Louis Riel's sister Eulalie in 1879. See Stanley, et al., eds., *The Collected Diaries of Louis Riel*, Vol. V, 262-3.

50. GA, Denney Papers, 'James McMillan File' (#491.000B). Allan was reported to have died in 1841 at St. Paul, Minnesota with no record of issue. See note 57.

51. There is record of a Suzanne McMullan (born ca. 1821) married to Pierre Sutherland, son of Pierre Sutherland and Angelique, an Assiniboine Indian. For a record of the union of Suzanne McMullan and Pierre Sutherland, see 'Table I: Genealogies of Red River Households, 1818–1870,' in Sprague and Frye, eds., *The Genealogy of the First Metis Nation*.

52. Peter C. Newman, *Caesars of the Wilderness* (Markham, Ontario: Penguin Books Canada Limited, 1987), 332; see also Brown, *Strangers in Blood*, 190-2.

53. HBCA, Winnipeg, 'General Dickson File.'

54. 'Batosh' (more commonly spelled 'Batoche') is another surname used to refer to the Letendre family, William McMillan's maternal kin.

55. HBCA, D.4/22, folio 80-80d, 'George Simpson Personal Correspondence,' Simpson to Chief Factor Alexander Christie, Lachine, 18 September 1836.

56. PAHPM, Conolly Manuscript, ca. 1917-1923, 55-7.

57. HBCA, Allan McMillan File. There is, however, an alternative account concerning the fate of Allan McMillan: 'McMillan did his work well, and got very little thanks for that. He was taken into the Company's service, but was looked down upon by some of the pale-faced fools in the service, so he left and went to St. Paul. He was killed by some curs. Poor Allan, he was a very good fellow.' PAHPM, Conolly Manuscript, 56-7.

58. PAHPM, 'Harriet Munnick Correspondence,' letter from Munnick to Hugh McMillan, 10 February 1970.

59. Marguerite was the daughter of former Nor'Wester Jean-Etienne Wadin, and prior to her marriage with McLoughlin had been the country wife of North West Company partner Alexander McKay, who had left Indian country about 1808. See Van Kirk, *'Many Tender Ties'* 121; see also Brown, *Strangers in Blood*, 142.

60. See Coues, ed., *The Manuscript Journals of Alexander Henry and David Thompson*, 968.

61. Josephine was born in 1870 and died in 1899. On May 21, 1873 old Marguerite 'Kilakotah' Labonté sold a 320 acre parcel of land to her daughter Victoire and husband Etienne Grégoire for $200, on the understanding that 'the said grantees will support and maintain me, the said Margaret Labonté, during my natural life in the same manner in which they have here-to-fore recently supported, maintained, and cared for me.' The parcel was all that remained of the Labonté claim fronting the Yamhill river, a tributary of the Willamette River some forty miles south of Vancouver. It is assumed that Kilakotah spent the rest of her life with her daughter in St. Louis. See PAHPM, 'Harriet D. Munnick Correspondence,' 'The Plum Thicket,' an account of the life of Kilakotah and her descendants, by Harriet D. Munnick, ca. 1969, 4.

62. See Dorge, 'The Metis and Canadien Councillors of Assiniboia,' in *The Beaver*, Summer, Fall, and Winter 1974.

63 64. National Archives of Canada, Hargrave Papers, MG 19 A21, Vol. XXI, as quoted in 'The Character Book of George Simpson, 1832,' in Glyndwr Williams, ed., *Hudson's Bay Miscellany 1670-1870*, 184, fn. 1.

# PART VI

# CHARTS

# CHAPTER 10

# THE GLENPEAN AND MURLAGGAN CHARTS

HUGH P. MacMILLAN AND DUNCAN (DARBY) MacDONALD

Since 1984, Duncan MacDonald, Honorary Secretary and Genealogist for Clan Donald Canada, has been recording the genealogies of the Scots of Glengarry, especially those of Clan Donald. By force of necessity he began to do charts for MacMillan, the second most numerous clan name in Glengarry. Lochaber and Glengarry (Scotland) are homelands of both the MacMillans and the clan Donald (MacDonald, MacDonell, etc.).

My first attempts at genealogical research began in 1954 soon after Muriel and I moved to Glengarry from Vancouver. Much later I made use of the few notes I had from my grandmother, when at age fifteen, I first began to ask her questions about our family. Had I been more clever there would have been thirty pages of notes rather than a meagre three pages. My father, who valued theology and philosophy more than he did history, still managed to give me valuable information. My wife, father, children, brothers, and friends suggested, and at times most emphatically, that I would be better advised to spend more time at my work and less on family history which paid nothing. They were right and it is a wonder that I

escaped the divorce court. As it turned out, this obsession with family history was the beginning of my career in the field of history. Perhaps it was preordained?

By 1958 I had assembled voluminous notes on our line back to my great-great-grandfather John Roy, who had come from Scotland in 1792-3. At the urging of Somerled MacMillan, clan bard and historian, I published my genealogical data on John Roy and his descendants in the 1960 issue of *The Clan Magazine*. I have been correcting errors ever since.

Elsie MacMillan in her excellent book *Butternuts & Maple Syrup* revised my data for inclusion in her story about the old 14th Concession of Lochiel. Mary Beaton, another fine MacMillan genealogist, has been of great help in setting me straight on numerous points. I was never totally satisfied with Somerled's antecedents for John Roy. I became convinced that John Roy was another brother of Allan, Alexander, Ranald and Archibald. I based this assumption on the information supplied by my grandmother and the notes I made from interviews with my father. My grandmother always claimed that I had a great-great uncle Ranald who went to the 'East' Indies. In 1970 my father recalled that his father, Hughie Archie Roy, had recalled his father telling him that his father's brother Ranald had come to visit from the West Indies about 1805. This is confirmed in a letter of 20 October 1805 when Archibald 'Murlaggan' wrote to Ewen Cameron of Fassifern:

> Ronald (Ranald) McMillan Glen Pean's brother, left this Febr'y last for Jamaica by way of N.Y. with an intention of coming back to this place to settle for good and all but I am sorry to say he has not been heard from since he left N.Y., and I saw a gentleman who told me he had read in the N.Y., papers of the ship in which he sailed being taken by a French privateer and his name mentioned as one of the passengers. This account is most likely true, but as he must by this time have got clear of them we look for him still in this quarter.

Somerled had it right that the 'Glenpean' brothers were descended from Ewen. I had not found my grandmother's notes at the time Somerled wrote his introduction to my 1960 charts.

Little is known about any descendants of Ranald or Archibald 'Glenpean' who went to the West Indies. Somerled had no record of Archibald until I came on his name in an 1807 letter to John Cameron of Inverskilivuline from his son Dougald. At this time Dougald was a Captain in the Loyal Black Rangers (militia) stationed on the island of Grenada. His father had recently immigrated to Canada after the 1802 emigration and was settled at Stonefield several miles down river on the Ottawa from Archibald 'Murlaggan.' In a letter to his father, Dougald wrote, 'Much to my surprise I encountered Archibald [Glenpean's brother] in Trinidad and he had with him Sandy [Allan Glenpean's son]. I only hope Sandy did not follow as his uncle was in some trouble.' It is probable that Sandy, perhaps even Archie, and others had gone to the West Indies with Ranald in 1805. Contact between Glengarry and the West Indies was

likely maintained into the third decade of the nineteenth century.

Mary Beaton came on proof of this in an obituary dated 12 Sept 1824 which reads 'd. on 24th July last in Is. of Grenada, Ewen McMillan, Esq. aged 38 yrs, a native of the township of Lancaster, UC, and son of Duncan McMillan of Corribuie, Invernessshire, Scotland. He was of the firm of Messrs John Simpson & Co estate of Upper Canferns Grenada.' This obituary lends credence to my belief in the Highlanders' propensity for enlightened nepotism. 'Corribuie' identifies Duncan and his son Ewen as Lochaber emigrants. There were likely others besides McMillans who left Glengarry for jobs in the West Indies. Early in this century, a Métis great-grandson of Allan Glenpean went from Winnipeg to Trinidad and Grenada. According to his nephew Rolland, he was on the same chase as my grandfather who hired a lawyer to try and locate the fortune Ranald was supposed to have left. I checked Chancery Court records with no success. It is strange how such tales persist in some families.

In 1960 I placed a letter to the editor of the Trinidad Guardian and the Jamaica Gleaner. This made me the second Glenpean family member to seek contact with our West Indian cousins. I enquired about descendants of Ranald, Archibald, and Alexander. Much to my surprise I drew forty to fifty replies. I made a trip to Jamaica, with little success, but was unable to get to Grenada. Since then I have met a number of cousins who have moved from the West Indies back to Canada. Stan Barrett has elaborated on this in chapter 7. I am urging scholars connected with this project to combine the disciplines of history and anthropology for a much closer look at these Lochaber emigrants. The ethnic mixing of many races is on the increase and our particular family group may make an interesting example. Black, East Indian, Chinese, French, Spanish, Plains Indians mixed with Highland Scots. This makes for an exotic addition to our Glenpean line.

By 1961 I had discovered James McMillan's connection to our line. My knowledge of the Métis offspring of Highland fur traders from Montreal and Glengarry, members of the North West Company, was very sketchy. It was my compulsive interest in family history that set me searching my uncle's farmhouse for the notes I took after quizzing my grandmother in 1940. It was amazing that the notes were still there.

In the late 1950s, a cousin had been at my uncle's farm visiting her sister. Both she and her sister had severe mental problems. They decided to clean our uncle's house while he was in Montreal. Their idea of housecleaning was to take all the furniture out of the house, pile it up in the garden and burn it. Fortunately I was able to put the fire out, but I was sure most of the old papers had burned. It was a pleasant surprise to learn that the notes and other valuable papers had survived. They were in a blanket box which I had missed before and which my two crazed cousins had not found as it was concealed from view under the eaves in the attic. I have found during my thirty-year career as a paper chaser that it is often by such accidents that relics, art, or historical papers get saved.

Next, my interest in family history focused on the fur trade. I began reading, researching, re-enacting and writing about the fur trade. I was by now convinced that my ancestor, John Roy, was a brother of Allan Glenpean. This meant that his son James was a first cousin of my great-grandfather Archie Roy, reason enough to make me a fur-trade history buff for life. My interest in this aspect of my family history led me to co-founding Canada's first North West Company museum at the village of Williamstown in Ontario's Glengarry County. This in turn led me to travelling in fur-trade canoes. Canoe brigades that I helped to organize over the next twenty-five years crisscrossed many of the old fur trade routes. Lecturing and writing about the fur trade became a part-time occupation. In the process I met many of my Métis relatives as well as a host of other enthusiasts with an interest in the fur trade. Many of these relatives and fur trade buffs have become close friends. This serves to illustrate that anyone can benefit from

an interest in family history. It tends to broaden our horizons and the research can be fun. For me it is the contemplation of the next investigation – be it historical documents, artifacts, or family history that spurs me on to solve one more mystery.

Lt. Col. Alexander McMillan was the first of the Glenpean brothers to arrive in North America. In the 1960s I made contact with some of his descendants before I became certain of my connection to the Glenpean line. Military records show that he was with DeLancey's Brigade, fighting for the British in the American Revolution. He went to Scotland in 1792 and returned to Canada with several young Highlanders including a younger brother, John Roy, who was my great-great-grandfather. As a captain in the Royal Canadian Volunteer Regiment, he recruited many of these young men into the regiment.

The Glenpean line left many descendants but few papers. The Murlaggan line left few descendants but a fine collection of papers, invaluable to the writers of this book. They were carefully preserved by direct descendants of Archibald 'Murlaggan,' and are with the National Archives of Canada in Ottawa. Other original material and copies of letters are with me. These will be filed with the Glengarry Historical Society for use of other researchers and copies will go to the Clan Research Centre in Scotland. I have made use of these papers in verifying information that I sent on to Duncan MacDonald for amending the charts.

Our Celtic ancestors used memory and oral tradition to keep records, including genealogies. They probably thought the Romans or the Greeks a bit dense since they needed to write everything down. The Celts relied on memory to maintain their genealogy for at least seven generations. When our ancestors lost the Gaelic, this created a gap that those of us engaged in Celtic genealogy keep trying to fill.

In our mobile society, it is difficult to keep in contact with relatives beyond brothers, sisters, and perhaps, first cousins. Family history enthusiasts, myself included, are the exception. We seek out and try to maintain contact with relatives as far removed as fourth or fifth cousins. Living in Mississauga, west of Toronto, are a number of Glenpean cousins who have never heard of each other, except perhaps through me. It has been my experience that such contacts with strangers who are related can be rewarding.

The Glenpean/Murlaggan charts, containing nearly 1700 entries, are designed by Duncan (Darby) MacDonald and can serve as a model. The blank pages in the back of this book are meant for you to enter genealogical information, no matter what connection you may have with the emigration of 1802. The Glengarry Highland Society, sponsors of this book, hope to set up a descendants program for the Lochaber emigrants, to maintain family history information in conjunction with the Clan Donald database.

Genealogical charts are the backbone of any family history. What makes a family or an emigration history come alive are the documents and stories. It is curiosity about the past that fuels the hopes of family historians. We rarely get all the details we want about these elusive ancestors, their hopes and dreams and what they were really like.

We hope that these charts will lead you to more family research. Any additions and/or corrections should be filed with The MacDonald Research Centre, 268 Bartholomew Street, Brockville, ON, Canada K6V 2S6.

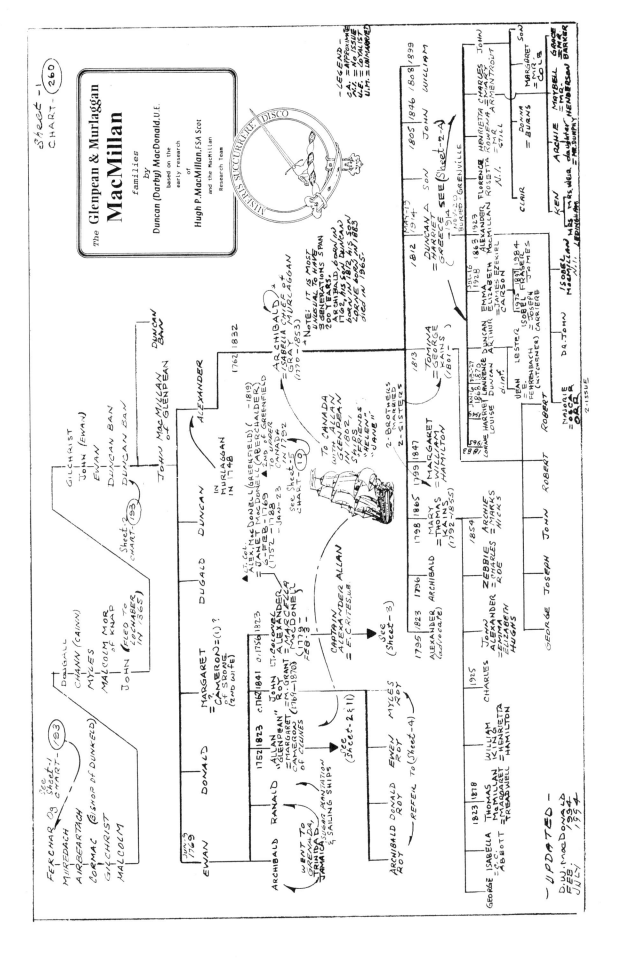

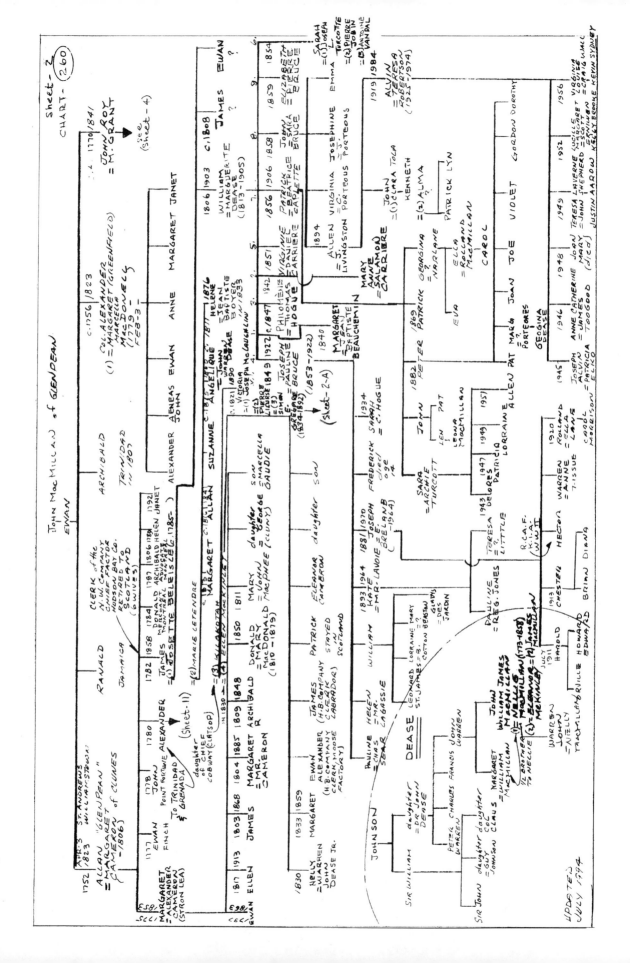

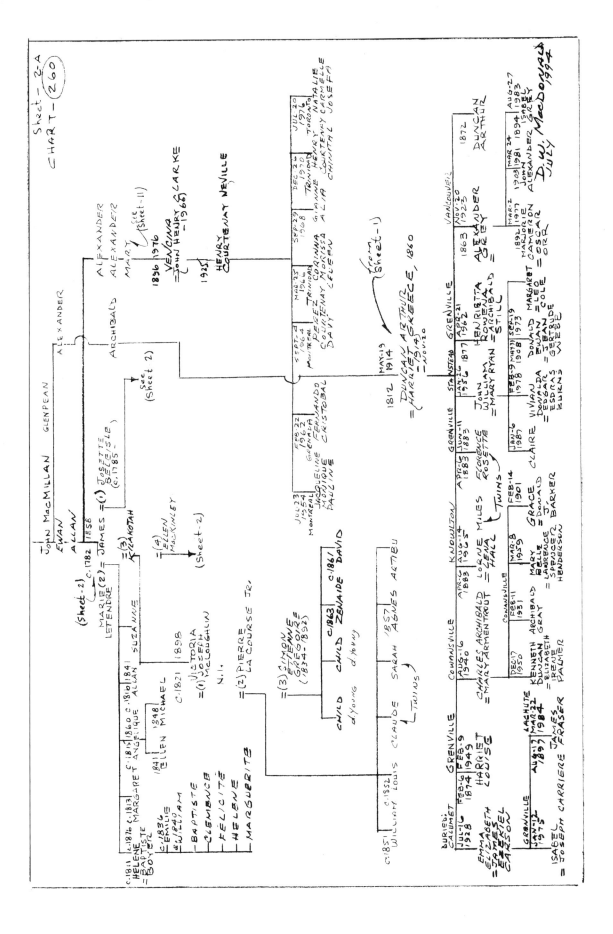

D.W. MacDonald
July 1994

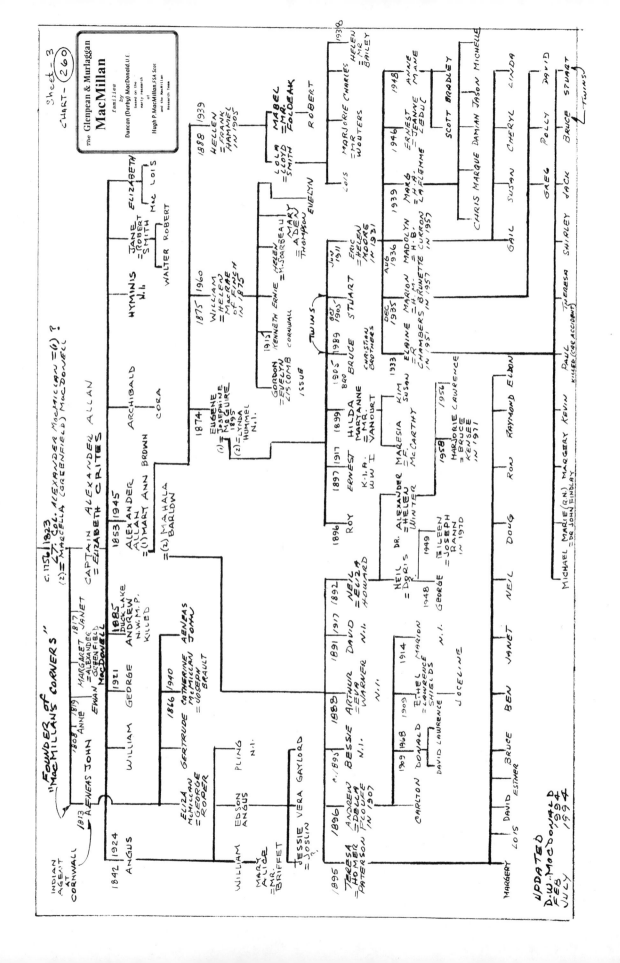

The Glenpean & Murlaggan
**MacMillan**
families
by
Duncan (Dorby) MacDonald
based on the
early research
of
Hugh P. MacMillan, F.S.A. Scot
and the MacMillan
Research Team

Sheet-3
Chart-260

UPDATED
D.W. MacDonald
FEB 1994
JULY

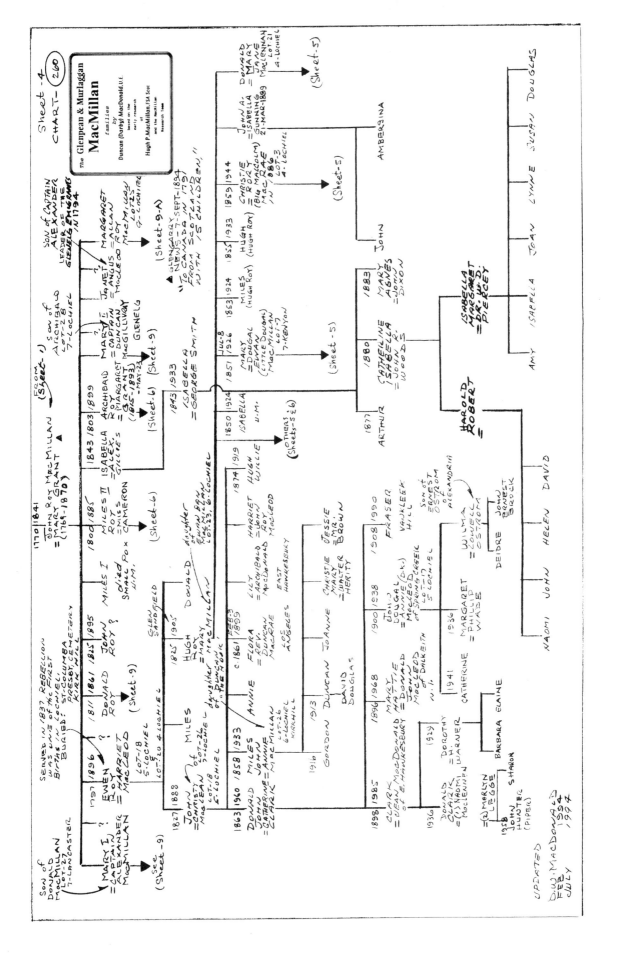

The Glenpean & Murlaggan
**MacMillan**
families
by
Duncan (Dorby) MacDonald, U.E.
based on the
early research
of
Hugh P. MacMillan, FSA Scot
and the MacMillan
Research Team

Sheet - 4
CHART - 26O

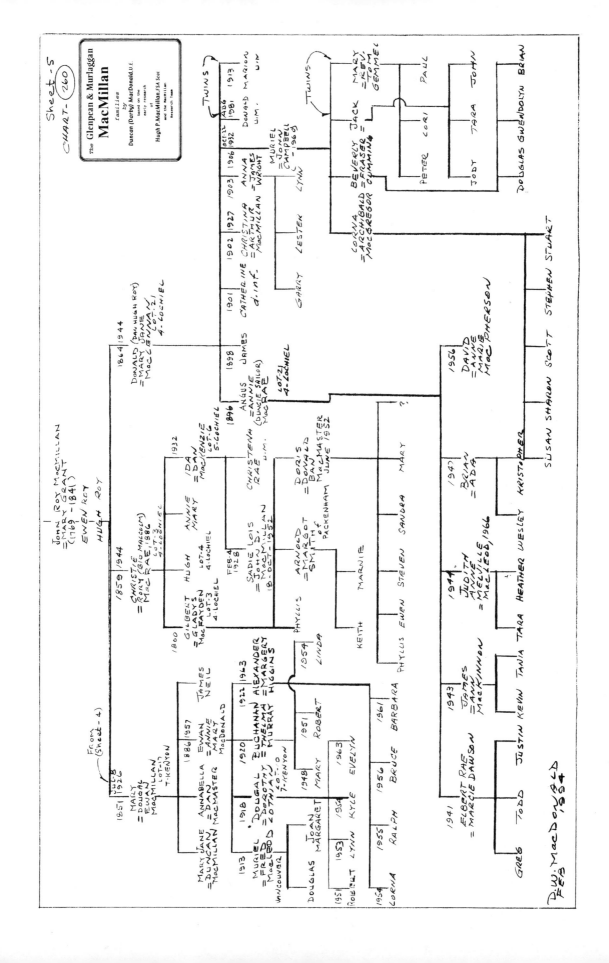

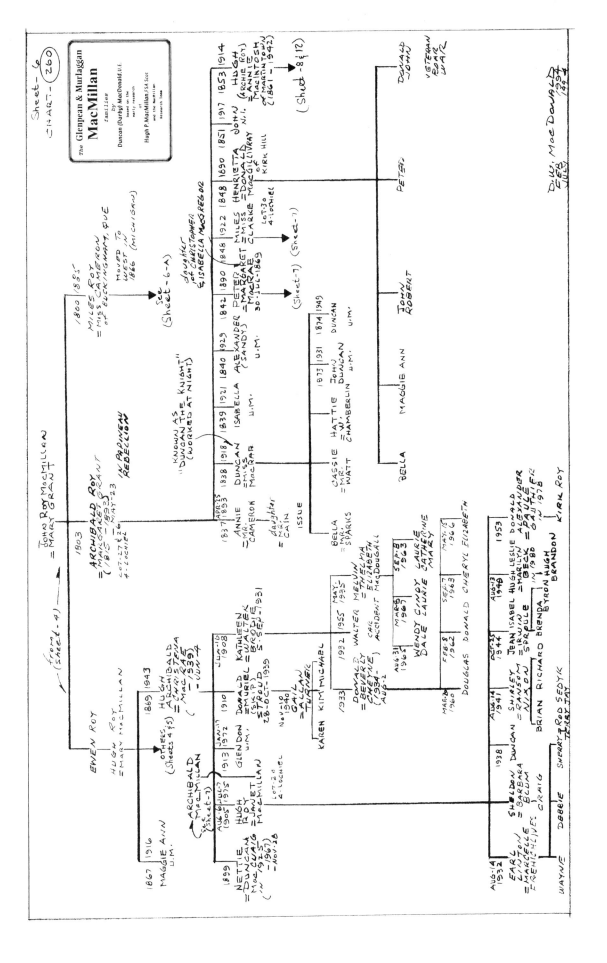

Sheet-6
CHART-(260)

The Glenpean & Murlaggan
**MacMillan**
families
by
Duncan (Darby) MacDonald,U.E.
based on the
early research
of
Hugh P. MacMillan,F.S.A. Scot.
and the MacMillan
Research Team

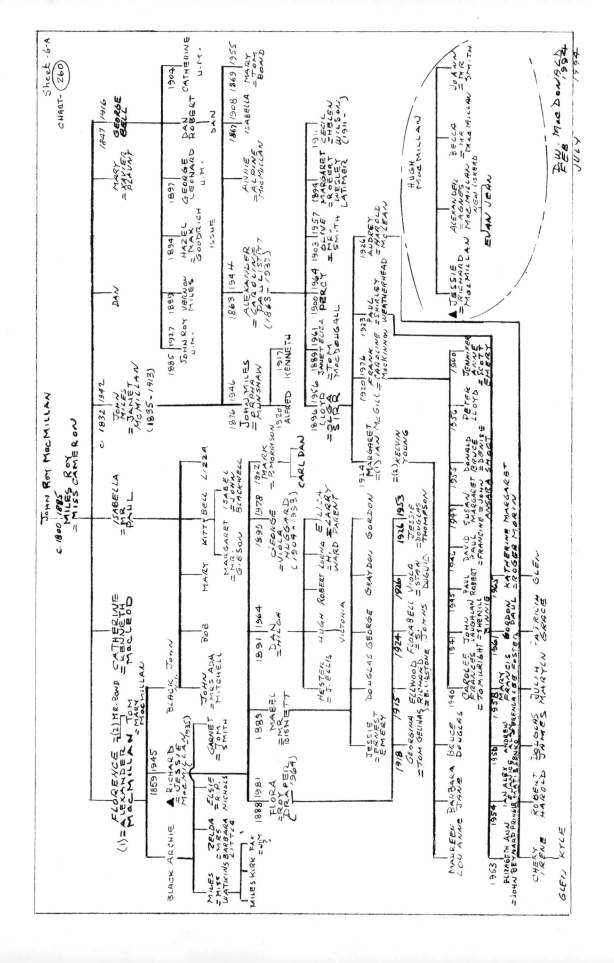

Sheet - 6-A
CHART- 260

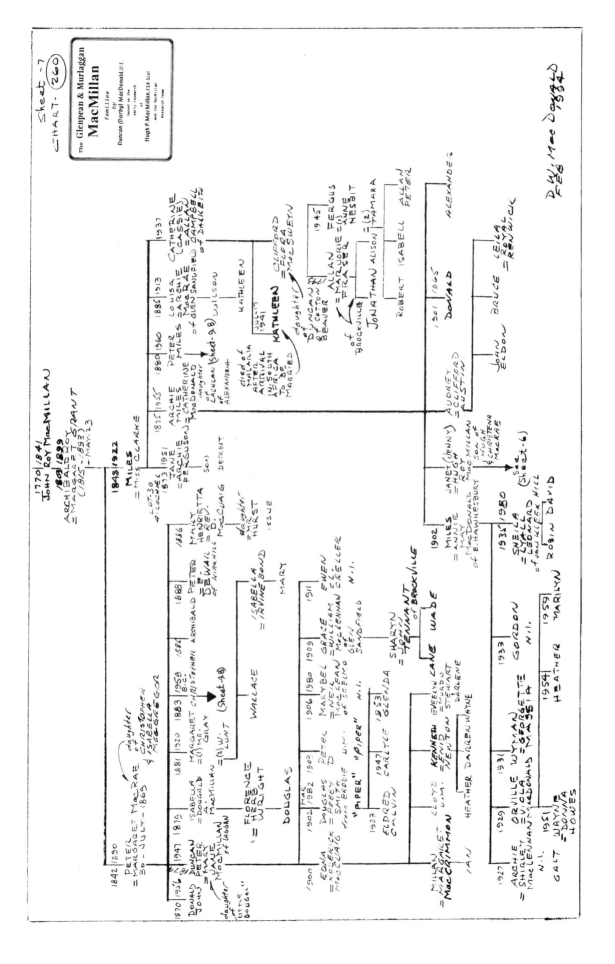

The Glenpean & Murlaggan
**MacMillan**
families
by
Duncan (Darby) MacDonald.U.E.
based on the
early research
of
Hugh P. MacMillan.FSA Scot
and the MacMillan
Research Team

D.W. MacDOUGALL
FEB 1994

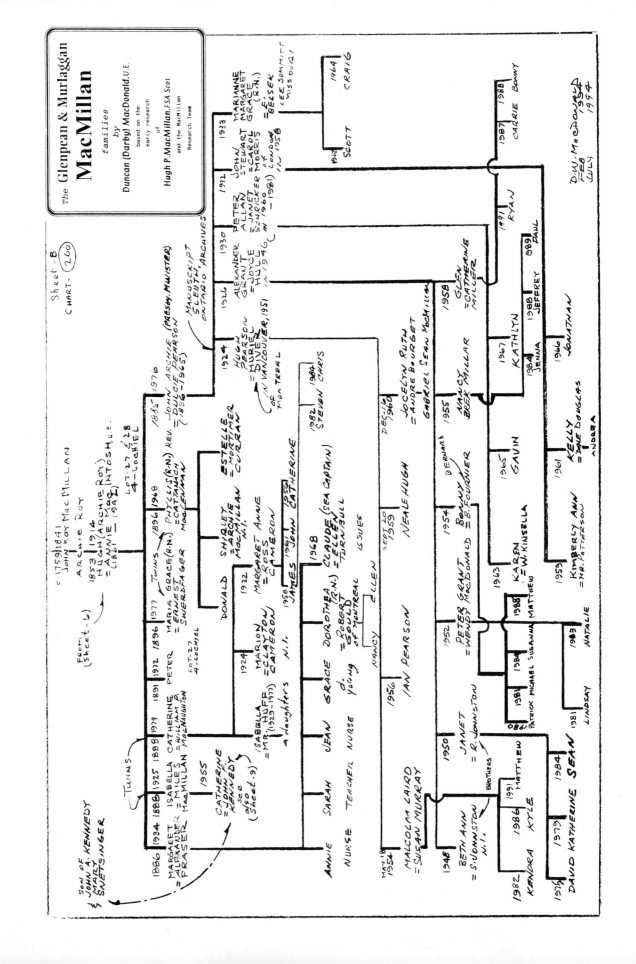

The Glenpean & Murlaggan
**MacMillan**
families
*by*
Duncan (Darby) MacDonald, U.E.
based on the
early research
*of*
Hugh P. MacMillan, F.S.A. Scot
and the MacMillan
Research Team

Sheet - 8
CHART - 260

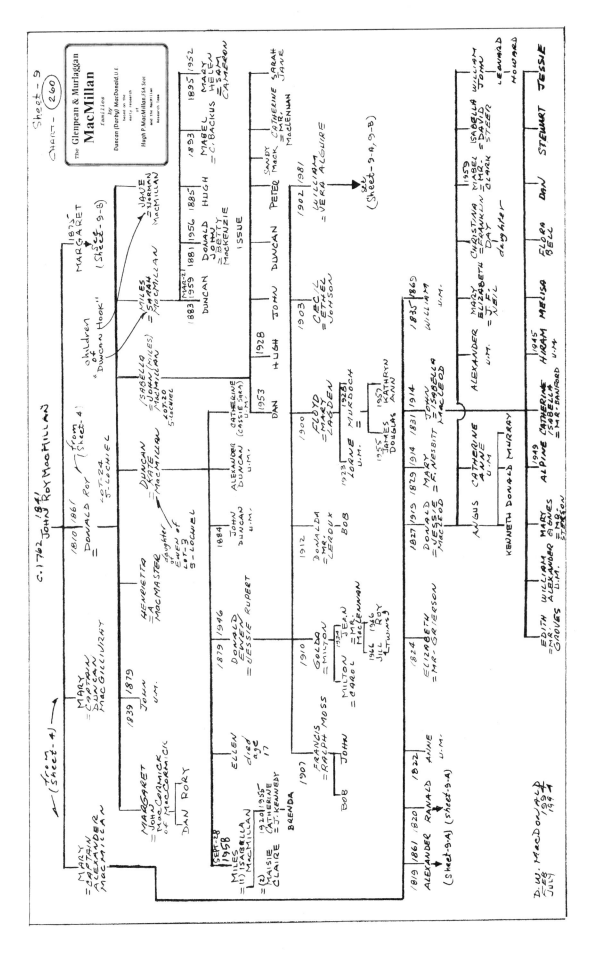

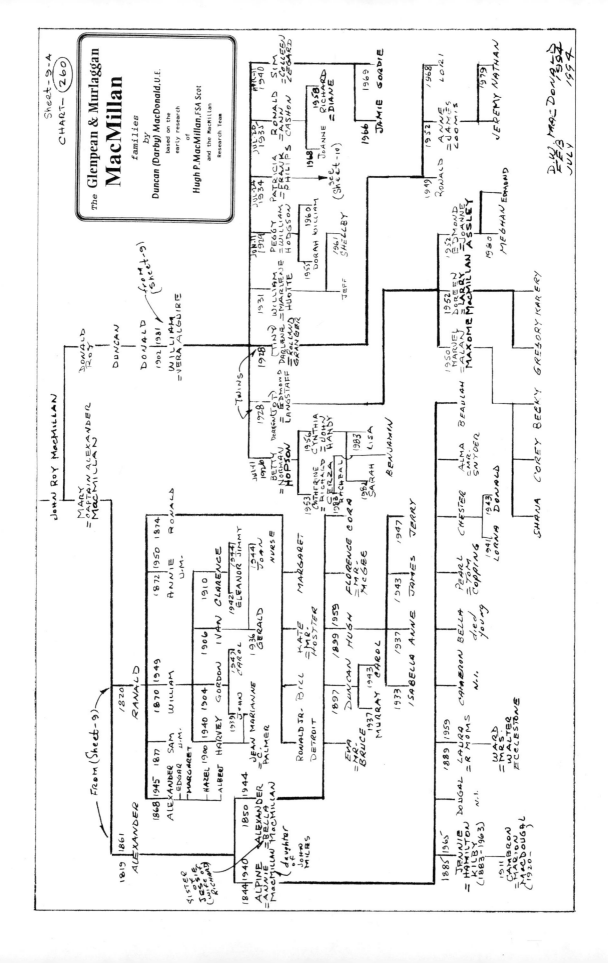

The Glenpean & Murlaggan
**MacMillan**
families
by
**Duncan (Darby) MacDonald, U.E.**
based on the
early research
of
**Hugh P. MacMillan, FSA Scot**
and the MacMillan
Research Team

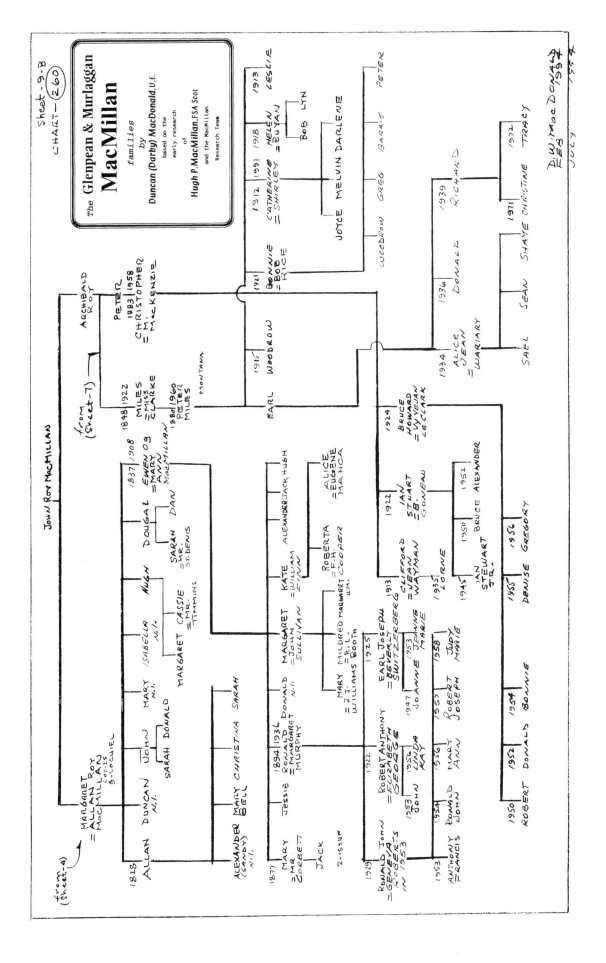

The Glenpean & Murlaggan
**MacMillan**
families
by
Duncan (Darby) MacDonald, U.E.
based on the
early research
of
Hugh P. MacMillan, FSA Scot
and the MacMillan
Research Team

JOHN ROY MACMILLAN

D.W. MacDONALD
FEB 1994

JULY 1994

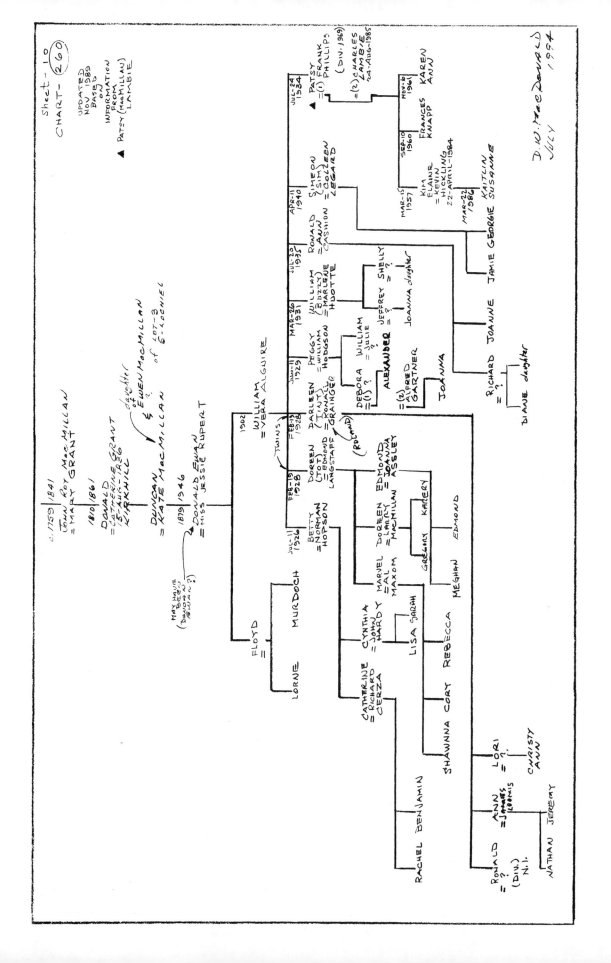

Sheet-10
CHART- (260)

UPDATED
NOV. 1989
BASED
ON
INFORMATION
FROM
▲ PATSY (MacMILLAN)
LAMBIE

c.1759/1841
JOHN ROY MacMILLAN
= MARY GRANT

1810/1861
DONALD
= CATHERINE GRANT
13-AUG-1836
KIRKHILL

DUNCAN
= KATE MacMILLAN
daughter of
EWEN MacMILLAN
of LOT-3
S. LOCHIEL

1879/1946
DONALD EWAN
= MISS JESSIE RUPERT

MAY HAVE
BEEN
(DUNCAN?)
(SWAN?)

D.W. MacDONALD
JULY
1994

The Glenpean & Murlaggan
# MacMillan
*families*
*by*
**Duncan (Darby) MacDonald**, U.E.
based on the
early research
of
**Hugh P. MacMillan**, FSA Scot
and the MacMillan
Research Team

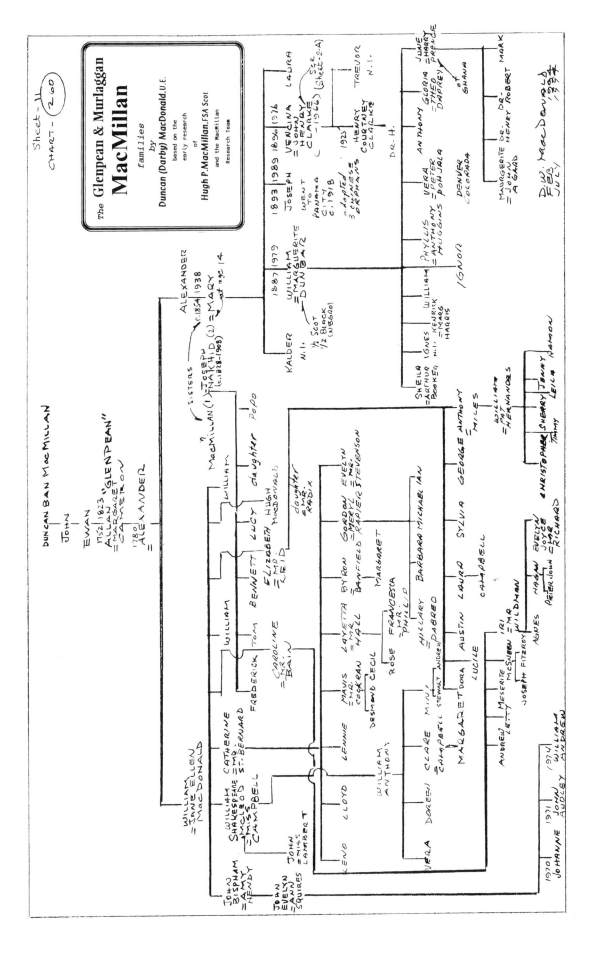

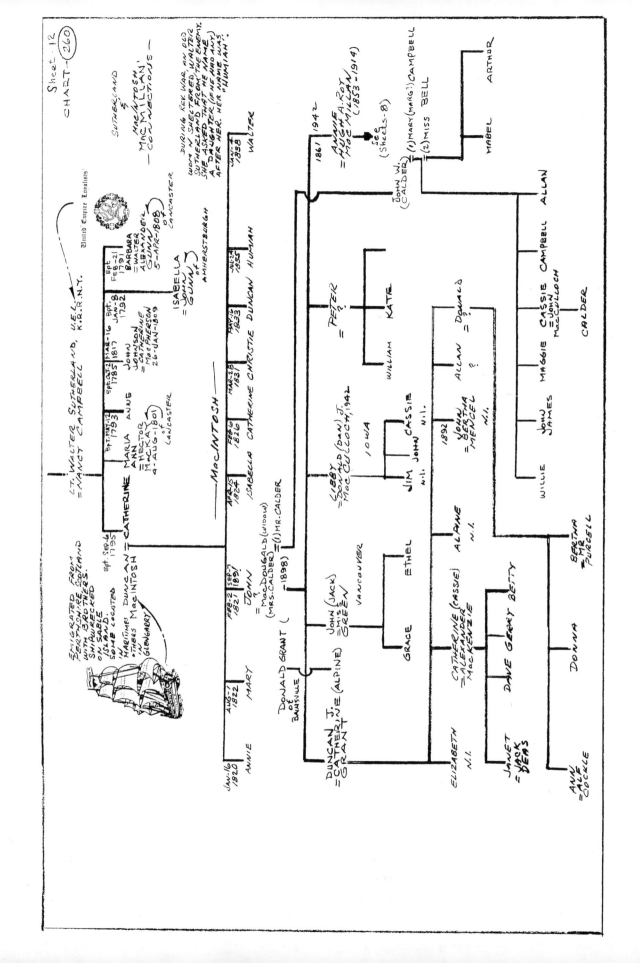

SUTHERLAND'S
&
MACINTOSH /
MAC MILLAN
CONNECTIONS

United Empire Loyalists

EMIGRATED FROM
PERTHSHIRE SCOTLAND
WITH BROTHERS.
SHIPWRECKED
ON SABLE
ISLAND.
SOME LOCATED
IN
MARITIMES DUNCAN
+ OTHERS MAC INTOSH
IN
GLENGARRY

LT. WALTER SUTHERLAND, U.E.L.
= NANCY CAMPBELL
K.R.R.N.Y.

DURING REV. WAR, AN OLD
WOMAN SHELTERED WALTER
SUTHERLAND FROM THE ENEMY.
SHE ASKED THAT HE NAME
A DAUGHTER (IF HE HAD ANY)
AFTER HER. HER NAME WAS
"HUMAN".

Bpt. May 12
1793
MARIA
ANN
= HECTOR
MACKAY
4-AUG-1801
of
LANCASTER

Bpt. Aug. 6
1795
CATHERINE = DUNCAN MACINTOSH

Bpt. Oct. 2
1785
JOHN
JOHNSON
= CATHERINE
MACPHERSON
26-JAN-1809

Bpt. Mar-16
1817

Bpt.
Jan-8
1792

Bpt.
Feb-21
1791
BARBARA
ALEXANDER
= WALTER
GUNN
5-APR-1808
of
LANCASTER

ISABELLA
= JOHN
GUNN
of
AMHERSTBURGH

MACINTOSH

Jan-16
1820
ANNIE

Aug-1
1822
MARY

Feb-2
1821
JOHN
= ?
= MAC DOUGALD (WIDOW)
(MRS. CALDER)
(1) MR. CALDER
(1898)

Sep-7
1897

Apr-15
1824
ISABELLA

Feb-10
1826
CATHERINE

Mar-18
1831
CHRISTIE

May-10
1833
DUNCAN

Jul-24
1855
HUMAN

Jan-1
1838
WALTER

1861 1942
ANNIE
= HUGH A. ROY
MAC MILLAN
(1853 - 1914)

JOHN W.
(CALDER)
(1) MARY (MARG?) CAMPBELL
(2) MISS BELL

see
(Sheets-B)

MABEL

ARTHUR

DONALD GRANT
of
BAINSVILLE

DUNCAN J.
= CATHERINE (ALPINE)
GRANT

JOHN (JACK)
= MISS
GREEN
VANCOUVER

GRACE

ETHEL

LIBBY
= DONALD (DAN) J.
MAC CULLOCH, 1942
IOWA

PETER
= ?

WILLIAM

KATE

JIM
N.I.
JOHN
N.I.
CASSIE
N.I.

1892
JOHN
= BERTHA
MENZEL
N.I.

ALLAN
= ?

DONALD
?

WILLIE

JOHN
JAMES

MAGGIE

CASSIE
= JOHN
MAC CULLOCH

CAMPBELL

ALLAN

CALDER

ELIZABETH
N.I.

CATHERINE (CASSIE)
= ALEXANDER
MAC KENZIE

ALPINE
N.I.

JANET
= JACK
DEAS

DAVE GERRY BETTY

BERTHA
= MR
PURCELL

DONNA

ANN
= ALF
COCKLE

## DESCENDANTS OF JOHN MacMILLAN
### OF GLENPEAN

The following computerized genealogical chart shows descendants of John MacMillan, common ancestor of the 'Glenpean' and 'Murlaggan' McMillans/MacMillans who migrated to Glengarry, Canada and to the Caribbean in the late eighteenth and early nineteenth centuries. The arabic numbers on the left side will help you to find your way through the listings. For example, in the first generation, Alexander, son of John MacMillan of Glenpean, is preceded by the number 2. You will find his entry is number 2 in the second generation. Alexander's son Archibald is number 4 in the third generation, and so on. The numbers in square brackets [ ] indicate to which generation of descent the person belongs. For instance, John[1] MacMillan shows that he is of the first generation. His son Alexander[2] is of the second generation, at least as far as this printed chart is concerned. In total, nine generations are listed below. The names in the round brackets ( ) are the ancestors of the listed person. For instance, the first name of the FOURTH GEN-ERATION is Mary. She is listed as Mary[4] MacMillan (Archibald[3], Alexander[2], John of Glenpean[1]. Born 1798. Died 1865. In other words Mary (1798-1865) was of the fourth [4] generation, counting John of Glenpean as [1]. She was the daughter of Archibald, who was son of Alexander, who in turn was son of John. Not surprisingly, names of many spouses and children are unknown.

### FIRST GENERATION

1.  John[1] MacMillan of Glenpean, son of Duncan ban MacMillan and Unknown Unknown. Res. Glenpean, Scotland.

    He married Unknown Unknown. Children:
    2   i.   Alexander[2].
        ii.  Margaret. She married Unknown Cameron of Strone.
    3   iii. Ewan.
        iv.  Donald.
        v.   Dugald.
        vi.  Duncan.

### SECOND GENERATION

2.  Alexander[2] 'Murlaggan' MacMillan (John of Glenpean[1]). Res. Murlaggan, Scotland.

    He married Unknown Unknown. Children:
    4   i.   Archibald[3].

3.  Ewan[2] MacMillan (John of Glenpean[1]). Died 1769.

    He married Unknown Unknown. Children:
        i.   Archibald[3]. Res. Grenada. Immigration, Grenada, Trinidad & Jamaica.
        ii.  Ranald. Res. Grenada. Immigration, Granada, Trinidad & Jamaica.
    5   iii. Allan 'Glenpean.'
    6   iv.  Lt. Col. Alexander.
    7   v.   John Roy.

### THIRD GENERATION

4.  Archibald[3] MacMillan (Alexander[2], John of Glenpean[1]). Born 1762. Died 1832. Immigration: 1802 Canada.

    He married Isabella Gray. Born 1770. Died 1853. Children:
        i.   Alexander[4]. Born 1795. Died 1823. Occupation: advocate.
        ii.  Archibald. Born 1796.
    8   iii. Mary.
        iv.  Margaret. Born 1799. Died 1847. She married William Hamilton.
        v.   John. Born 1805. Died 1846.
        vi.  Wiliam. Born 1808. Died 1899.
    9   vii. Duncan.
    10  viii. Tomina.
        ix.  Unknown.

5.  Allan (Glenpean)[3] MacMillan (Ewan[2], John of Glenpean[1]). Born ca. 1752. Died 3 Apr 1823. Burial St. Andrews, Williamstown.

    He married Margaret Cameron. Died 1806. Children:
    11  i.   Margaret[4].
        ii.  Ewan. Born 1777. Res. Finch, Ont.
        iii. John. Born 1778. Res. Pointe Fortune, Que.
    12  iv.  Alexander.
    13  v.   James.
        vi.  Donald. Born 1784. Died Montréal. Occupation: merchant.
        vii. Archibald. Born 1787. Died 1806 Montréal. Occupation: advocate.
        viii. Helen. Born 1789.
        ix.  Janet. Born 1792.

6.  Lt. Col. Alexander[3] MacMillan (Ewan[2], John of Glenpean[1]). Born ca. 1756. Died 1823.

    He married a: Unknown Unknown.

129

He married b: Marcella MacDonell, dau. Lt. Col.
Alexander MacDonell (Greenfield) and Janet MacDonell
(Aberchalder). Born 3 Feb 1779. Children:

14    i.   Captain Alexander Allan[4].

     ii.   Anne. Born 1808.

15   iii.  Aeneas John.

     iv.  Janet. Born 1817.

     v.   Ewan. Born 1819.

     vi.  Margaret.

7.  John Roy[3] MacMillan (Ewan[2], John of Glenpean[1]).
Born ca. 1762. Died 1841.

He married Mary Grant. Born 1769. Died 1870.
Immigration: 1791 at age 22. Children:

16    i.   Ewen Roy[4].

17   ii.   Myles Roy II.

18  iii.  Archibald Roy.

19   iv.  Donald Roy.

20   v.   Mary I.

     vi.  John Roy.

     vii.  Miles I. Died smallpox.

21  viii.  Isabella.

     ix.  Mary II. She married Capt. Duncan
MacGillivray, son of Archibald MacGillivray.

     x.   Janet. She married Angus MacLeod, son of
Captain Alexander MacLeod.

22   xi.  Margaret.

     xii.  Unknown.

     xiii.  Unknown.

     xiv.  Unknown.

     xv.  Unknown.

## FOURTH GENERATION

8.  Mary[4] MacMillan (Archibald[3], Alexander[2], John of
Glenpean[1]). Born 1798. Died 1865.

She married Thomas Kains, son of Unknown Kains. Born
1792. Died 1855. Children:

     i.   George[5].

     ii.   Isabella. She married C.C. Abbott.

     iii.  Thomas McMillan. Born 1823. Died 1878. He
married Margaret Treadwell.

     iv.  William King. He married Henrietta Hamilton.

     v.   Charles. Died 1925.

     vi.  John Alexander. He married Emma Elizabeth
Hughes.

     vii.  Zebbie. She married Charles Roe.

     viii.  Archie. Born 1854. He married Marks Hicks.

9.  Duncan[4] MacMillan (Archibald[3], Alexander[2], John
of Glenpean[1]). Born 1812. Died 1901 Grenville, Que.

He married Harriet Greece. Children:

23    i.   Alexander Grey[5].

     ii.   Lawrence Duncan. Born 6 Jan 1868. Died 27
Dec 1870. Burial: Grenville.

27  iii.  Duncan Arthur.

     iv.  Harriet Louise. Born 6 Feb 1874. Died 9 Feb
1949. Burial: Grenville.

     v.   Henrietta Rowena. Born 1877. Died 21 Apr
1962. Burial: Apr 1962 Grenville. She married
Archibald Still.

     vi.  Lorne Miles. Born 6 Apr 1883. Died 14 Aug 1965
in Grimsby Ont. Burial: Aug 1965 in Knowlton,
Que. He married Lena Hall.

24   vii.  Emma Elizabeth.

25  viii.  Charles Archibald.

     ix.  Florence Rosetta. Born 6 Apr 1883. Died 11 Jun
1883. Burial: Jun 1883 Grenville.

26   x.   John William.

10.  Tomina[4] MacMillan (Archibald[3], Alexander[2], John
of Glenpean[1]). Born 1813.

She married George Kains, son of Unknown Kains. Born
1801. Children:

     i.   George[5].

     ii.   Joseph.

     iii.  John.

     iv.  Robert.

     v.   Robert.

11.  Margaret[4] MacMillan (Allan (Glenpean)[3], Ewan[2],
John of Glenpean[1]). Born 1775. Died 1853.

She married Alexander Cameron of Stron Lea. Children:

     i.   Ewan[5]. Born 1797. Died 1863.

     ii.   James. Born 1803. Died 1868.

     iii.  Margaret. Born 1804. Died 1885. She married
Unknown Cameron.

     iv.  Archibald R. Born 1809. Died 1848.

     v.   Mary. Born 1811. She married John MacPhee.

     vi.  Ellen. Born 1817. Died 1913.

     vii.  Donald. Died 1850. He married Mary
MacDonald.

     viii.  Unknown.

     ix.  Unknown. He married Marcella Gaudie.

12.  Alexander[4] MacMillan (Allan (Glenpean)[3], Ewan[2],
John of Glenpean[1]). Born 1780. Res. Trinidad.

He married Unknown Unknown. Children:

28    i.   William[5].

29   ii.   Alexander.

13.  James[4] MacMillan (Allan (Glenpean)[3], Ewan[2], John
of Glenpean[1]). Born 1782. Died 1858. Occupation:
Clerk, North-West Co.

He married a: Josette Beleisle. Born ca. 1785. Children:

30    i.   William[5]. Born ca. 1806. Died 29 Sept 1903.

     ii.   James. Born ca. 1808.

     iii.   Ewan.

He married b: Marie Letendre. Born ca. 1790. Children:

     iv.   Hélène. Born 1811.

31    v.   Margaret. Born 16 Sept 1813.

32    vi.   Angelique. Born ca. 1814.

     vii.   Allan. Born 1 Jan 1816. Died 1841.

     viii.   Suzanne.

He married c: Kilakotah, daughter of sub-chief Coboway Clatsop. Children:

33    ix.   Victoire. Born 1821.

He married d: Eleanor McKinley 1830. Children:

     x.   James.

     xi.   Ewan Alexander. Occupation: Clerk, Hudson's Bay Co.

     xii.   Nellie. Born 1830.

     xiii.   Margaret. Born 1833. Died 1859.

     xiv.   Patrick. Residence Scotland.

     xv.   Eleanor Cameron.

     xvi.   Unknown.

     xvii.   Unknown.

14. Captain Alexander Allan[4] MacMillan (Lt. Col. Alexander[3], Ewan[2], John of Glenpean[1]).

He married a: Elizabeth Crites U.E. Children:

34    i.   Alexander Allan U.E.[5].

35    ii.   Angus.

     iii.   William.

     iv.   George. Died 1921.

     v.   Andrew. Died 1885 Duck Lake. Occupation: North West Mounted Police.

36    vi.   Archibald.

     vii.   Hyminis.

37    viii.   Jane.

38    ix.   Elizabeth.

He married b: Unknown Unknown.

15. Aeneas John[4] MacMillan (Lt. Col. Alexander[3], Ewan[2], John of Glenpean[1]). Born 1813. Died Cornwall. Founder MacMillan's Corners. Occupation: Indian Agent.

He married Unknown Unknown. Children:

     i.   Eliza[5]. She married George Roper.

     ii.   Gertrude.

     iii.   Catherine. Born 1866. Died 1940. She married Joseph Brault.

     iv.   Aeneas John.

16. Ewen Roy[4] MacMillan (John Roy[3], Ewan[2], John of Glenpean[1]). Born 1797. Died 1896. Burial Kirk Hill.

He married Harriet MacLeod. Res. Lot 18, 5 Lochiel (20, 4th). Children:

39    i.   Hugh Roy[5].

40    ii.   John.

17. Myles Roy[4] MacMillan II (John Roy[3], Ewan[2], John of Glenpean[1]). Born 1800. Died 1885 Cheboygan, Mich.

He married Unknown Cameron. Children:

41    i.   John Miles[5].

     ii.   Mary. She married Xavier Plaunt.

42    iii.   Isabella.

43    iv.   Florence.

     v.   Catherine (Kitty). She married Kenneth Macleod.

44    vi.   George Bell.

18. Archibald Roy[4] MacMillan (John Roy[3], Ewan[2], John of Glenpean[1]). Born 1803. Died 1899.

He married Margaret Grant, daughter of Duncan Grant. Born 1815. Died 23 May 1893. Children:

45    i.   Annie[5].

46    ii.   Duncan.

     iii.   Isabella. Born 1839. Died 1921.

     iv.   Alexander (Sandy). Born 1840. Died 1929 Lot 26, Conc. 4 Lochiel.

47    v.   Peter.

48    vi.   Miles.

49    vii.   Henrietta.

     viii.   John. Born 1851. Died 1917.

50    ix.   Hugh Archie Roy.

19. Donald Roy[4] MacMillan (John Roy[3], Ewan[2], John of Glenpean[1]). Born 1810. Died 1861 Lot 24, Conc. 5 Lochiel.

He married Catherine Grant 15 Aug 1836 in Kirk Hill. Children:

51    i.   Margaret[5].

     ii.   John. Born 1839. Died 1879.

     iii.   Henrietta. She married A. MacMaster.

52    iv.   Duncan.

53    v.   Isabella.

54    vi.   Miles.

     vii.   Jane. She married Norman MacMillan, son of Duncan 'The Hook' MacMillan.

20. Mary[4] MacMillan I (John Roy[3], Ewan[2], John of Glenpean[1]). Died Lot 27, Conc. 7 Lancaster.

She married Capt. Alexander MacMillan, son of Donald MacMillan. Res. Lot 27, Conc. 7 Lancaster. Children:

55    i.   Alexander[5].

56    ii.   Ronald.

     iii.   Anne.

     iv.   Elizabeth. She married Unknown Grierson.

57    v.   Donald.

     vi.   Mary. She married F. Nesbitt.

58    vii.  John.

      viii. William. Born 1835. Died 1869.

21.   Isabella[4] MacMillan (John Roy[3], Ewan[2], John of Glenpean[1]). Died 1843.

      She married Alexander Gillies. Children:

59    i.    Isabella.

22.   Margaret[4] MacMillan (John Roy[3], Ewan[2], John of Glenpean[1]).

      She married Allan Roy MacMillan. Res. Lot 25, Conc. 9 Lochiel. Children:

60    i.    Allan[5].

      ii.   Duncan.

61    iii.  John.

      iv.   Mary.

      v.    Isabella.

62    vi.   Hugh.

63    vii.  Dougal.

64    viii. Ewen Og.

**FIFTH GENERATION**

23.   Alexander Grey[5] MacMillan (Duncan[4], Archibald[3], Alexander[2], John of Glenpean[1]). Born 1863. Died 20 Nov 1923. Burial Vancouver.

      He married Unknown Unknown. Children:

      i.    Marjorie[6]. Born 1892. Died 2 Mar 1977. Burial: Mar 1977 Vancouver. She married Oscar Orr.

      ii.   Isobel Gray. Born 1894. Died 27 Aug 1983 in Vancouver.

      iii.  Dr. John Alexander. Born 1903. Died 24 Mar 1981. Burial Vancouver.

24.   Emma Elizabeth[5] MacMillan (Duncan[4], Archibald[3], Alexander[2], John of Glenpean[1]). Died 16 Jun 1928. Burial Calumet, Ont.

      She married James Ezekiel Carson. Children:

      i.    James Fraser[6]. Born 17 Aug 1897. Died 22 Mar 1984. Burial Lachute.

      ii.   Isobel. Died 12 Jan 1975. Burial Grenville Roman Catholic cem. She married Joseph Carrière.

25.   Charles Archibald[5] MacMillan (Duncan[4], Archibald[3], Alexander[2], John of Glenpean[1]). Died 16 Aug 1940. Burial Cowansville United Church cem.

      He married Mary Armentrout. Children:

65    i.    Kenneth Duncan[6].

66    ii.   Archibald Gray.

      iii.  Maybell. Died 8 Mar 1959. Burial: Mar 1959 Cowansville Union cem. She married Lawrence Spencer Henderson.

      iv.   Grace. Born 14 Feb 1901. She married Donald J. Barker.

26.   John William[5] MacMillan (Duncan[4], Archibald[3], Alexander[2], John of Glenpean[1]). Died 26 Jan 1956. Burial Crystal Lake, Stanstead, Que.

      He married Mary Ryan. Children:

      i.    Claire[6]. Died 6 Jan 1987. Burial: Jan 1987 Crystal Lake, Stanstead.

      ii.   Vivian Donalda. Died 9 Feb 1978. Burial: Feb 1978 Thunder Bay. She married Edgar Esdras Burns.

      iii.  Margaret. She married Leo Cole.

      iv.   Donald Ewan. Born 31 May 1908. Died 19 Sept 1973. Burial: Sept 1973 Mountain View, Thunder Bay. He married Jean Gertrude Webb.

27.   Duncan Arthur[5] MacMillan (Duncan[4], Archibald[3], Alexander[2], John of Glenpean[1]). Born 1872.

      He married Unknown Unknown. Children:

      i.    Lester[6].

      ii.   Jean. She married E. Fehrenbach.

28.   William[5] MacMillan (Alexander[4], Allan (Glenpean)[3], Ewan[2], John of Glenpean[1]).

      He married Jane Ellen MacDonald. Children:

67    i.    William Shakespeare MacLeod[6].

68    ii.   John Bisham.

69    iii.  Catherine.

70    iv.   Caroline.

71    v.    Elizabeth.

      vi.   William.

      vii.  Hugh MacDonald.

      viii. William.

29.   Alexander[5] MacMillan (Alexander[4], Allan (Glenpean)[3], Ewan[2], John of Glenpean[1]).

      He married Unknown Unknown. Children:

72    i.    Mary[6].

73    ii.   Unknown.

30.   William[5] MacMillan (James[4], Allan (Glenpean)[3], Ewan[2], John of Glenpean[1]). Born ca. 1806. Died 29 Sept 1903 Red River.

      He married Marguerite Dease, daughter of John Warren Dease. Born 1813. Died 1905. Children:

      i.    Margaret[6]. Born 12 Jan 1840. She married Jean-Baptiste Beauchemin.

      ii.   Marie-Anne. Born 18 Jan 1842. She married Salomon Carrière.

      iii.  Philomène. Born ca. 1847. She married Thomas Hogue.

74    iv.   Joseph. Born 4 Dec 1849. Died 1922.

      v.    Virginie. Born ca. 1851. She married Daniel

Carrière.

vi. Sarah. Born 5 March 1854. She married a: Joseph Turcotte; b: Pierre Jobin; and c: Antoine Vandal.

75 viii. Patrick. Born 18 May 1856. Died 1906.

76 ix. John. Born ca. 1857.

x. Elisabeth. Born ca. 1859. She married Pierre Bruce.

31. Helen[5] MacMillan (James[4], Allan (Glenpean)[3], Ewan[2], John of Glenpean[1]). Born 1811. Died 1876.

She married Baptiste Boyer 1833. Children:

i. Emilie[6]. Born ca. 1836.

ii. William. Born ca. 1840.

iii. Baptiste.

iv. Clémence.

v. Félicité.

vi. Hélène.

vii. Marguerite.

32. Angélique[5] MacMillan (James[4], Allan (Glenpean)[3], Ewan[2], John of Glenpean[1]). Born ca. 1814. Died 1860.

She married John Warren Dease, Jr. Children:

i. Ellen[6]. Born ca. 1841.

ii. Michael. Born ca. 1848.

33. Victoire[5] MacMillan (James[4], Allan (Glenpean)[3], Ewan[2], John of Glenpean[1]). Born ca. 1821. Died 1898.

She married a: Joseph McLoughlin.

She married b: Pierre LaCourse Jr. Children:

i. William[6]. Born ca. 1851.

ii. Louis. Born ca. 1852.

iii. Claude. Born ca. 1854. Twin of Sarah.

iv. Sarah. Born ca. 1854. Twin of Claude.

v. Agnes. Born 1857. Died 1860.

vi. Artibule Isaac. Born ca. 1860.

She married c: Simon-Etienne Grégoire. Born 1834. Died 1892. Children:

vii. Unknown.

viii. Unknown.

ix. Zenaide. Born ca. 1863.

x. David. Born ca. 1866.

34. Alexander Allan[5] MacMillan U.E. (Captain Alexander Allan[4], Lt. Col. Alexander[3], Ewan[2], John of Glenpean[1]). Born 1819. Died 1899.

He married a: Mary Ann Brown. Children:

77 i. Eugene U.E.[6].

78 ii. William.

79 iii. Helen.

He married b: Mahala Barlow. Children:

iv. Arthur. Born 1888. He married Eva Warner.

v. David. Born 1891. Died 1917.

80 vi. Neil.

81 vii. Teresa.

viii. Bessie. Born ca. 1895. Died young.

82 ix. Andrew.

35. Angus[5] MacMillan (Captain Alexander Allan[4], Lt. Col. Alexander[3], Ewan[2], John of Glenpean[1]). Born 1842. Died 1924.

He married Unknown Unknown. Children:

83 i. William[6].

84 ii. Edson Angus.

iii. Pling.

36. Archibald[5] MacMillan (Captain Alexander Allan[4], Lt. Col. Alexander[3], Ewan[2], John of Glenpean[1]).

He married an Unknown Unknown. Children:

i. Cora[6].

37. Jane[5] MacMillan (Captain Alexander Allan[4], Lt. Col. Alexander[3], Ewan[2], John of Glenpean[1]).

She married Robert Smith. Children:

i. Walter[6].

ii. Robert.

38. Elizabeth[5] MacMillan (Captain Alexander Allan[4], Lt. Col. Alexander[3], Ewan[2], John of Glenpean[1]).

She married Unknown Unknown. Children:

i. Mac[6].

ii. Lois.

39. Hugh Roy[5] MacMillan (Ewen Roy[4], John Roy[3], Ewan[2], John of Glenpean[1]). Born 1825. Died 1905 Glen Sandfield.

He married Mary MacMillan, daughter of Ewan ban MacMillan. Res. Lot 18, Conc. 5 Lochiel (20, 4th). Children:

i. Isabelle[6]. Born 1850. Died 1924.

85 ii. Mary.

iii. Miles (Hugh Roy). Born 1853. Died 1924.

iv. Hugh (Hugh Roy). Born 1855. Died 1933.

86 v. Christie.

87 vi. John A.

88 vii. Donald (Danny Hugh Roy).

viii. Maggie Ann. Born 1867. Died 1916.

89 ix. Hughie Archibald.

40. John[5] MacMillan (Ewen Roy[4], John Roy[3], Ewan[2], John of Glenpean[1]). Born 1827. Died 1888 Lot 18, Conc. 5 Lochiel.

He married Christy MacLean. Res. Lot 26, Conc. 7 Lochiel. Children:

90 i. Miles John[6].

ii. Flora. Born ca. 1861. Died 3 Feb 1899. She married Rev. Duncan MacRae.

91   iii. Donald John.

     iv. Annie.

     v. Lily. She married Archibald MacDonald.

     vi. Harriet. She married John Roy MacLeod.

     vii. Hugh Willie. Born 1874. Died 1919.

41.  John Miles[5] MacMillan (Myles Roy II[4], John Roy[3], Ewan[2], John of Glenpean[1]).

He married Janet McMillan. Born 1835. Died 1913. Children:

92   i. Alexander[6].

    ii. Isabella. Born 1867. Died 1908.

    iii. Mary. Born 1869. Died 1955. She married Tom Bond.

93   iv. John Miles.

94   v. Annie.

42.  Isabella[5] MacMillan (Myles Roy II[4], John Roy[3], Ewan[2], John of Glenpean[1]).

She married Unknown Paul. Children:

    i. John[6]. He married Ada Unknown.

    ii. Bob.

    iii. Mary.

95   iv. Kitty Bell.

    v. Lizza.

43.  Florence[5] MacMillan (Myles Roy II[4], John Roy[3], Ewan[2], John of Glenpean[1]).

She married a: Alexander MacMillan. Children:

96   i. 'Black' Archie[6].

    ii. 'Black' John (Jack).

97   iii. Richard.

She married b: Unknown Bond. Children:

    iv. Tom. He married Mary MacMillan.

44.  George Bell[5] MacMillan (Myles Roy II[4], John Roy[3], Ewan[2], John of Glenpean[1]). Born 1847. Died 1916.

He married Unknown Unknown. Children:

    i. John Roy[6]. Born 1885. Died 1927.

    ii. Vernon Miles. Born 1889.

    iii. Hazel. Born 1894.

    iv. George Leonard. Born 1897.

98   v. Dan Robert.

    vi. Catherine. Born 1904.

45.  Annie[5] MacMillan (Archibald Roy[4], John Roy[3], Ewan[2], John of Glenpean[1]). Born 1837. Died 25 Apr 1893.

She married Unknown Cameron. Residence in South Branch. Children:

    i. Unknown[6]. She married Unknown Cain.

46.  Duncan[5] MacMillan (Archibald Roy[4], John Roy[3], Ewan[2], John of Glenpean[1]). Born 1838. Died 1918. Aka 'Duncan The Night.'

He married Unknown MacRae. Children:

    i. Bella[6]. She married Unknown Sparks.

    ii. Cassie. She married Unknown Watt.

    iii. Hattie. She married W. Chamberlin.

    iv. John Duncan. Born 1873. Died 1931.

    v. Duncan. Born 1874. Died 1949.

47.  Peter[5] MacMillan (Archibald Roy[4], John Roy[3], Ewan[2], John of Glenpean[1]). Born 1842. Died 1890.

He married Margaret MacRae, daughter of Christopher MacRae and Isabella MacGregor 30 Jul 1869. Children:

    i. Donald John[6]. Born 1870. Died 1956 Kirk Hill.

99   ii. Duncan Peter.

100  iii. Isabella.

101  iv. Margaret.

102  v. Christopher.

    vi. Archibald. Born 1885.

103  vii. Mary Henrietta.

    viii. Peter. Born 1888. He married E. Dewar.

48.  Miles[5] MacMillan (Archibald Roy[4], John Roy[3], Ewan[2], John of Glenpean[1]). Born 1848. Died 1922.

He married Unknown Clarke. Residence in South Branch. Children:

    i. Jane[6]. Born 1873. Died 1951. She married Archie Ferguson.

104  ii. Archibald Miles.

105  iii. Peter Miles.

106  iv. Louisa.

107  v. Catherine (Cassie).

49.  Henrietta[5] MacMillan (Archibald Roy[4], John Roy[3], Ewan[2], John of Glenpean[1]). Born 1848. Died 1890 Kirk Hill.

She married Donald MacGillivray. Res. Kirk Hill. Children:

    i. Bella[6].

    ii. Maggie Ann.

    iii. John Robert.

    iv. Peter.

    v. Donald John. Veteran Boer War.

50.  Hugh Archie Roy[5] MacMillan (Archibald Roy[4], John Roy[3], Ewan[2], John of Glenpean[1]). Born 1853. Died 1914.

He married Annie MacIntosh U.E., daughter of John MacIntosh U.E. and Unknown MacDougald. Born 1861. Died 1942 Martintown. Children:

108  i. Rev. John Archibald U.E.[6].

109  ii. Margaret U.E.

110  iii. Isabella U.E.

111  iv. Catherine U.E.

v. Peter U.E. Born 1891. Died 1972 Lot 27, Conc. 4 Lochiel.

vi. Maria Grace U.E. Born 1896. Died 1977. She married Ernest Swerdfager.

112 vii. Phyllis U.E.

51. Margaret[5] MacMillan (Donald Roy[4], John Roy[3], Ewan[2], John of Glenpean[1]).

She married John MacCormick. Children:

i. Dan[6].

ii. Rory.

52. Duncan[5] MacMillan (Donald Roy[4], John Roy[3], Ewan[2], John of Glenpean[1]).

He married Kate MacMillan, daughter of Ewen MacMillan. Children:

i. Catherine (Cassie Sara)[6].

ii. Alexander Duncan (Alex Duncie).

113 iii. Donald Ewen.

iv. John Duncan. Born, 1884.

v. Ellen. Died age 17 years.

114 vi. Myles Angus.

53. Isabella[5] MacMillan (Donald Roy[4], John Roy[3], Ewan[2], John of

She married John (Miles) MacMillan. Children:

i. Dan[6]. Died 1953.

ii. Hugh. Died 1928.

iii. John.

iv. Duncan.

v. Peter.

vi. Sandy Mack.

vii. Catherine. She married Unknown Maclennan.

viii. Sarah Jane.

54. Miles[5] MacMillan (Donald Roy[4], John Roy[3], Ewan[2], John of Glenpean[1]). Born 1849. Died 1915.

He married Sarah MacMillan, daughter of Duncan 'The Hook' MacMillan. Children:

i. Donald John[6]. Born 1881. Died 1956. He married Betty MacKenzie.

ii. Duncan. Born 1883. Died 21 Mar 1959.

iii. Hugh. Born 1885.

iv. Mabel. Born 1893. She married C. Backus.

v. Mary Ellen. She married Sam Cameron.

55. Alexander[5] MacMillan (Mary I[4], John Roy[3], Ewan[2], John of Glenpean[1]). Born 1819. Died 1861.

He married Unknown Unknown. Children:

115 i. Alpine[6].

116 ii. Alexander.

56. Ronald[5] MacMillan (Mary I[4], John Roy[3], Ewan[2], John of Glenpean[1]). Born 1820.

He married Unknown Unknown. Children:

117 i. Alexander[6].

118 ii. William.

iii. Annie. Born 1872. Died 1950.

119 iv. Ronald.

v. Sam. Born 1877.

57. Donald[5] MacMillan (Mary I[4], John Roy[3], Ewan[2], John of Glenpean[1]).

He married Jessie Macleod. Children:

120 i. Angus[6].

ii. Catherine Anne.

iii. Alexander.

iv. Mary Elizabeth. She married J.F. Neil.

121 v. Christina.

vi. Mabel. Died 1959. She married Unknown Clark.

vii. Isabella. She married David Steer.

122 viii. William John.

58. John[5] MacMillan (Mary I[4], John Roy[3], Ewan[2], John of Glenpean[1]).

He married Isabella Macleod. Children:

i. Edith[6]. She married Unknown Groves.

ii. William Alexander.

iii. Mary Agnes. She married Unknown Sterson.

iv. Alpine. Died 1949.

v. Catherine Isabella. She married Unknown Banford.

vi. Hiram. Died 1945.

vii. Melissa.

viii. FloraBell.

ix. Dan.

x. Stewart.

xi. Jessie.

59. [5] Isabella Gillies (Isabella[4], John Roy[3], Ewan[2], John of Glenpean[1]). Born 1843. Died 1933.

She married George Smith. Children:

i. Arthur[6]. Born 1877.

123 ii. Catherine Isabella.

iii. Mary Agnes. Born 1883. She married John Dixon.

60. Allan[5] MacMillan (Margaret[4], John Roy[3], Ewan[2], John of Glenpean[1]). Born 1828.

He married Unknown Unknown. Children:

i. Alexander (Sandy)[6].

ii. MaryBell.

iii. Christina.

iv. Sarah.

61. John[5] MacMillan (Margaret[4], John Roy[3], Ewan[2], John of Glenpean[1]).

He married Unknown Unknown. Children:

 i. Sarah[6].

 ii. Donald.

62. Hugh[5] MacMillan (Margaret[4], John Roy[3], Ewan[2], John of Glenpean[1]).

 He married Unknown Unknown. Children:

  i. Margaret[6].

  ii. Cassie. She married Unknown Timmins.

63. Dougal[5] MacMillan (Margaret[4], John Roy[3], Ewan[2], John of Glenpean[1]).

 He married Unknown Unknown. Children:

  i. Sarah[6]. She married Unknown Denis.

  ii. Dan.

64. Ewen og[5] MacMillan (Margaret[4], John Roy[3], Ewan[2], John of Glenpean[1]). Born 1837. Died 1908.

 He married Mary Ann MacMillan. Children:

124 i. Mary[6].

  ii. Jessie.

125 iii. Ronald.

  iv. Donald.

126 v. Margaret.

127 vi. Kate.

  vii. Alexander.

  viii. Jack.

  ix. Hugh.

### SIXTH GENERATION

65. Kenneth Duncan[6] MacMillan (Charles Archibald[5], Duncan[4], Archibald[3], Alexander[2], John of Glenpean[1]). Died 17 Dec 1950. BurialCowansville Union cem.

 He married Elizabeth Irene Palmer. Children:

  i. Unknown[7]. She married Unknown Weir.

  ii. Unknown. She married Unknown Ledingham.

66. Archibald Gray[6] MacMillan (Charles Archibald[5], Duncan[4], Archibald[3], Alexander[2], John of Glenpean[1]). Died 11 Feb 1931 Cowansville.

 He married Unknown Unknown. Children:

  i. Unknown[7]. She married Unknown Dunphy.

67. William Shakespeare MacLeod[6] MacMillan (William[5], Alexander[4], Allan (Glenpean)[3], Ewan[2], John of Glenpean[1]). Res. Grenada.

 He married a: Unknown Campbell. Children:

128 i. William Anthony[7].

 Associated b: Unknown Unknown. Children:

  ii. John. He married Unknown Lambert.

68. John Bisham[6] MacMillan (William[5], Alexander[4], Allan (Glenpean)[3], Ewan[2], John of Glenpean[1]).

He married a: Amy Hendy. Children:

 i. John Evelyn[7].

He married b: Ann Squires. Children:

 ii. Johanne. Born 1970.

 iii. John Audley. Born 1971.

 iv. William Andrew. Born 1974.

69. Catherine[6] MacMillan (William[5], Alexander[4], Allan (Glenpean)[3], Ewan[2], John of Glenpean[1]).

 She married Unknown Bernard. Children:

  i. Leno[7].

  ii. Lloyd.

  iii. Lennie.

129 iv. Mavis.

130 v. Layetta.

131 vi. Byron.

132 vii. Gordon.

  viii. Evelyn. She married Unknown Stevenson.

70. Caroline[6] MacMillan (William[5], Alexander[4], Allan (Glenpean)[3], Ewan[2], John of Glenpean[1]).

 She married Unknown Bain. Children:

  i. Andrew[7].

  ii. Letty.

  iii. Meserite.

133 iv. McSneen.

134 v. Iri.

71. Elizabeth[6] MacMillan (William[5], Alexander[4], Allan (Glenpean)[3], Ewan[2], John of Glenpean[1]).

 She married Unknown Leid. Children:

  i. Dora[7].

  ii. Lucile.

  iii. Austin.

135 iv. Laura.

  v. Sylvia.

  vi. George.

136 vii. Anthony.

72. Unknown[6] MacMillan (Alexander[5], Alexander[4], Allan (Glenpean)[3], Ewan[2], John of Glenpean[1]).

 She married Joseph Nakhid (his 1st marriage). Born ca. 1828. Died 1908. Children:

  i. Frederick[7].

  ii. Tom.

  iii. Bennett.

  iv. Lucy.

  v. Unknown.

  vi. Popo.

73. Mary[6] MacMillan (Alexander[5], Alexander[4], Allan (Glenpean)[3], Ewan[2], John of Glenpean[1]). Born ca. 1854. Died 1938.

She married Joseph Nakhid (his second marriage). Children:

    i. Kalder[7].

137  ii. William.

    iii. Joseph. Born 1893. Died 1989 Panama City.

138  iv. Vencina.

    v. Laura.

74. Joseph[6] MacMillan (William[5], James[4], Allan (Glenpean)[3], Ewan[2], John of Glenpean[1]). Born 4 Dec 1849. Died 1922.

He married Appolline Bruce. Born 1853. Died 1922. Children:

    i. Pauline[7]. She married Charles Sear.

    ii. Helen. She married Unknown Lagassie.

139  iii. William.

140  iv. Joseph.

141  v. Kate.

    vi. Frederick. Died age 14.

    vii. Sarah. Died 1934. She married C. Hogue.

75. Patrick[6] MacMillan (William[5], James[4], Allan (Glenpean)[3], Ewan[2], John of Glenpean[1]). Born 1856. Died 1906.

He married Beatrice Caplette. Children:

    i. Sara[7].

    ii. John.

    iii. Patrick. Born 1869.

142  iv. Peter.

143  v. Georgina.

76. John[6] MacMillan (William[5], James[4], Allan (Glenpean)[3], Ewan[2], John of Glenpean[1]). Born 1858.

He married Sara Bruce. Children:

144  i. Allen[7].

    ii. Virginia. She married C. Porteous.

    iii. Josephine. She married J. Porteous.

    iv. Emma.

77. Eugene[6] MacMillan U.E. (Alexander Allan U.E.[5], Captain Alexander Allan[4], Lt. Col. Alexander[3], Ewan[2], John of Glenpean[1]). Born 1874.

He married a: Josephine McGuire 1895. Children:

    i. Roy[7]. Born 1896.

    ii. Ernest. Born 1897. Died 1917 (WWI).

145  iii. Hilda MaryAnne.

    iv. Stuart U.E. Born Oct 1905.

    v. Bruce U.E. Born Oct 1905. Died 1989.

    vi. Eric.

He married b: Lynda Hummel.

78. William[6] MacMillan (Alexander Allan U.E.[5], Captain Alexander Allan[4], Lt. Col. Alexander[3], Ewan[2], John of Glenpean[1]). Born 1875. Died 1960.

He married Helen MacRae 1875. Children:

    i. Gordon[7]. He married Evelyn Liscomb.

    ii. Kenneth. Born 1915. Res. Cornwall.

    iii. Ernie.

    iv. Helen. She married M. Scarbeau.

    v. Mary. She married Aden Thompson.

    vi. Evelyn.

79. Hellen[6] MacMillan (Alexander Allan U.E.[5], Captain Alexander Allan[4], Lt. Col. Alexander[3], Ewan[2], John of Glenpean[1]). Born 1888. Died 1939.

She married Frank Hammel 1905. Children:

147  i. Lola[7].

148  ii. Mabel.

80. Neil[6] MacMillan (Alexander Allan U.E.[5], Captain Alexander Allan[4], Lt. Col. Alexander[3], Ewan[2], John of Glenpean[1]). Born 1892.

He married Eliza Howard. Children:

149  i. Neil[7].

150  ii. Alexander.

81. Teresa[6] MacMillan (Alexander Allan U.E.[5], Captain Alexander Allan[4], Lt. Col. Alexander[3], Ewan[2], John of Glenpean[1]). Born 1895.

She married Homer Patterson. Children:

    i. Margery[7].

    ii. Lois.

    iii. David.

    iv. Esther.

    v. Bruce.

    vi. Ben.

    vii. Janet.

    viii. Neil.

    ix. Doug.

    x. Ron.

    xi. Raymond.

    xii. Edon.

82. Andrew[6] MacMillan (Alexander Allan U.E.[5], Captain Alexander Allan[4], Lt. Col. Alexander[3], Ewan[2], John of Glenpean[1]). Born 1896.

He married Della Plouffe 1907. Children:

    i. Carlton[7].

151  ii. Donald.

152  iii. Ethel.

    iv. Marion. Born 1914.

83. William[6] MacMillan (Angus[5], Captain Alexander Allan[4], Lt. Col. Alexander[3], Ewan[2], John of Glenpean[1]).

He married an Unknown Unknown. Children:

    i. Mary Alice[7]. She married Unknown Briffet.

84. Edson Angus[6] MacMillan (Angus[5], Captain Alexander

Allan[4], Lt. Col. Alexander[3], Ewan[2], John of Glenpean[1]).

He married Unknown Unknown. Children:

    i. Gaylord[7].
    ii. Vera.
    iii. Jessie.

85. Mary[6] MacMillan (Hugh Roy[5], Ewen Roy[4], John Roy[3], Ewan[2], John of Glenpean[1]). Born 1851. Died 8 Jul 1926 Lot 7, Conc. 7 Kenyon.

She married Dougal Ewan ('Little Dougal') MacMillan. Res. Lot 7, Conc. 7 Kenyon. Children:

153   i. Ewen Alexander[7].
    ii. Mary Jane. She married Duncan MacMillan.
    iii. AnnaBella. She married Dan MacMaster.
    iv. James Neil.

86. Christie[6] MacMillan (Hugh Roy[5], Ewen Roy[4], John Roy[3], Ewan[2], John of Glenpean[1]). Born 1859. Died 1944.

She married Rory (Big Malcolm) MacRae 1886. Res. Lot 3, Conc. 4 Lochiel. Children:

154   i. Gilbert[7].
    ii. Hugh. Res. Lot 4, Conc. 4 Lochiel.
    iii. Annie Mary.
155   iv. Ida.

87. John A.[6] MacMillan (Hugh Roy[5], Ewen Roy[4], John Roy[3], Ewan[2], John of Glenpean[1]). Born 12 May 1861. Died 25 Nov 1924.

He married Isabelle Gunning, 21 Mar 1889. Children:

    i. John[7].
    ii. Ambersina. Res. Hawaii.

88. Donald (Danny Hugh Roy)[6] MacMillan (Hugh Roy[5], Ewen Roy[4], John Roy[3], Ewan[2], John of Glenpean[1]). Born 1864 Glen Sandfield. Died 1944 Lot 21, Conc. 4 Lochiel.

He married Mary Jane MacLennan. Born Glen Sandfield. Children:

156   i. Angus[7].
    ii. James. Born 1898.
    iii. Catherine. Born 1901.
    iv. Christena. Born 1902. Died 1927. She married Arthur MacMillan.
157   v. Anna.
158   vi. Muriel.
    vii. Donald. Born 1913. Died Aug 1981.
    viii. Marion. Born 1913.

89. Hughie Archibald[6] MacMillan (Hugh Roy[5], Ewen Roy[4], John Roy[3], Ewan[2], John of Glenpean[1]). Born 1869. Died 1943.

He married Christena MacRae. Died 4 Jun 1939.

Children:

    i. Nettie[7]. Born 1899. She married Duncan MacCuaig 1925.
159   ii. Hugh Roy.
160   iii. Kathleen.
161   iv. Donald.
    v. Glendon. Born 1913. Died 17 Jan 1972 (WWII).

90. Miles John[6] MacMillan (John[5], Ewen Roy[4], John Roy[3], Ewan[2], John of Glenpean[1]). Born 1858. Died 1933 Lot 26, Conc. 6 Lochiel, (Kirkhill).

He married Annie MacMillan, daughter of Duncan 'The Hook' MacMillan. Children:

162   i. Duncan[7].
    ii. Gordon. Born 1916.
    iii. JoAnne.
    iv. Christie Mary. She married Walter Herity.
    v. Jessie. She married Unknown Brown.

91. Donald John[6] MacMillan (John[5], Ewen Roy[4], John Roy[3], Ewan[2], John of Glenpean[1]). Born 1863. Died 1960.

He married Catherine Clark. Children:

    i. Mary Hattie[7]. Born 1896. Died 1968. She married Donald John MacLeod.
163   ii. Clark.
164   iii. John Dougal.
    iv. Fraser. Born 1908. Res. Vankleek Hill.

92. Alexander[6] MacMillan (John Miles[5], Myles Roy II[4], John Roy[3], Ewan[2], John of Glenpean[1]). Born 1863. Died 1944.

He married Caroline Paulistitt. Born 1863. Died 1937. Children:

    i. Janet Eliza[7]. Born 1889. Died 1961. She married Tom MacDougall.
    ii. Margaret. Born 1894. She married Robert Wesley Latimer.
165   iii. Lloyd.
    iv. Percy. Born 1900. Died 1964.
    v. Olive. Born 1903. Died 1957. She married Unknown Smith.
    vi. Cecil. Born 1911. He married Helen Wilson.

93. John Miles[6] MacMillan (John Miles[5], Myles Roy II[4], John Roy[3], Ewan[2], John of Glenpean[1]). Born 1876. Died 1946.

He married Orpha Munshaw. Children:

    i. Kenneth[7]. Born 1917.
    ii. Alfred. Born 1920.

94. Annie[6] MacMillan (John Miles[5], Myles Roy II[4], John Roy[3], Ewan[2], John of Glenpean[1]).

She married Alpine MacMillan (115).

95. Kitty Bell[6] Paul (Isabella[5], Myles Roy II[4], John Roy[3], Ewan[2], John of Glenpean[1]).

   She married Unknown Unknown. Children:

       i. Margaret[7]. She married Unknown Gibson.

       ii. Isabel. She married John Blackwell.

96. Black Archie[6] MacMillan (Florence[5], Myles Roy II[4], John Roy[3], Ewan[2], John of Glenpean[1]).

   He married Unknown Unknown. Children:

   169    i. Miles[7].

       ii. Zelda. He married Barbara Unknown.

       iii. Elsie. She married R.P. Nichols.

       iv. Garnet. She married Tom Smith.

97. Richard[6] MacMillan (Florence[5], Myles Roy II[4], John Roy[3], Ewan[2],John of Glenpean[1]). Born 1859. Died 1945.

   He married Jessie MacMillan, daughter of Hugh MacMillan and Unknown Unknown. Died, 1935. Children:

   170    i. Flora[7].

   171    ii. Mabel.

   172    iii. Dan.

       iv. George. Born 1899. Died 1980. He married Viola Huggard.

   173    v. Mark.

98. Dan Robert[6] MacMillan (George Bell[5], Myles Roy II[4], John Roy[3], Ewan[2], John of Glenpean[1]).

   He married an Unknown Unknown. Children:

       i. Dan[7].

99. Duncan Peter[6] MacMillan (Peter[5], Archibald Roy[4], John Roy[3], Ewan[2], John of Glenpean[1]). Born 1874. Died 1947.

   He married Mary Jane MacMillan, daughter of 'Little Dougal' MacMillan. Res. Laggan. Children:

   174    i. Edna[7].

   175    ii. Douglas.

       iii. Peter D. Born 1903. Occupation: Piper.

       iv. MaryBel. Born 1906. Died 1980. She married Neil MacLean.

   176    v. Grace.

       vi. Ewen. Born 1911. He married L. Creller.

100. Isabella[6] MacMillan (Peter[5], Archibald Roy[4], John Roy[3], Ewan[2], John of Glenpean[1]). Born 1879.

   She married Dougal A. MacMillan. Children:

   177    i. Florence[7].

101. Margaret[6] MacMillan (Peter[5], Archibald Roy[4], John Roy[3], Ewan[2], John of Glenpean[1]). Born 1881. Died 1920.

   She married a: W. Lunt. Children:

       i. Wallace[7].

178    ii. Isabella.

   She married b: Unknown Gray.

102. Christopher[6] MacMillan (Peter[5], Archibald Roy[4], John Roy[3], Ewan[2], John of Glenpean[1]). Born 1883. Died 1958 B.C.

   He married M. MacKenzie. Children:

   179    i. Clifford[7].

   180    ii. Ian Stuart.

   181    iii. Bruce Howard.

103. Mary Henrietta[6] MacMillan (Peter[5], Archibald Roy[4], John Roy[3], Ewan[2], John of Glenpean[1]). Born 1886.

   She married Rev.D. MacCuaig. Occupation: Minister. Children:

       i. Unknown[7]. She married Unknown Hurst.

104. Archibald Miles[6] MacMillan (Miles[5], Archibald Roy[4], John Roy[3], Ewan[2], John of Glenpean[1]). Born 1875. Died 1955.

   He married Catherine MacDonald, daughter of Lachlan MacDonald. Children:

   182    i. Janet[7].

       ii. Donald. Born 1901. Died 1965.

   183    iii. Miles.

   184    iv. Audrey.

       v. Alexander. Residence in Alexandria.

105. Peter Miles[6] MacMillan (Miles[5], Archibald Roy[4], John Roy[3], Ewan[2], John of Glenpean[1]). Born 1880. Died 1960 Montana.

   He married Unknown Unknown. Children:

   185    i. Earl[7].

   186    ii. Catherine.

       iii. Leslie. Born 1913.

       iv. Woodrow. Born 1915.

   187    v. Helen.

   188    vi. Bonnie.

106. Louisa[6] MacMillan (Miles[5], Archibald Roy[4], John Roy[3], Ewan[2], John of Glenpean[1]). Born 1885. Died 1913.

   She married Archie MacRae. Born Glen Sandfield. Children:

   189    i. Wilson[7].

107. Catherine (Cassie)[6] MacMillan (Miles[5], Archibald Roy[4], John Roy[3],Ewan[2], John of Glenpean[1]). Died 1937.

   She married Allan Campbell. Res. Dalkeith. Children:

   190    i. Clifford[7].

       ii. Kathleen. Died 17 Jul 1941 (malaria).

108. Rev. John Archibald[6] MacMillan U.E. (Hugh Archie Roy[5], Archibald Roy[4], John Roy[3], Ewan[2], John of

Glenpean[1]). Born 1885. Died 1977. Occupation: Presbyterian Minister.

He married Dulcie Pearson. Born 1896. Died 1965. Children:

191    i.   Hugh Pearson U.E.[7]. Born 1924.

192    ii.   Alexander Grant U.E.

193    iii.   Peter Allan U.E.

194    iv.   John Stewart U.E.

195    v.   Marianne Margaret Grace U.E.

109. Margaret[6] MacMillan U.E. (Hugh Archie Roy[5], Archibald Roy[4], John Roy[3], Ewan[2], John of Glenpean[1]). Born 1886. Died 1934.

She married Alexander Fraser. Children:

   i.   Annie U.E.[7]. Occupation: Nurse.

   ii.   Sarah U.E. Occupation: Teacher.

   iii.   Jean U.E.. Occupation: Nurse.

   iv.   Grace U.E.

196    v.   Dorothea U.E.

   vi.   Claude U.E. Died 1968. Occupation: Sea Captain. He married Ellen Turnbull.

110. Isabella[6] MacMillan U.E. (Hugh Archie Roy[5], Archibald Roy[4], John Roy[3], Ewan[2], John of Glenpean[1]). Born 1888. Died 1925.

She married Myles Angus MacMillan (114).

111.    Catherine[6] MacMillan U.E. (Hugh Archie Roy[5], Archibald Roy[4], John Roy[3], Ewan[2], John of Glenpean[1]). Born 1888. Died 1979.

She married William P. MacNaughton. Children:

   i.   Isabella U.E.[7]. She married Unknown Huff.

198    ii.   Margaret Anne U.E.

   iii.   Marion U.E. Born 1924. She married Clayton Cameron.

112. Phyllis[6] MacMillan U.E. (Hugh Archie Roy[5], Archibald Roy[4], John Roy[3], Ewan[2], John of Glenpean[1]). Born 1896. Died 1968. Occupation: Nurse.

She married Cattanach MacLennan. Children:

   i.   Donald U.E.[7].

   ii.   Shirley U.E. She married Archibald MacMillan.

   iii.   Estelle U.E. She married Mortimer Curran.

113. Donald Ewen[6] MacMillan (Duncan[5], Donald Roy[4], John Roy[3], Ewan[2], John of Glenpean[1]). Born 1879. Died 1946.

He married Jessie Rupert. Children:

199    i.   Floyd[7].

200    ii.   William.

   iii.   Cecil. Born 1903. He married Ethel Johnson.

201    iv.   Francis.

202    v.   Golda.

   vi.   Donalda. Born 1912. She married Unknown Leroux.

114. Myles Angus[6] MacMillan (Duncan[5], Donald Roy[4], John Roy[3], Ewan[2], John of Glenpean[1]). Born 23 Nov 1892 Lochiel, Glengarry. Died 28 Sep 1958, Toronto.

He married a: Isabella MacMillan U.E. (110). Children:

197    i.   Catherine U.E.[7].

He married b: Florence May Clare 23 Nov 1929, Brooklyn, N.Y. Born 1897. Died 1987. Children:

203    ii.   Florence.

115. Alpine[6] MacMillan (Alexander[5], Mary I[4], John Roy[3], Ewan[2], John of Glenpean[1]). Born 1844. Died 1940.

He married Annie MacMillan (94). Children:

167    i.   Laura[7].

166    ii.   Jennie.

   iii.   Dougal.

   iv.   Cameron.

   v.   Bella. (died young).

   vi.   Pearl. She married Tom Copping.

168    vii.   Chester.

   viii.   Alma. She married Unknown Snyder.

   ix.   Beaulah.

116. Alexander[6] MacMillan (Alexander[5], Mary I[4], John Roy[3], Ewan[2], John of Glenpean[1]). Born 1850. Died 1944.

He married Bella MacMillan, daughter of Hugh MacMillan and Unknown Unknown. Children:

   i.   Eva[7]. She married Unknown Bruce.

204    ii.   Duncan.

205    iii.   Hugh.

   iv.   Florence. She married Unknown McGee.

   v.   Cora.

117. Alexander[6] MacMillan (Ronald[5], Mary I[4], John Roy[3], Ewan[2], John of Glenpean[1]). Born 1868. Died 1945.

He married Unknown Unknown. Children:

   i.   Edgar[7].

   ii.   Margaret.

   iii.   Hazel.

   iv.   Albert.

118. William[6] MacMillan (Ronald[5], Mary I[4], John Roy[3], Ewan[2], John of Glenpean[1]). Born 1870. Died 1949.

He married Unknown Unknown. Children:

206    i.   Harvey[7].

207    ii.   Gordon.

208    iii.   Ivan.

209    iv.   Clarence.

119. Ronald[6] MacMillan (Ronald[5], Mary I[4], John Roy[3], Ewan[2], John of Glenpean[1]). Born 1874.

He married Unknown Unknown. Children:

    i. Ronald Jr.[7]. Residence in Detroit.

    ii. Bill.

    iii. Kate. She married Unknown Hostter.

    iv. Margaret.

120. Angus[6] MacMillan (Donald[5], Mary I[4], John Roy[3], Ewan[2], John of Glenpean[1]).

He married Unknown Unknown. Children:

    i. Kenneth[7].

    ii. Donald.

    iii. Murray.

121. Christina[6] MacMillan (Donald[5], Mary I[4], John Roy[3], Ewan[2], John of Glenpean[1]).

She married Franklin Day. Children:

    i. Unknown[7].

122. William John[6] MacMillan (Donald[5], Mary I[4], John Roy[3], Ewan[2], John of Glenpean[1]).

He married an Unknown Unknown. Children:

210    i. Leonard[7].

123. Catherine Isabella[6] Smith (Anonymous[5], Isabella[4], John Roy[3], Ewan[2], John of Glenpean[1]). Born 1880.

She married John R. Woods. Children:

211    i. Harold Robert[7].

212    ii. Isabella Margaret.

124. Mary[6] MacMillan (Ewen og[5], Margaret[4], John Roy[3], Ewan[2], John of Glenpean[1]).

She married Unknown Corbet. Children:

    i. Jack[7].

125. Ronald[6] MacMillan (Ewen og[5], Margaret[4], John Roy[3], Ewan[2], John of Glenpean[1]). Born 1894. Died 1936.

He married Margaret Murphy. Children:

213    i. Robert Anthony[7].

214    ii. Earl Joseph.

215    iii. Ronald John.

126. Margaret[6] MacMillan (Ewen og[5], Margaret[4], John Roy[3], Ewan[2], John of Glenpean[1]).

She married John Sullivan. Children:

    i. Mary[7]. She married J.J. Williams.

    ii. Mildred. She married R.L. Booth.

    iii. Margaret.

127. Kate[6] MacMillan (Ewen og[5], Margaret[4], John Roy[3], Ewan[2], John of Glenpean[1]).

She married William Finn. Children:

    i. Roberta[7]. She married F.H. Cooper.

    ii. Alice. She married Eugene Manca.

SEVENTH GENERATION

128. William Anthony[7] MacMillan (William Shakespeare MacLeod[6], William[5], Alexander[4], Allan (Glenpean)[3], Ewan[2], John of Glenpean[1]).

He married Unknown Unknown. Children:

    i. Vera[8].

    ii. Doreen.

216    iii. Clare.

    iv. Mini.

129. Mavis[7] Bernard (Catherine[6], William[5], Alexander[4], Allan (Glenpean)[3], Ewan[2], John of Glenpean[1]).

She married Unknown Cockran. Children:

    i. Desmond[8].

    ii. Cecil.

130. Layetta[7] Bernard (Catherine[6], William[5], Alexander[4], Allan (Glenpean)[3], Ewan[2], John of Glenpean[1]).

She married Unknown Hall. Children:

    i. Rose[8].

    ii. Francesca. She married Unknown Phillip.

131. Byron[7] Bernard (Catherine[6], William[5], Alexander[4], Allan (Glenpean)[3], Ewan[2], John of Glenpean[1]).

He married Unknown Banfield. Children:

    i. Margaret[8].

132. Gordon[7] Bernard (Catherine[6], William[5], Alexander[4], Allan (Glenpean)[3], Ewan[2], John of Glenpean[1]).

He married Meryl Rapier. Children:

    i. Hillary[8].

    ii. Barbara.

    iii. Michael.

    iv. Ian.

133. McSneen[7] Bain (Caroline[6], William[5], Alexander[4], Allan (Glenpean)[3], Ewan[2], John of Glenpean[1]).

He married an Unknown Unknown. Children:

    i. Joseph[8].

    ii. Fitzroy.

134. Iri[7] Bain (Caroline[6], William[5], Alexander[4], Allan (Glenpean)[3], Ewan[2], John of Glenpean[1]).

She married Unknown Wildman. Children:

    i. Agnes[8].

217    ii. Hagan.

    iii. Evelyn Joyce. She married Unknown Richard.

135. Laura[7] Leid (Elizabeth[6], William[5], Alexander[4], Allan (Glenpean)[3], Ewan[2], John of Glenpean[1]).

She married Unknown Unknown. Children:

      i. Campbell[8].

136. Anthony[7] Leid (Elizabeth[6], William[5], Alexander[4], Allan (Glenpean)[3], Ewan[2], John of Glenpean[1]).

    He married Unknown Miles. Children:

218    i. William[8].

137. William[7] Nakhid (Mary[6], Alexander[5], Alexander[4], Allan (Glenpean)[3], Ewan[2], John of Glenpean[1]). Born 1887. Died 1979.

    He married Marguerite Dunbar. Children:

      i. Sheila[8]. She married Arthur Booker.

      ii. Ignes.

      iii. Kenrick. He married Margaret Harris.

      iv. William.

      v. Ignor.

      vi. Phyllis. She married Anthony Huggins.

      vii. Vera. She married Peter Pohjala.

      viii. Anthony.

      ix. Gloria. She married Theo Daprey.

219    x. June.

138. Vencina[7] Nakhid (Mary[6], Alexander[5], Alexander[4], Allan (Glenpean)[3], Ewan[2], John of Glenpean[1]). Born 1896. Died 1976.

    She married John Henry Clarke. Died 1966. Children:

      i. Trevor[8].

220    ii. Henry Courtney.

139. William[7] MacMillan (Joseph[6], William[5], James[4], Allan (Glenpean)[3], Ewan[2], John of Glenpean[1]).

    He married Unknown Unknown. Children:

      i. Leonard St. James[8].

      ii. Lorraine. She married B. Cotton.

      iii. Mary. She married Unknown Beaston.

      iv. Gladys. She married Unknown Desjardins.

140. Joseph[7] MacMillan (Joseph[6], William[5], James[4], Allan (Glenpean)[3], Ewan[2], John of Glenpean[1]). Born 1881. Died 1970.

    He married E. Breland. Died 1964. Children:

221    i. Harold[8].

222    ii. Chester.

      iii. Hector. Occupation: R.C.A.F. Died WWII.

      iv. Warren.

223    v. Rolland.

141. Kate[7] MacMillan (Joseph[6], William[5], James[4], Allan (Glenpean)[3], Ewan[2], John of Glenpean[1]). Born 1893. Died 1964.

    She married Unknown Lavoie. Children:

      i. Pauline[8]. She married Reginald Jones.

      ii. Teresa. She married Unknown Little.

142. Peter[7] MacMillan (Patrick[6], William[5], James[4], Allan (Glenpean)[3], Ewan[2], John of Glenpean[1]). Born 1882.

    He married Unknown Unknown. Children:

      i. Pat[8].

224    ii. Marg.

      iii. Joan.

      iv. Joe.

      v. Violet.

      vi. Gordon.

      vii. Dorothy.

143. Georgina[7] MacMillan (Patrick[6], William[5], James[4], Allan (Glenpean)[3], Ewan[2], John of Glenpean[1]).

    She married Unknown Narlane. Children:

      i. Eva[8].

225    ii. Ella.

144. Allen[7] MacMillan (John[6], William[5], James[4], Allan (Glenpean)[3], Ewan[2], John of Glenpean[1]).

    He married J. Livingston. Children:

226    i. John[8].

227    ii. Alvin.

145. Hilda MaryAnne[7] MacMillan (Eugene U.E.[6], Alexander Allan U.E.[5], Captain Alexander Allan[4], Lt. Col. Alexander[3], Ewan[2], John of Glenpean[1]). Born 1899.

    She married Unknown Vanourt. Children:

      i. Kim Susan[8].

      ii. Maresia. She married F. McCarthy.

146. Eric[7] MacMillan (Eugene U.E.[6], Alexander Allan U.E.[5], Captain Alexander Allan[4], Lt. Col. Alexander[3], Ewan[2], John of Glenpean[1]). Born Jun 1911.

    He married Helen Moors, 1931. Children:

228    i. Elaine[8].

229    ii. Marion.

230    iii. Madolyn.

231    iv. Marg.

      v. Ernest. Born 1946. He married Jeanne Leduc.

232    vi. Anne Mane.

147. Lola[7] Hammel (Hellen[6], Alexander Allan U.E.[5], Captain Alexander Allan[4], Lt. Col. Alexander[3], Ewan[2], John of Glenpean[1]).

    She married Lloyd Smith. Children:

      i. Lois[8].

      ii. Marjorie. She married Unknown Wouters.

      iii. Charles.

      iv. Helen. She married Unknown Bailey.

148. Mabel[7] Hammel (Hellen[6], Alexander Allan U.E.[5], Captain Alexander Allan[4], Lt. Col. Alexander[3], Ewan[2], John of Glenpean[1]).

She married Unknown Foldeak. Children:

    i. Robert[8].

149. Neil[7] MacMillan (Neil[6], Alexander Allan U.E.[5], Captain Alexander Allan[4], Lt. Col. Alexander[3], Ewan[2], John of Glenpean[1]).

He married an Unknown Unknown. Children:

    i. George[8]. Born 1948.

    ii. Eileen. Born 1949. She married Joseph Rann 1970.

150. Dr. Alexander[7] MacMillan (Neil[6], Alexander Allan U.E.[5], Captain Alexander Allan[4], Lt. Col. Alexander[3], Ewan[2], John of Glenpean[1]).

He married Helen Winter. Children:

    i. Marjorie[8]. She married Bruce Kensee 1971.

    ii. Lawrence. Born 1956.

151. Donald[7] MacMillan (Andrew[6], Alexander Allan U.E.[5], Captain Alexander Allan[4], Lt. Col. Alexander[3], Ewan[2], John of Glenpean[1]). Born 1909. Died 1968.

He married Unknown Unknown. Children:

    i. David[8].

    ii. Lawrence.

152. Ethel[7] MacMillan (Andrew[6], Alexander Allan U.E.[5], Captain Alexander Allan[4], Lt. Col. Alexander[3], Ewan[2], John of Glenpean[1]).

She married Lawrence Shields. Children:

    i. Joceline[8].

153. Ewen Alexander[7] MacMillan (Mary[6], Hugh Roy[5], Ewen Roy[4], John Roy[3], Ewan[2], John of Glenpean[1]). Born 1886. Died 1957.

He married Annie Mary MacDonald. Children:

233    i. Muriel[8].

234    ii. Dougal.

235    iii. Buchanan.

236    iv. Alexander.

154. Gilbert[7] MacRae (Christie[6], Hugh Roy[5], Ewen Roy[4], John Roy[3], Ewan[2], John of Glenpean[1]). Born 1900. Res. Lot 3, Conc. 4 Lochiel.

He married Gladys MacFayden. Children:

    i. Phyllis[8].

237    ii. Arnold.

238    iii. Doris.

155. Ida[7] MacRae (Christie[6], Hugh Roy[5], Ewen Roy[4], John Roy[3], Ewan[2], John of Glenpean[1]). Died 1932.

She married Dan MacKenzie. Res. Lot 6, Conc. 5 Lochiel. Children:

    i. Sadie Lois[8]. Born 4 Feb 1928. She married John D. MacMillan 18 Oct 1952.

    ii. Christena Rae.

156. Angus[7] MacMillan (Donald (Danny Hugh Roy)[6], Hugh Roy[5], Ewen Roy[4], John Roy[3], Ewan[2], John of Glenpean[1]). Born 1896.

He married Annie 'Duncie Sailor' MacRae. Res. Lot 21, Conc. 4 Lochiel. Children:

239    i. Elbert Rae[8].

240    ii. James.

241    iii. Judith Anne.

242    iv. Brian.

    v. David. Born 1956. He married Anne Marie MacPherson.

157. Anna[7] MacMillan (Donald (Danny Hugh Roy)[6], Hugh Roy[5], Ewen Roy[4], John Roy[3], Ewan[2], John of Glenpean[1]). Born 1903.

She married James Wright. Children:

    i. Garry[8].

    ii. Lester.

    iii. Lynn.

158. Muriel[7] MacMillan (Donald (Danny Hugh Roy)[6], Hugh Roy[5], Ewen Roy[4], John Roy[3], Ewan[2], John of Glenpean[1]). Born 1906. Died 22 Oct 1932.

She married John Campbell. Died 1960. Children:

243    i. Lorna[8].

244    ii. Beverly (R.N.).

245    iii. Jack.

246    iv. Mary.

159. Hugh Roy[7] MacMillan (Hughie Archibald[6], Hugh Roy[5], Ewen Roy[4], John Roy[3], Ewan[2], John of Glenpean[1]). Born 6 Aug 1905. Died 7 Jul 1975.

He married Janet MacMillan (182). Children:

247    i. Earl Linton[8].

248    ii. Sheldon.

    iii. Duncan. Born 1938.

249    iv. Shirley.

250    v. Jean Isabel.

251    vi. Hugh Leslie.

252    vii. Donald Alexander.

160. Kathleen[7] MacMillan (Hughie Archibald[6], Hugh Roy[5], Ewen Roy[4], John Roy[3], Ewan[2], John of Glenpean[1]). Born 16 Jun 1908.

She married Walter Broadie, 5 Sep 1931. Children:

    i. Walter[8]. Born 1932. Died 1955.

253    ii. Donald.

254    iii. Melvin.

161. Donald[7] MacMillan (Hughie Archibald[6], Hugh Roy[5], Ewen Roy[4], John Roy[3], Ewan[2], John of Glenpean[1]). Born 1910.

He married Muriel (Skippy) Stroud. Children:

255    i. Gail[8].

162. Duncan[7] MacMillan (Miles John[6], John[5], Ewen Roy[4], John Roy[3], Ewan[2], John of Glenpean[1]). Born 1913.

He married an Unknown Unknown. Children:
    i. David Douglas[8].

163. Clark[7] MacMillan (Donald John[6], John[5], Ewen Roy[4], John Roy[3], Ewan[2], John of Glenpean[1]). Born 1898. Died 1985. Occupation: R.C.A.F.

He married Jean MacDonald. Residence in east Hawkesbury. Children:
256  i. Dorothy[8].
257  ii. Donald Clark.

164. John Dougal[7] MacMillan (Donald John[6], John[5], Ewen Roy[4], John Roy[3], Ewan[2], John of Glenpean[1]). Born 1900. Died 1938.

He married Annie D.K. MacLeod. Residence in Spring Creek. Children:
    i. Catherine[8]. Died 1941.
    ii. Margaret. Born 1936.
258  iii. Wilma.

165. Lloyd[7] MacMillan (Alexander[6], John Miles[5], Myles Roy II[4], John Roy[3], Ewan[2], John of Glenpean[1]). Born 1896. Died 1956.

He married Olga Sirr. Children:
    i. Frank[8]. Born 1920. Died 1976.
259  ii. Paul.
260  iii. Margaret.
261  iv. Audrey.

166. Jennie[7] MacMillan (Alpine[6], Alexander[5], Mary I[4], John Roy[3], Ewan[2], John of Glenpean[1]). Born 1895. Died 1965.

She married Hamilton Kilby. Born 1883. Died 1963. Children:
    i. Cameron[8]. Born 1911. He married Marion MacDougal.

167. Laura[7] MacMillan (Alpine[6], Alexander[5], Mary I[4], John Roy[3], Ewan[2], John of Glenpean[1]). Born 1889. Died 1959.

She married R. Moms. Children:
    i. Ward[8]. He married Unknown Unknown.

168. Chester[7] MacMillan (Alpine[6], Alexander[5], Mary I[4], John Roy[3], Ewan[2], John of Glenpean[1]).

He married Unknown Unknown. Children:
    i. Lorna[8]. Born 1941.
    ii. Donald. Born 1943.

169. Miles[7] MacMillan (Black Archie[6], Florence[5], Myles Roy II[4], John Roy[3], Ewan[2], John of Glenpean[1]).

He married Unknown Watkins. Children:
    i. Miles[8].

    ii. Kirk.
    iii. Fax.

170. Flora[7] MacMillan (Richard[6], Florence[5], Myles Roy II[4], John Roy[3], Ewan[2], John of Glenpean[1]). Born 1888. Died 1981.

She married Roy Draper. Died 1964. Children:
    i. Ellwood Richard[8]. Born 1915. He married B. Lidstone.
    ii. Georgina. Born 1918. She married Tom Gelinas.
    iii. Flora Bell. Born 1924. She married S. Johns.
    iv. Viola. Born 1926. She married Stan Duguid.
    v. Jessie. Born 1926. Died 1953. She married Douglas Thompson.

171. Mabel[7] MacMillan (Richard[6], Florence[5], Myles Roy II[4], John Roy[3], Ewan[2], John of Glenpean[1]). Born 1889.

She married Unknown Bisnett. Children:
    i. Jessie[8]. She married Ernest Emery.
    ii. Douglas.
    iii. George.
    iv. Graydon.
    v. Gordon.

172. Dan[7] MacMillan (Richard[6], Florence[5], Myles Roy II[4], John Roy[3], Ewan[2], John of Glenpean[1]). Born 1891. Died 1964.

He married Hilda Unknown. Children:
    i. Hester[8]. She married J. Ellis.
262  ii. Hugh.
    iii. Robert.
    iv. Lorna. She married H. Ward.
    v. Eilica. She married Larry Parent.

173. Mark[7] MacMillan (Richard[6], Florence[5], Myles Roy II[4], John Roy[3],Ewan[2], John of Glenpean[1]).

He married P. Morrison. Children:
    i. Carl[8].
    ii. Dan.

174. Edna[7] MacMillan (Duncan Peter[6], Peter[5], Archibald Roy[4], John Roy[3], Ewan[2], John of Glenpean[1]). Born 1900.

She married Roderick MacCuaig. Children:
263  i. Millan[8].
    ii. Lloyd. Res. Vankleek Hill.
264  iii. Kenneth.
265  iv. Evelyn.

175. Douglas[7] MacMillan (Duncan Peter[6], Peter[5], Archibald Roy[4], John Roy[3], Ewan[2], John of Glenpean[1]). Born 1902. Occupation: Piper.

He married Pebby Smith. Res. Brodie, Ont. Children:
    i. Eldred Calvin[8]. Born 1933.

ii. Carlyle. Born 1947.

iii. Glenda. Born 1953.

176. Grace[7] MacMillan (Duncan Peter[6], Peter[5], Archibald Roy[4], John Roy[3], Ewan[2], John of Glenpean[1]). Born 1909.

She married William MacLennan. Res. Glen Sandfield, Ont. Children:

266 i. Sharyn[8].

177. Florence[7] MacMillan (Isabella[6], Peter[5], Archibald Roy[4], John Roy[3], Ewan[2], John of Glenpean[1]).

She married Herb Wright. Children:

i. Douglas[8].

178. Isabella[7] Lunt (Margaret[6], Peter[5], Archibald Roy[4], John Roy[3], Ewan[2], John of Glenpean[1]).

She married Irvine Bond. Res. Vankleek Hill. Children:

i. Mary[8].

179. Clifford[7] MacMillan (Christopher[6], Peter[5], Archibald Roy[4], John Roy[3], Ewan[2], John of Glenpean[1]). Born 1913.

He married Jean Wayman. Children:

i. Lorne[8]. Born 1935.

180. Ian Stuart[7] MacMillan (Christopher[6], Peter[5], Archibald Roy[4], John Roy[3], Ewan[2], John of Glenpean[1]). Born 1922.

He married B. Goneau. Children:

i. Ian Stewart Jr.[8]. Born 1945.

ii. Bruce. Born 1950.

iii. Alexander. Born 1952.

181. Bruce Howard[7] MacMillan (Christopher[6], Peter[5], Archibald Roy[4], John Roy[3], Ewan[2], John of Glenpean[1]). Born 1924.

He married VyVejean LeClark. Children:

i. Robert[8]. Born 1950.

ii. Donald. Born 1952.

iii. Bonnie. Born 1954.

iv. Denise. Born 1955.

v. Gregory. Born 1956.

182. Janet[7] MacMillan (Archibald Miles[6], Miles[5], Archibald Roy[4], John Roy[3], Ewan[2], John of Glenpean[1]). Res. Lot 20, Conc. 4 Lochiel.

She married Hugh Roy MacMillan (159).

183. Miles[7] MacMillan (Archibald Miles[6], Miles[5], Archibald Roy[4], John Roy[3], Ewan[2], John of Glenpean[1]). Born 1902.

He married Annie May MacDonald. Res. E. Hawkesbury. Children:

i. Archibald[8]. Born 1927. He married Shirley MacLennan.

267 ii. Orville.

iii. Wyman. Born 1931. He married Georgette Massia.

iv. Gordon. Born 1933.

268 v. Sheila.

184. Audrey[7] MacMillan (Archibald Miles[6], Miles[5], Archibald Roy[4], John Roy[3], Ewan[2], John of Glenpean[1]).

She married Clifford Austin. Children:

i. John Eldon[8].

ii. Bruce.

iii. Leila. She married Royal Renwick.

185. Earl[7] MacMillan (Peter Miles[6], Miles[5], Archibald Roy[4], John Roy[3], Ewan[2], John of Glenpean[1]).

He married Unknown Unknown. Children:

269 i. Alice Jean[8].

ii. Donald. Born 1936.

270 iii. Richard.

186. Catherine[7] MacMillan (Peter Miles[6], Miles[5], Archibald Roy[4], John Roy[3], Ewan[2], John of Glenpean[1]). Born 1912. Died 1991.

She married Unknown Unknown (Shirley?). Children:

i. Joyce[8].

ii. Melvin.

iii. Darlene.

187. Helen[7] MacMillan (Peter Miles[6], Miles[5], Archibald Roy[4], John Roy[3], Ewan[2], John of Glenpean[1]). Born 1918.

She married Unknown Buyan. Children:

i. Bob[8].

ii. Lyn.

188. Bonnie[7] MacMillan (Peter Miles[6], Miles[5], Archibald Roy[4], John Roy[3], Ewan[2], John of Glenpean[1]). Born 1921.

She married Bob Rice. Children:

i. Woodrow[8].

ii. Greg.

iii. Barrie.

iv. Peter.

189. Wilson[7] MacRae (Louisa[6], Miles[5], Archibald Roy[4], John Roy[3], Ewan[2], John of Glenpean[1]).

He married an Unknown Unknown. Children:

i. Kathleen[8].

190. Clifford[7] Campbell (Catherine (Cassie)[6], Miles[5], Archibald Roy[4], John Roy[3], Ewan[2], John of Glenpean[1]).

He married Flora MacSweyn, daughter of Duncan MacSweyn. Children:

271 i. Allan[8].

272 ii. Fergus.

191. Hugh Pearson[7] MacMillan U.E. (Rev. John Archibald
U.E.[6], Hugh Archie Roy[5], Archibald Roy[4], John
Roy[3], Ewan[2], John of Glenpean[1]). Born 12 Mar 1924.
Res. Guelph. Occupation: Retired Archivist.

He married Muriel Diver 1951, Vancouver. Children:
- 273　i.　Malcolm Laird U.E.[8].
- 　　ii.　Ian Pearson U.E. Born 1956.
- 　　iii.　Neale Hugh U.E. Born 1959.
- 274　iv.　Jocelyn Ruth U.E.

192. Alexander Grant[7] MacMillan U.E. (Rev. John Archibald
U.E.[6], Hugh Archie Roy[5], Archibald Roy[4], John
Roy[3], Ewan[2], John of Glenpean[1]).Born 1926.

He married Joyce Hull 1946. Children:
- 　　i.　Beth Ann U.E.[8]. Born 1948. She married
Stephen Johnston.
- 275　ii.　Janet U.E.
- 276　iii.　Peter Grant U.E.
- 277　iv.　Bonny U.E.
- 278　v.　Nancy U.E.
- 279　vi.　Glen U.E.

193. Peter Allan[7] MacMillan U.E. (Rev. John Archibald
U.E.[6], Hugh Archie Roy[5], Archibald Roy[4], John
Roy[3], Ewan[2], John of Glenpean[1]). Born 1930.

He married Janet Schricker 1960. Died 1981. Children:
- 　　i.　Karen U.E.[8]. Born 1963. She married W.
Kinsella.
- 　　ii.　Gavin U.E. Born 1965.
- 　　iii.　Kathlyn U.E. Born 1967.

194. John Stewart[7] MacMillan U.E. (Rev. John Archibald
U.E.[6], Hugh Archie Roy[5], Archibald Roy[4], John
Roy[3], Ewan[2], John of Glenpean[1]). Born 1932.

He married Carol Morris 1956. Children:
- 　　i.　Kimberly Ann U.E.[8]. Born 1959. She married
Unknown Patterson.
- 280　ii.　Kelly U.E.
- 　　iii.　Jonathan U.E. Born 1966.

195. Marianne Margaret Grace[7] MacMillan R.N.,U.E. (Rev.
John Archibald U.E.[6], Hugh Archie Roy[5], Archibald
Roy[4], John Roy[3], Ewan[2], John of Glenpean[1]).
Born 1933. Res. Lee Summit, Missouri.

She married Edward Lee Belser. Children:
- 　　i.　Scott U.E.[8]. Born 1962.
- 　　ii.　Craig U.E. Born 1964.

196. Dorothea[7] Fraser U.E. (Margaret U.E.[6], Hugh Archie
Roy[5], Archibald Roy[4], John Roy[3], Ewan[2], John of
Glenpean[1]).

She married Robert Gould. Children:
- 　　i.　Nancy[8].
- 　　ii.　Ellen.

197. Catherine[7] MacMillan U.E. (Myles Angus[6],
Duncan[5], Donald Roy[4], John Roy[3], Ewan[2], John
of Glenpean[1]). Born 1920. Died 1955.

She married John F. Kennedy, son of John A. Kennedy
and Mary Snetsinger. Children:
- 　　i.　Brenda[8].

198. Margaret Anne[7] MacNaughton U.E. (Catherine
U.E.[6], Hugh Archie Roy[5],Archibald Roy[4], John
Roy[3], Ewan[2], John of Glenpean[1]). Born 1922.

She married Ross Cameron. Children:
- 　　i.　Catherine U.E.[8]. Born 1956.
- 　　ii.　James U.E. Born 1958.
- 　　iii.　John U.E. Born 1961.

199. Floyd[7] MacMillan (Donald Ewen[6], Duncan[5],
Donald Roy[4], John Roy[3], Ewan[2], John of
Glenpean[1]). Born 1900.

He married Mary Lagden. Children:
- 　　i.　Lorne[8]. Born 1923.
- 281　ii.　Murdoch.

200. William[7] MacMillan (Donald Ewen[6], Duncan[5],
Donald Roy[4], John Roy[3], Ewan[2], John of
Glenpean[1]). Born 1902. Died 1981.

He married Vera Alguire. Children:
- 282　i.　Betty[8].
- 283　ii.　Doreen (Tot).
- 284　iii.　Darleen (Tiny).
- 285　iv.　Peggy.
- 286　v.　William (Buzzy).
- 287　vi.　Patricia (Patsy).
- 288　vii.　Ronald.
- 289　viii.　Simeon (Sim).

201. Francis[7] MacMillan (Donald Ewen[6], Duncan[5],
Donald Roy[4], John Roy[3], Ewan[2], John of
Glenpean[1]). Born 1907.

He married an Unknown Unknown. Children:
- 　　i.　Bob[8].
- 　　ii.　John.

202. Golda[7] MacMillan (Donald Ewen[6], Duncan[5],
Donald Roy[4], John Roy[3], Ewan[2], John of
Glenpean[1]). Born 1910.

She married Milton Unknown. Children:
- 　　i.　Milton[8].
- 290　ii.　Jean.

203. Florence[7] MacMillan (Myles Angus[6], Duncan[5],
Donald Roy[4], John Roy[3], Ewan[2], John of
Glenpean[1]). Born 1930.

She married Donald MacKenzie. Children:
- 291　i.　Randall[8].
- 　　ii.　Sharon.

    iii. Scott. Born 1960.

    iv. Donald. Born 1965.

204. Duncan[7] MacMillan (Alexander[6], Alexander[5], Mary I[4], John Roy[3], Ewan[2], John of Glenpean[1]). Born 1897.

He married Unknown Unknown. Children:

    i. Murray[8]. Born 1937.

    ii. Carol. Born 1943.

205. Hugh[7] MacMillan (Alexander[6], Alexander[5], Mary I[4], John Roy[3], Ewan[2], John of Glenpean[1]). Born 1899. Died 1959.

He married Unknown Unknown. Children:

    i. Isabella[8]. Born 1933.

    ii. Anne. Born 1937.

    iii. James. Born 1943.

    iv. Jerry. Born 1947.

206. Harvey[7] MacMillan (William[6], Ronald[5], Mary I[4], John Roy[3], Ewan[2], John of Glenpean[1]). Born 1900. Died 1940.

He married Unknown Unknown. Children:

    i. MariAnne[8].

    ii. Jean. She married C. Palmer.

207. Gordon[7] MacMillan (William[6], Ronald[5], Mary I[4], John Roy[3], Ewan[2], John of Glenpean[1]). Born 1904.

He married Unknown Unknown. Children:

    i. John[8]. Born 1939.

    ii. Carol. Born, 1947.

208. Ivan[7] MacMillan (William[6], Ronald[5], Mary I[4], John Roy[3], Ewan[2], John of Glenpean[1]). Born 1906.

He married Unknown Unknown. Children:

    i. Gerald[8]. Born 1936.

    ii. Joan. Born 1944.

209. Clarence[7] MacMillan (William[6], Ronald[5], Mary I[4], John Roy[3], Ewan[2], John of Glenpean[1]). Born 1910.

He married Unknown Unknown. Children:

    i. Eleanor[8]. Born 1942.

    ii. Jimmy. Born 1944.

210. Leonard[7] MacMillan (William John[6], Donald[5], Mary I[4], John Roy[3],Ewan[2], John of Glenpean[1]).

He married an Unknown Unknown. Children:

    i. Howard[8].

211. Harold Robert[7] Woods (Catherine Isabella[6], Anonymous[5], Isabella[4],John Roy[3], Ewan[2], John of Glenpean[1]).

He married Unknown Unknown. Children:

    i. Naomi[8].

    ii. John.

    iii. Helen.

    iv. David.

212. Isabella Margaret[7] Woods (Catherine Isabella[6], Anonymous[5], Isabella[4], John Roy[3], Ewan[2], John of Glenpean[1]).

She married Dr. W.D. Piercey. Children:

    i. Amy[8].

    ii. Isabella.

    iii. Joan.

    iv. Lynne.

    v. Susan.

    vi. Douglas.

213. Robert Anthony[7] MacMillan (Ronald[6], Ewen og[5], Margaret[4], John Roy[3], Ewan[2], John of Glenpean[1]). Born 1922.

He married Elizabeth George. Children:

    i. John[8]. Born 1953.

    ii. Linda Kay. Born 1956.

214. Earl Joseph[7] MacMillan (Ronald[6], Ewen og[5], Margaret[4], John Roy[3], Ewan[2], John of Glenpean[1]). Born 1925.

He married Beverly Switzerberg. Children:

    i. JoAnne[8]. Born 1947.

    ii. Jeanne Marie. Born 1953.

215. Ronald John[7] MacMillan (Ronald[6], Ewen og[5], Margaret[4], John Roy[3], Ewan[2], John of Glenpean[1]). Born 1929.

He married Geneva Roberts, 1953. Children:

    i. Anthony Francis[8]. Born 1953.

    ii. Ronald John. Born 1954.

    iii. Mary Ann. Born 1956.

    iv. Robert Joseph. Born 1957.

    v. Judy Marie. Born 1958.

**EIGHTH GENERATION**

216. Clare[8] MacMillan (William Anthony[7], William Shakespeare MacLeod[6], William[5], Alexander[4], Allan (Glenpean)[3], Ewan[2], John of Glenpean[1]).

She married Unknown Campbell. Children:

    i. Margaret[9].

217. Hagan[8] Wildman (Iri[7], Caroline[6], William[5], Alexander[4], Allan (Glenpean)[3], Ewan[2], John of Glenpean[1]).

He married an Unknown Unknown. Children:

    i. Peter[9].

    ii. John.

218. William[8] Leid (Anthony[7], Elizabeth[6], William[5], Alexander[4], Allan (Glenpean)[3], Ewan[2], John of Glenpean[1]).

He married Pat Hernandes. Children:
  i. Christopher[9].
  ii. Timmy.
  iii. Sherry.
  iv. Leila.
  v. Jenny.
  vi. Ramon.

219. June[8] Nakhid (William[7], Mary[6], Alexander[5], Alexander[4], Allan (Glenpean)[3], Ewan[2], John of Glenpean[1]).

  She married Harry Prence. Residence in Ghana. Children:
  i. Marguerite[9]. Residence in Trinidad. Occupation: Teacher.
  ii. Dr. Henry. Res. Trinidad.
  iii. Dr. Robert.
  iv. Mark.

220. Henry Courtney[8] Clarke (Vencina[7], Mary[6], Alexander[5], Alexander[4], Allan (Glenpean)[3], Ewan[2], John of Glenpean[1]). Born 1925.

  He married an Unknown Unknown. Children:
  i. Dr. Henry[9].

221. Harold[8] MacMillan (Joseph[7], Joseph[6], William[5], James[4], Allan (Glenpean)[3], Ewan[2], John of Glenpean[1]). Born Jul 1911.

  He married an Unknown Unknown. Children:
  i. Orville[9].
  ii. Howard Edward.

222. Chester[8] MacMillan (Joseph[7], Joseph[6], William[5], James[4], Allan (Glenpean)[3], Ewan[2], John of Glenpean[1]). Born 1913.

  He married an Unknown Unknown. Children:
  i. Brian[9].
  ii. Diana.

223. Rolland[8] MacMillan (Joseph[7], Joseph[6], William[5], James[4], Allan (Glenpean)[3], Ewan[2], John of Glenpean[1]). Born 1920.

  He married Ella Lane. Children:
  i. Carol Morrison[9].

224. Marg.[8] MacMillan (Peter[7], Patrick[6], William[5], James[4], Allan (Glenpean)[3], Ewan[2], John of Glenpean[1]).

  She married Unknown Porteous. Children:
  i. Georgina Dease[9].

225. Ella[8] Narlane (Georgina[7], Patrick[6], William[5], James[4], Allan (Glenpean)[3], Ewan[2], John of Glenpean[1]).

  She married Rolland MacMillan. Children:
  i. Carol[9].

226. John[8] MacMillan (Allen[7], John[6], William[5], James[4], Allan (Glenpean)[3], Ewan[2], John of Glenpean[1]).

  He married a: Clara Tola. Children:
  i. Kenneth[9].

  He married b: Alma Unknown. Children:
  ii. Patrick.
  iii. Lyn.

227. Alvin[8] MacMillan (Allen[7], John[6], William[5], James[4], Allan (Glenpean)[3], Ewan[2], John of Glenpean[1]). Born 1919. Died 1984.

  He married Teresa Robertson. Born 1925. Died 1974. Children:
  i. Joseph Alvin[9]. Born 1945. He married Patricia Elko.
  ii. Anne Catherine. Born 1946. She married James Toogood.
  iii. Joan Mary. Born 1948.
292 iv. Teresa Laverne.
293 v. Lucille Margaret.
294 vi. Virginia Louise.

228. Elaine[8] MacMillan (Eric[7], Eugene U.E.[6], Alexander Allan U.E.[5], Captain Alexander Allan[4], Lt. Col. Alexander[3], Ewan[2], John of Glenpean[1]). Born 1933.

  She married R. Chambers. Children:
  i. Michael[9].
  ii. Marie.
  iii. Margery.
  iv. Kevin.
  v. Paul. (Died in car accident).
  vi. Theresa.
  vii. Shirley.
  viii. Jack.
  ix. Bruce.
  x. Stuart.

229. Marion[8] MacMillan (Eric[7], Eugene U.E.[6], Alexander Allan U.E.[5], Captain Alexander Allan[4], Lt. Col. Alexander[3], Ewan[2], John of Glenpean[1]). Born Dec 1935.

  She married H.M. Brunette. Children:
  i. Greg[9].
  ii. Polly.
  iii. David.

230. Madolyn[8] MacMillan (Eric[7], Eugene U.E.[6], Alexander Allan U.E.[5], Captain Alexander Allan[4], Lt. Col. Alexander[3], Ewan[2], John of Glenpean[1]). Born Aug 1936.

  She married H.B. Curron. Children:
  i. Gail[9].
  ii. Susan.

iii. Cheryl.

iv. Linda.

231. Marg.[8] MacMillan (Eric[7], Eugene U.E.[6], Alexander Allan U.E.[5], Captain Alexander Allan[4], Lt. Col. Alexander[3], Ewan[2], John of Glenpean[1]). Born 1939.

She married H.A. LaFlamme. Children:

    i. Chris[9].

    ii. Marque.

    iii. Damian.

    iv. Jason.

    v. Michelle.

232. Anne Mane[8] MacMillan (Eric[7], Eugene U.E.[6], Alexander Allan U.E.[5], Captain Alexander Allan[4], Lt. Col. Alexander[3], Ewan[2], John of Glenpean[1]). Born 1948.

She married Unknown Unknown. Children:

    i. Scott[9].

    ii. Bradley.

233. Muriel[8] MacMillan (Ewen Alexander[7], Mary[6], Hugh Roy[5], Ewen Roy[4], John Roy[3], Ewan[2], John of Glenpean[1]). Born 1913.

She married Fred MacLeod. Children:

    i. Douglas[9].

    ii. Joan Margaret.

234. Dougal[8] MacMillan (Ewen Alexander[7], Mary[6], Hugh Roy[5], Ewen Roy[4], John Roy[3], Ewan[2], John of Glenpean[1]). Born, 1918. Died, 1978.

He married Dorothy Lothian. Born 1918. Died 1978. Children:

    i. Robert[9]. Born 1951.

    ii. Lynn. Born 1953.

    iii. Kyle. Born 1954.

    iv. Evelyn. Born 1963.

235. Buchanan[8] MacMillan (Ewen Alexander[7], Mary[6], Hugh Roy[5], Ewen Roy[4], John Roy[3], Ewan[2], John of Glenpean[1]). Born 1920.

He married Thelma Murray. Children:

    i. Mary[9]. Born 1948.

    ii. Robert. Born 1951.

    iii. Linda. Born 1954.

236. Alexander[8] MacMillan (Ewen Alexander[7], Mary[6], Hugh Roy[5], Ewen Roy[4], John Roy[3], Ewan[2], John of Glenpean[1]). Born 1922. Died 1963.

He married Margery Higgins. Children:

    i. Lorna[9]. Born 1954.

    ii. Ralph. Born 1955.

    iii. Bruce. Born 1956.

    iv. Barbara. Born 1961.

237. Arnold[8] MacRae (Gilbert[7], Christie[6], Hugh Roy[5], Ewen Roy[4], John Roy[3], Ewan[2], John of Glenpean[1]).

He married Margot Smith. Children:

    i. Keith[9].

    ii. Marnie.

238. Doris[8] MacRae (Gilbert[7], Christie[6], Hugh Roy[5], Ewen Roy[4], John Roy[3], Ewan[2], John of Glenpean[1]).

She married Donald ban MacMaster, Jun 1952. Children:

    i. Phyllis[9].

    ii. Ewen.

    iii. Steven.

    iv. Sandra.

    v. Mary.

239. Elbert Rae[8] MacMillan (Angus[7], Donald (Danny Hugh Roy)[6], Hugh Roy[5], Ewen Roy[4], John Roy[3], Ewan[2], John of Glenpean[1]). Born 1941.

He married Marcia Dawson. Children:

    i. Greg[9].

    ii. Todd.

    iii. Justin.

240. James[8] MacMillan (Angus[7], Donald (Danny Hugh Roy)[6], Hugh Roy[5], Ewen Roy[4], John Roy[3], Ewan[2], John of Glenpean[1]). Born 1943.

He married Ann MacKinnon. Children:

    i. Kevin[9].

    ii. Tania.

241. Judith Anne[8] MacMillan (Angus[7], Donald (Danny Hugh Roy)[6], Hugh Roy[5], Ewen Roy[4], John Roy[3], Ewan[2], John of Glenpean[1]). Born 1944.

She married Melville MacLeod, 1966. Children:

    i. Tara[9].

    ii. Heather.

242. Brian[8] MacMillan (Angus[7], Donald (Danny Hugh Roy)[6], Hugh Roy[5], Ewen Roy[4], John Roy[3], Ewan[2], John of Glenpean[1]). Born 1947.

He married Ada Unknown. Children:

    i. Wesley[9].

    ii. Kristopher.

243. Lorna[8] Campbell (Muriel[7], Donald (Danny Hugh Roy)[6], Hugh Roy[5], Ewen Roy[4], John Roy[3], Ewan[2], John of Glenpean[1]).

She married Archibald MacGregor. Children:

    i. Susan[9].

    ii. Sharon.

    iii. Scott.

    iv. Stephen.

    v. Stuart.

244. Beverly[8] Campbell (R.N.) (Muriel[7], Donald (Danny

Hugh Roy)[6], Hugh Roy[5], Ewen Roy[4], John Roy[3], Ewan[2], John of Glenpean[1]).

She married Fraser Cumming. Children:

    i. Douglas[9].

    ii. Gwendolyn.

    iii. Brian.

245. Jack[8] Campbell (Muriel[7], Donald (Danny Hugh Roy)[6], Hugh Roy[5], Ewen Roy[4], John Roy[3], Ewan[2], John of Glenpean[1]).

He married Unknown Unknown. Children:

    i. Jody[9].

    ii. Tara.

    iii. Johnny.

246. Mary[8] Campbell (Muriel[7], Donald (Danny Hugh Roy)[6], Hugh Roy[5], Ewen Roy[4], John Roy[3], Ewan[2], John of Glenpean[1]).

She married Rev. Tom Gemmell. Occupation: Minister. Children:

    i. Peter[9].

    ii. Lori.

    iii. Paul.

247. Earl Linton[8] MacMillan (Hugh Roy[7], Hughie Archibald[6], Hugh Roy[5], Ewen Roy[4], John Roy[3], Ewan[2], John of Glenpean[1]). Born 14 Aug 1932.

He married Marcelle Frehichlives. Children:

    i. Wayne[9].

    ii. Debbie.

295   iii. Sherry.

248. Sheldon[8] MacMillan (Hugh Roy[7], Hughie Archibald[6], Hugh Roy[5], Ewen Roy[4], John Roy[3], Ewan[2], John of Glenpean[1]).

He married Barbara Blum. Children:

    i. Craig[9].

249. Shirley[8] MacMillan (Hugh Roy[7], Hughie Archibald[6], Hugh Roy[5], Ewen Roy[4], John Roy[3], Ewan[2], John of Glenpean[1]). Born 14 Aug 1941.

She married Ransom Nixon. Children:

    i. Brian[9].

    ii. Richard.

250. Jean Isabel[8] MacMillan (Hugh Roy[7], Hughie Archibald[6], Hugh Roy[5], Ewen Roy[4], John Roy[3], Ewan[2], John of Glenpean[1]). Born 25 Oct 1944.

She married Irwin Sproule. Children:

    i. Brenda[9].

    ii. Byron.

251. Hugh Leslie[8] MacMillan (Hugh Roy[7], Hughie Archibald[6], Hugh Roy[5], Ewen Roy[4], John Roy[3], Ewan[2], John of Glenpean[1]). Born 13 Aug 1949.

He married Marilyn Beck 1980. Children:

    i. Hugh Brandon[9].

252. Donald Alexander[8] MacMillan (Hugh Roy[7], Hughie Archibald[6], Hugh Roy[5], Ewen Roy[4], John Roy[3], Ewan[2], John of Glenpean[1]). Born 1953.

He married Paule Gauthier 1978. Children:

    i. Kirk Roy[9].

253. Donald[8] Broadie (Kathleen[7], Hughie Archibald[6], Hugh Roy[5], Ewen Roy[4], John Roy[3], Ewan[2], John of Glenpean[1]). Born 1933.

He married Beverly Cheyne. Born 2 Aug 1934. Children:

    i. Douglas[9]. Born 20 Mar 1960.

    ii. Donald. Born 8 Feb 1962.

    iii. Cheryl. Born 7 Sep 1963.

    iv. Elizabeth. Born 15 May 1966.

254. Melvin[8] Broadie (Kathleen[7], Hughie Archibald[6], Hugh Roy[5], Ewen Roy[4], John Roy[3], Ewan[2], John of Glenpean[1]). Born May 1935.

He married Thelma Elizabeth MacDougall. Children:

    i. Laurie Catherine Mary[9]. Born 8 Sep 1963.

    ii. Wendy Dale. Born 31 Aug 1965.

    iii. Cindy Laurie. Born 8 Mar 1967.

255. Gail[8] MacMillan (Donald[7], Hughie Archibald[6], Hugh Roy[5], Ewen Roy[4], John Roy[3], Ewan[2], John of Glenpean[1]). Born 10 Nov 1940.

She married Allan Turner. Children:

    i. Karen[9].

    ii. Kim.

    iii. Michael.

256. Dorothy[8] MacMillan (Clark[7], Donald John[6], John[5], Ewen Roy[4], John Roy[3], Ewan[2], John of Glenpean[1]). Born 1929.

She married H. Warner. Children:

    i. Barbara[9].

    ii. Elaine.

257. Donald Clark[8] MacMillan (Clark[7], Donald John[6], John[5], Ewen Roy[4], John Roy[3], Ewan[2], John of Glenpean[1]). Born 1936.

He married a: Naomi MacLennan. Res. Williamstown, Ont.

He married b: Marlyn Legge. Children:

    i. John Hunter[9]. Born 1958. Occupation: Piper.

    ii. Sharon.

258. Wilma[8] MacMillan (John Dougal[7], Donald John[6], John[5], Ewen Roy[4], John Roy[3], Ewan[2], John of Glenpean[1]).

She married Lowell Ostrom, son of Ernest Ostrom. Children:

    i. Deidre[9]. Born 1959.

    ii. John Ernest Brock.

259. Paul[8] MacMillan (Lloyd[7], Alexander[6], John Miles[5], Myles Roy II[4], John Roy[3], Ewan[2], John of Glenpean[1]). Born 1923.

He married Shirley Weatherhead. Children:

    i. Andrew Alan[9]. Born 1950. He married Brenda Lee Foster.

    ii. Elizabeth Ann. Born 1953. She married John Beynard Pringle.

    iii. Ian Alexander. Born 1954. He married Janice Matiesenko.

    iv. Mary Francis. Born 1958.

    v. Gordon Paul. Born 1961.

    vi. Katherine Margaret. Born 1965. She married Roger Morin.

260. Margaret[8] MacMillan (Lloyd[7], Alexander[6], John Miles[5], Myles Roy II[4], John Roy[3], Ewan[2], John of Glenpean[1]). Born 1924.

She married a: Ian McGill.

She married b: Kelvin Young. Children:

    i. Maureen Lou Anne[9].

    ii. Barbara Jane.

    iii. Bruce Douglas.

261. Audrey[8] MacMillan (Lloyd[7], Alexander[6], John Miles[5], Myles Roy II[4], John Roy[3], Ewan[2], John of Glenpean[1]). Born 1926.

She married Harold McLean. Children:

296    i. Chery Irene[9].

    ii. Robert Harold.

    iii. Douglas James.

    iv. Julia Marylyn.

    v. Patricia Grace.

    vi. Glen.

262. Hugh[8] MacMillan (Dan[7], Richard[6], Florence[5], Myles Roy II[4], John Roy[3], Ewan[2], John of Glenpean[1]).

He married an Unknown Unknown. Children:

    i. Victoria[9].

263. Millan[8] MacCuaig (Edna[7], Duncan Peter[6], Peter[5], Archibald Roy[4], John Roy[3], Ewan[2], John of Glenpean[1]).

He married Margaret MacCrimmon. Children:

    i. Ian[9].

264. Kenneth[8] MacCuaig (Edna[7], Duncan Peter[6], Peter[5], Archibald Roy[4], John Roy[3], Ewan[2], John of Glenpean[1]).

He married Enid Newton. Children:

    i. Heather[9].

    ii. Darren.

    iii. Wayne.

265. Evelyn[8] MacCuaig (Edna[7], Duncan Peter[6], Peter[5], Archibald Roy[4], John Roy[3], Ewan[2], John of Glenpean[1]).

She married Murdo Stewart. Children:

    i. Darlene[9].

266. Sharyn[8] MacLennan (Grace[7], Duncan Peter[6], Peter[5], Archibald Roy[4], John Roy[3], Ewan[2], John of Glenpean[1]).

She married John Tennant. Res. Brockville, Ont. Children:

    i. Lane[9].

    ii. Wade.

267. Orville[8] MacMillan (Miles[7], Archibald Miles[6], Miles[5], Archibald Roy[4], John Roy[3], Ewan[2], John of Glenpean[1]). Born 1929.

He married Viola MacDonald. Children:

    i. Donna Howes[9]. Born 1951.

    ii. Heather. Born 1954.

    iii. Marilyn. Born 1959.

268. Sheila[8] MacMillan (Miles[7], Archibald Miles[6], Miles[5], Archibald Roy[4], John Roy[3], Ewan[2], John of Glenpean[1]). Born 1935. Died 1980.

She married Lyall Leonard. Res. Vankleek Hill. Children:

    i. Robin[9].

    ii. David.

269. Alice Jean[8] MacMillan (Earl[7], Peter Miles[6], Miles[5], Archibald Roy[4], John Roy[3], Ewan[2], John of Glenpean[1]). Born 1934.

She married Unknown Wariary. Children:

    i. Sael[9].

    ii. Sean.

    iii. Shaye.

270. Richard[8] MacMillan (Earl[7], Peter Miles[6], Miles[5], Archibald Roy[4], John Roy[3], Ewan[2], John of Glenpean[1]). Born 1939.

He married Unknown Unknown. Children:

    i. Christine[9]. Born 1971.

    ii. Tracy. Born 1972.

271. Allan[8] Campbell (Clifford[7], Catherine (Cassie)[6], Miles[5], Archibald Roy[4], John Roy[3], Ewan[2], John of Glenpean[1]). Born 1943. Res. Brockville, Ont.

He married Marjorie Fraser. Children:

    i. Jonathan[9].

    ii. Alison.

272. Fergus[8] Campbell (Clifford[7], Catherine (Cassie)[6], Miles[5], Archibald Roy[4], John Roy[3], Ewan[2], John of Glenpean[1]). Born 1945.

He married a: Anne Nesbit.

He married b: Unknown Unknown. Children:

    i.  Robert[9].

    ii.  Isabel.

    iii.  Allan Peter.

He married c: Tamara Unknown.

273. Malcolm Laird[8] MacMillan U.E. (Hugh Pearson U.E.[7], Rev. John Archibald U.E.[6], Hugh Archie Roy[5], Archibald Roy[4], John Roy[3], Ewan[2], John of Glenpean[1]). Born 1954.

He married Susan Murray. Children:

    i.  Kendra U.E.[9]. Born 1982.

    ii.  Kyle U.E. Born 1986.

    iii.  Matthew U.E. Born 1991.

274. Jocelyn Ruth[8] MacMillan U.E. (Hugh Pearson U.E.[7], Rev. John Archibald U.E.[6], Hugh Archie Roy[5], Archibald Roy[4], John Roy[3], Ewan[2], John of Glenpean[1]). Born 16 Dec 1960.

She married André Bourget. Children:

    i.  Gabriel U.E.[9]. Born 1991.

    ii.  Rachelle U.E. Born 1992.

    iii.  Daniel U.E. Born 1994.

275. Janet[8] MacMillan U.E. (Alexander Grant U.E.[7], Rev. John Archibald U.E.[6], Hugh Archie Roy[5], Archibald Roy[4], John Roy[3], Ewan[2], John of Glenpean[1]). Born 1950.

She married Richard Johnston. Children:

    i.  David U.E.[9]. Born 1975.

    ii.  Katherine U.E. Born 1979.

    iii.  Sean U.E. Born 1984.

276. Peter Grant[8] MacMillan U.E. (Alexander Grant U.E.[7], Rev. John Archibald U.E.[6], Hugh Archie Roy[5], Archibald Roy[4], John Roy[3], Ewan[2],John of Glenpean[1]). Born 1952.

He married Wendy MacDonald. Children:

    i.  Lindsay U.E.[9]. Born 1981.

    ii.  Natalie U.E. Born 1983.

277. Bonny[8] MacMillan U.E. (Alexander Grant U.E.[7], Rev. John Archibald U.E.[6], Hugh Archie Roy[5], Archibald Roy[4], John Roy[3], Ewan[2], John of Glenpean[1]). Born 1954.

She married Bernard Fournier. Children:

    i.  Patrick U.E.[9]. Born 1980.

    ii.  Michael U.E. Born 1981.

    iii.  Susanna U.E. Born 1984.

    iv.  Matthew U.E. Born 1988.

278. Nancy[8] MacMillan U.E. (Alexander Grant U.E.[7], Rev. John Archibald U.E.[6], Hugh Archie Roy[5], Archibald Roy[4], John Roy[3], Ewan[2], John of Glenpean[1]). Born 1955.

She married Brek (Derek) Millar. Children:

    i.  Jenna U.E.[9]. Born 1984.

    ii.  Jeffrey U.E. Born 1988.

    iii.  Paul U.E. Born 1989.

279. Glen[8] MacMillan U.E. (Alexander Grant U.E.[7], Rev. John Archibald U.E.[6], Hugh Archie Roy[5], Archibald Roy[4], John Roy[3], Ewan[2], John of Glenpean[1]). Born 1958.

He married Catherine Miller. Children:

    i.  Carrie U.E.[9]. Born 1987.

    ii.  Bonny U.E. Born 1988.

    iii.  Ryan U.E. Born, 1991.

280. Kelly[8] MacMillan U.E. (John Stewart U.E.[7], Rev. John Archibald U.E.[6], Hugh Archie Roy[5], Archibald Roy[4], John Roy[3], Ewan[2], John of Glenpean[1]). Born 1961.

She married Kelly Douglas. Children:

    i.  Andrea U.E.[9].

281. Murdoch[8] MacMillan (Floyd[7], Donald Ewen[6], Duncan[5], Donald Roy[4],John Roy[3], Ewan[2], John of Glenpean[1]). Born 1928.

He married Unknown Unknown. Children:

    i.  James Douglas[9]. Born 1955.

    ii.  Kathryn Ann. Born 1957.

282. Betty[8] MacMillan (William[7], Donald Ewen[6], Duncan[5], Donald Roy[4],John Roy[3], Ewan[2], John of Glenpean[1]). Born 11 Jul 1926.

She married Norman Hopson. Children:

297    i.  Catherine[9].

298    ii.  Cynthia.

283. Doreen (Tot)[8] MacMillan (William[7], Donald Ewen[6], Duncan[5], Donald Roy[4], John Roy[3], Ewan[2], John of Glenpean[1]). Born 19 Feb 1928.

She married Edmond Langstaff. Children:

299    i.  Marvel[9].

300    ii.  Doreen.

301    iii.  Edmond.

284. Darleen (Tiny)[8] MacMillan (William[7], Donald Ewen[6], Duncan[5], Donald Roy[4], John Roy[3], Ewan[2], John of Glenpean[1]). Born 19 Feb 1928.

She married Roland Granger. Children:

    i.  Ronald[9]. Born 1949.

302    ii.  Anne.

303    iii.  Lori.

285. Peggy[8] MacMillan (William[7], Donald Ewen[6], Duncan[5], Donald Roy[4],John Roy[3], Ewan[2], John of Glenpean[1]). Born 11 Jun 1929.

She married William Hodgson. Children:

304    i.  Debora[9].

    ii.  William. He married Julie Unknown.

286. William (Buzzy)[8] MacMillan (William[7], Donald

Ewen[6], Duncan[5], Donald Roy[4], John Roy[3], Ewan[2], John of Glenpean[1]). Born 26 Mar 1931.

He married Marlene Huotte. Children:

305   i.   Jeffrey[9].

306   ii.   Shelly (Shelby).

287. Patricia (Patsy)[8] MacMillan (William[7], Donald Ewen[6], Duncan[5], Donald Roy[4], John Roy[3], Ewan[2], John of Glenpean[1]). Born 24 Jul 1934.

She married a: Frank Phillips. Children:

307   i.   Kim Elaine[9].

      ii.   Frances Knapp. Born 10 Sept 1960.

      iii.   Karen Ann. Born 6 Nov 1961.

She married b: Charles Lambie 24 Aug 1985.

288. Ronald[8] MacMillan (William[7], Donald Ewen[6], Duncan[5], Donald Roy[4], John Roy[3], Ewan[2], John of Glenpean[1]). Born 20 Jul 1935.

He married Ann Cashion. Children:

308   i.   Richard[9].

      ii.   Joanne. Born 1968.

289. Simeon (Sim)[8] MacMillan (William[7], Donald Ewen[6], Duncan[5], Donald Roy[4], John Roy[3], Ewan[2], John of Glenpean[1]). Born 11 Apr 1940.

He married Colleen Legard. Children:

      i.   Jamie[9]. Born 1966.

      ii.   Georgie. Born 1969.

290. Jean[8] Unknown (Golda[7], Donald Ewen[6], Duncan[5], Donald Roy[4], John Roy[3], Ewan[2], John of Glenpean[1]).

She married Unknown MacLennan. Children:

      i.   Jill[9]. Born 1966.

      ii.   Roy. Born 1966.

291. Randall[8] MacKenzie (Florence[7], Myles Angus[6], Duncan[5], Donald Roy[4], John Roy[3], Ewan[2], John of Glenpean[1]). Born 1956.

He married Athanasia Ouzoyannis, 1982. Children:

      i.   Alexandra[9]. Born 1988.

**NINTH GENERATION**

292. Teresa Laverne[9] MacMillan (Alvin[8], Allen[7], John[6], William[5], James[4], Allan (Glenpean)[3], Ewan[2], John of Glenpean[1]). Born 1949.

She married John Shepherd. Children:

      i.   Justin Aarow[10].

293. Lucille Margaret[9] MacMillan (Alvin[8], Allen[7], John[6], William[5], James[4], Allan (Glenpean)[3], Ewan[2], John of Glenpean[1]). Born 1952.

She married Scott Erniwen. Children:

      i.   Kelly Brooke[10].

294. Virginia Louise[9] MacMillan (Alvin[8], Allen[7],

John[6], William[5], James[4], Allan (Glenpean)[3], Ewan[2], John of Glenpean[1]). Born 1956.

She married Craig Wall. Children:

      i.   Kevin Sydney[10].

295. Sherry[9] MacMillan (Earl Linton[8], Hugh Roy[7], Hughie Archibald[6], Hugh Roy[5], Ewen Roy[4], John Roy[3], Ewan[2], John of Glenpean[1]).

She married Rod Sedyk. Children:

      i.   Terry Jay[10].

296. Chery Irene[9] McLean (Audrey[8], Lloyd[7], Alexander[6], John Miles[5], Myles Roy II[4], John Roy[3], Ewan[2], John of Glenpean[1]).

She married an Unknown Unknown. Children:

      i.   Glen Kyle[10].

297. Catherine[9] Hopson (Betty[8], William[7], Donald Ewen[6], Duncan[5], Donald Roy[4], John Roy[3], Ewan[2], John of Glenpean[1]). Born 1953.

She married Richard Cerza. Children:

      i.   Rachel[10]. Born 1983.

      ii.   Benjamin.

298. Cynthia[9] Hopson (Betty[8], William[7], Donald Ewen[6], Duncan[5], Donald Roy[4], John Roy[3], Ewan[2], John of Glenpean[1]). Born 1956.

She married John Hardy. Children:

      i.   Sarah[10]. Born 1982.

      ii.   Lisa. Born 1983.

299. Marvel[9] Langstaff (Doreen (Tot)[8], William[7], Donald Ewen[6], Duncan[5], Donald Roy[4], John Roy[3], Ewan[2], John of Glenpean[1]). Born 1950.

She married Allan Maxome. Children:

      i.   Shawnna[10].

      ii.   Corey.

      iii.   Rebecca (Becky).

300. Doreen[9] Langstaff (Doreen (Tot)[8], William[7], Donald Ewen[6], Duncan[5], Donald Roy[4], John Roy[3], Ewan[2], John of Glenpean[1]). Born 1952.

She married Larry MacMillan. Children:

      i.   Gregory[10].

      ii.   Karery.

301. Edmond[9] Langstaff (Doreen (Tot)[8], William[7], Donald Ewen[6], Duncan[5], Donald Roy[4], John Roy[3], Ewan[2], John of Glenpean[1]). Born 1952.

He married Joanna Ashley. Children:

      i.   Meghan[10]. Born 1980.

      ii.   Edmond.

302. Anne[9] Granger (Darleen (Tiny)[8], William[7], Donald Ewen[6], Duncan[5], Donald Roy[4], John Roy[3], Ewan[2], John of Glenpean[1]). Born 1952.

She married James Loomis. Children:

i. Jeremy[10].

ii. Nathan. Born, 1979.

303. Lori[9] Granger (Darleen (Tiny)[8], William[7], Donald Ewen[6], Duncan[5], Donald Roy[4], John Roy[3], Ewan[2], John of Glenpean[1]). Born 1968.

She married Unknown Unknown. Children:

i. Christy Ann[10].

304. Debora[9] Hodgson (Peggy[8], William[7], Donald Ewen[6], Duncan[5], Donald Roy[4], John Roy[3], Ewan[2], John of Glenpean[1]).

She married a: Unknown Unknown. Children:

i. Alexander[10].

She married b: Alfred Gartner. Children:

ii. Joanna.

305. Jeffrey[9] MacMillan (William (Buzzy)[8], William[7], Donald Ewen[6], Duncan[5], Donald Roy[4], John Roy[3], Ewan[2], John of Glenpean[1]).

He married Unknown Unknown. Children:

i. Joanna[10].

306. Shelly (Shelby)[9] MacMillan (William (Buzzy)[8], William[7], Donald Ewen[6], Duncan[5], Donald Roy[4], John Roy[3], Ewan[2], John of Glenpean[1]).Born 1961.

She married Unknown Unknown. Children:

i. Unknown[10].

307. Kim Elaine[9] Phillips (Patricia (Patsy)[8], William[7], Donald Ewen[6], Duncan[5], Donald Roy[4], John Roy[3], Ewan[2], John of Glenpean[1]). Born 15 Mar 1957.

She married Kevin Hickling 22 Apr 1984. Children:

i. Kaitlin Susanne[10]. Born 22 Mar 1986.

308. Richard[9] MacMillan (Ronald[8], William[7], Donald Ewen[6], Duncan[5], Donald Roy[4], John Roy[3], Ewan[2], John of Glenpean[1]). Born 1958.

He married Unknown Unknown. Children:

i. Diane[10].

ii. Unknown.

# PART VII

# BIOGRAPHICAL SKETCHES

CHAPTER 11

# TWO
# MacMILLAN
# CHARACTERS

HUGH P. MacMILLAN

$\mathcal{S}$pace in this book does not permit biographical sketches of the many descendants of the Lochaber emigrants who became prominent. More sketches will appear in the forthcoming *Biographical Dictionary of Glengarry* being prepared by Dr. Royce MacGillivray of the University of Waterloo, the first such biographical dictionary of any county in Canada.

George MacMillan and his wife Viola were prominent for years in mining and stock broking circles. George's great-grandfather, Miles Roy, and Miles' brother, Archie Roy, were sons of John Roy. Miles followed the timber trade up the Ottawa Valley and ended up in northern Michigan in the 1860s. The little crossroads called McMillan's Corners in the Upper Peninsula was named after him. His grandson Richard was George's father. Richard's brother 'Black Jack' McMillan took the last pine timber raft down the Bonnechere River at Renfrew, Ontario about 1905. He was the first to teach George and Viola about prospecting. I saw them both over the years and admired their abilities.

When George died in 1978, the *Northern Miner*

printed the following obituary (5 October):

A tough, competent prospector, one who knew his rocks and his minerals, died suddenly last week at his farm near Tottenham, Ontario. He was in his 80th year. Just about everyone in the exploration business knew and will miss the jovial countenance of George. All are saddened at the knowledge that his huge shock of white hair will no longer be around, along with his warm broad grin, and his quiet 'Ohohohoho!' – the latter often in recollection of some bygone deadly poker game in the tough days when 500 shares of Opemiska Cooper, then quoted at 3 or 4 cents, would often be the stakes. There are few mining camps that did not feel the tread of George's boots in the bush... In George's relationship with his wife, one that was extremely public because both chose to lead a highly public life, he supported her, guided her and, as a matter of record, loved her as his wife... In commenting on George and Viola, even in the sad times of death, it is necessary to re-awaken the tragedy of the Windfall affair... One of the truths of the matter is that what started out as merely criticism of the

**157**

Prospectors George and Viola MacMillan, late 1930s, somewhere in Northern Ontario. (Courtesy of the executors of the estate of Viola MacMillan, Bradford, Ontario)

MacMillans grew into prosecution and finally persecution, which has persisted even though more than a decade has passed... Easy it was, and easy it is, to be critical of other people but in the matter of the MacMillans everyone got into the act... The bureacracy, just begging to put the tether on mining, flailed away with great energy and little thought. The everyday press donned its shiniest halo... The mining press was also guilty... It was not the MacMillans who were responsible for what happened. ... the matter was out of hand. The MacMillans' problem was to arrest it. She couldn't before it was too late. In any event George is now gone – a friend, a kindly person, and probably the only person who gave Viola support when she needed it most – the mark of a real man.

Viola died in 1993, and the *Globe and Mail* (31 August) had the following to say:

Viola MacMillan, a pioneer in a rough and rugged land and who staked her claim in the '30s rush and in Canadian mining history, has died in Toronto. She was 90. She was a miner, prospector, a central figure in a large stock scandal, and a member of the Order of Canada. Her nephew [George] commented, 'When she started she didn't have five cents.' Two years ago Mrs MacMillan was inducted into the Mining Hall of Fame... Her greatest contribution to the industry was to transform the Prospectors and Developers Association from a small group of less than 100 to over 4000. Mrs. MacMillan was convicted of fraudulent manipulation of stock exchange transactions in 1967 and was sentenced to nine months, but she served only six weeks. Her nephew said, 'She never felt she did anything wrong, what she did was done every day.' The federal government appears to have agreed with that assessment because in 1978 Mrs MacMillan was granted a full pardon. In 1989 she contributed $1.25 million towards the acquisition of the William Pinch Mineral Collection in New York. The collection is now on view on the Viola MacMillan Gallery at the Canadian Museum of Nature in Ottawa.

John Picton in the *Toronto Star* (31 August) added:

She was known in her heyday as the 'Queen Bee' of prospectors, a grande dame who helped develop Canadian mines that produced gold and other metals worth more than $100 million. She was the colourful and legendary Viola MacMillan who died last Thursday at age 90. She was born in Muskoka... [and] worked on the land during WWI and later as a maid and Bell operator. She married George MacMillan in 1923 and went with him into the bush. They were based in Timmins. She remembered seeing Ken Thomson selling newspapers on a street corner. 'She was an intelligent woman who worked in a man's business, and she was tough,' said Ed Thompson, a former president of the Prospectors & Developers Association.

In 1990 I was interviewing Viola in connection with this book. She had recently been fitted with a pacemaker and it improved her long-term memory. 'Why, Hugh,' she said, 'I just recall when I got out of jail in 1967 that the warden never gave me back my mink coat, I'm going to go after them for it.' When I pointed out the seven-year limit on prosecutions, she forgot about it. When she got to thinking of Roy Thomson (Lord Thomson of Fleet) she recalled, 'Hugh, I remember when George and I were just barely surviving in Timmins, about 1930, we discovered that Roy Thomson, whom we saw often, was so hard up he couldn't pay for his room. George and I just had one room and one bed for ourselves. I said to George, "We must do something for him. He can't sleep with us, so here is what we will do. I'll go out and buy a single cot and sleep on that, while you sleep with Roy in our double bed."' We don't have a record of what George thought about this arrangement but it continued for several months.

# PART VIII

# CONCLUSION

# CHAPTER 12

# HOW THIS BOOK
# CAME TO BE

HUGH P. MacMILLAN

*I* confess that the idea for this chapter is not original. Writers often attempt to explain how or why they have written a book, but a particularly fine instance of this came to my attention recently. Alfred Silver's *Red River Story* and *Where the Ghost Horse Runs* are historical novels set in the Canadian west during the early part of the nineteenth century, and I recommend them highly. Being one of those readers who like to look at the end of a book first, I discovered Silver's 'Author's Note' in *Where the Ghost Horse Runs*. In his informative and amusing manner, he explained how he mined historical sources to create a novel with plenty of action, skilfully blending historical fact with conjecture. Since chapter 8 of this book is about our western Canadian Métis connections and the early fur trade, I shall let an excerpt from Alfred Silver speak for me and help us to understand the connection between the Grants and the McMillans:

> I wouldn't have been able even to start on this book, much less that earlier one (remember?) if it hadn't been for an amateur historian named Margaret Arnett MacLeod. Among her many other

endeavours, including editing the letters of Letitia Hargrave and contributing to the delightful *Women of Red River*, Mrs MacLeod also developed a passionate obsession with researching Cuthbert Grant. When someone asked me for an explanation for Mrs. MacLeod's obsession, since she wasn't a descendant of Grant's nor did she appear to have any other vested interest, the only theory I could come up with was the gap left in her life by her only son. Lieutenant Alan MacLeod was a World War I flyer and was unusual among recipients of the Victoria Cross in that it wasn't awarded posthumously. He came home to Winnipeg with all his arms and legs intact and died in the influenza epidemic of 1919. Mrs MacLeod's husband also died before his time. The result of Mrs MacLeod's loneliness was a book entitled *Cuthbert Grant of Grantown* (well, snappy titles ain't exactly in the purview of scholastic publishing). It was written in collaboration with a budding young professional historian [W.L. Morton], because by that time she was unable to read her notes, her vision was too weak. The book has an interesting tension in it, because

Margaret had a romantic concept of Grant, and her collaborator appears to have been rather, well... jealous. Unfortunately there were further editions after Margaret MacLeod's death, allowing her collaborator (we used to shoot collaborators) to insert an introduction asserting that the dotty old half-blind lady's vision of Grant was flawed, because Grant was not, in fact, 'heroic' (whatever that means). One reason given is that Grant 'on occasion, at least, drank more than his position of responsibility allowed.' Another is that Grant was used by the North West Co and the Hudson's Bay Co for their own ends, while 'heroes, even when young, are not used; they pursue their own objects.' I suppose we will have to eliminate that brandy-sodden Churchill from the list of fit subjects for biography, not to mention that eager young Corsican who was so effectively used by Robespierre and by Josephine de Beuharnais's sugar daddy.

My sentiments about the collaborator mirror those of Silver. Let us keep Cuthbert Grant as a hero, warts and all. Cuthbert (1793-1854), known as the Warden of the Plains, was leader of the Métis in 1816 when they killed Governor Semple of the Hudson's Bay Company and twenty of his men in the battle of Seven Oaks near present-day Winnipeg. Isaac Cowie, a writer on the subject of Red River, said that:

> Under Grant, the Métis of the buffalo hunting brigades were organized as a disciplined force, which repelled every hostile Indian attack so successfully as to win renown as the most skilful and bravest warriors of the Prairies... They protected themselves from overwhelming numbers of Sioux... guarding the agricultural settlers of the Red River Colony from molestation by the bloodthirsty 'Tigers of the Plains' and other warlike tribes.

I admire Margaret Arnett MacLeod, and although I have read nearly everything she wrote, I never had the good fortune to meet her. Over twenty years ago,

I spent much time trying to track the papers of Cuthbert Grant in Manitoba and North Dakota. This was part of my work, but I also had a personal interest, aside from the fact my McMillan Métis relations around Red River would have known Cuthbert and likely were on many of his well-organized buffalo hunts. I was easily persuaded to use this portion of Alfred Silver's 'Author's Note' because of this personal interest. The following digression makes the point.

In 1971, our house in Toronto was torched in the middle of the night by a firebug. When the fifteen-year-old arsonist was caught a year after setting this forty second fire, he told the police it was random choice. He did not know us and could as easily have torched the house across the street. What attracted him, he claimed, was a huge canoe sitting on a trailer in front of the house. He didn't touch the canoe, as he claimed it was 'magical.' What he did do was pour gasoline over our two cars then toss a match on them. Luckily, a passing taxi driver saw the flames outside the darkened house. With great presence of mind, he kicked in the front door shouting 'Get out! Your house is on fire.' I thought it a dream as I saw no flames or smoke until I looked out the back window. Better I had left the canoe in the back yard where it usually was kept! As fate would have it, we were to leave that morning to paddle our fur-trade canoe through the Minesing swamp, part of the North West Company's alternate route during the War of 1812. We wanted to be the first to make the trip since the war. Four teenage boys, friends of my sons, were asleep upstairs ready for the big adventure. Our oldest son Malcolm went back into the house looking for his sister who had picked a good night to sleep at a friend's place. His mother saw him go in and rushed to get him out seconds before our station wagon blew up, spreading the flames into the house. We didn't canoe the Minesing that day.

We did manage to salvage much of the contents of the house and stored things with relatives and friends. Years later odds and ends keep resurfacing. Recently I went through some papers that my sister-in-law returned to me. Looking for information that I could use for this book, I came on five pages of smoke-blackened notes from interviews with my father in 1970. He had a retentive memory which needed prodding. He recalled that in 1907 when he was twenty-two, his own father, my grandfather, told him the following: 'My grandmother Mary Grant was related to a fur trader Cuthbert Grant who was out west. He was supposed to have visited here when he came back from Scotland.' I immediately thought of Alfred Silver's two novels that had Cuthbert Grant as a heroic figure, shortcomings and all. It makes for a natural tie-in. It points up the value of keeping track of old or new papers. I have a bad habit of mislaying things (just ask my wife) but as a person who has handled thousands of pieces of paper over many years, I have lost very little. (But where are those other papers I need for this chapter?)

At one time when I was younger and perhaps more foolish, I worried about my failings: no aptitude for, and little interest in, organized sports; failure to make use of some modest musical talent despite having a mother who was a music teacher; dropping out of first year college. I couldn't resist occasionally drinking too much, probably a reaction against too much Calvinism at home. I left home at the age of sixteen, having lied about my age in order to join the Royal Canadian Air Force and thus to escape being a P.K. (Preacher's Kid). Father must have intervened as the Air Force told me, not so politely, that there was a discrepancy in my age, and to go back to school. I eventually escaped by volunteering for the infantry. My military career was undistinguished; I didn't get overseas and was busted from sergeant back to private. The only action I saw, if you can call it that, was chasing after Japanese fire balloons in a jeep with a bren gun. This was while taking training in American weapons in the mountains of British Columbia, having signed up to go fight the Japanese in 1945. The atomic bomb ended that aspect of my brief military career. I escaped the military by asking for a discharge to go back to school. Carleton University was just

starting up in Ottawa. I thought I wanted to be a writer in the field of history. With this in mind, I signed up for some English courses and, of all things, accounting. After a year I had passing grades in English but failed in accounting. Armed with this meagre bit of education, I left school for a job in Montreal as the office 'gopher' with a Dutch export firm. In spite of my naivety it became clear the manager was shafting the owners. I led an office revolt of the three employees and got fired for my effort. Enough of my down side. We'll move to more positive things.

As Glengarry county is close to Montreal, I spent the summer of 1947 working on my uncle's farm and contemplating my next move. To stay and help run the family farm was an appealing option, in part because of my new-found interest in family history. However, I craved adventure and chose to go for a two month harvest excursion to Saskatchewan, stooking grain and later driving a team of horses to haul loads of sheaves to the thresher. Moving west, I spent two months on a cattle ranch in Alberta. My next move was to the Pacific coast. I landed in Vancouver with the idea of going to sea and writing at the same time since I was by now taking a writing course by mail. My timing was bad as there was a seamen's strike in progress and I had to settle for a coastal towboat where I started as a deck hand. I soon developed a thick skin as I was the butt of many a joke about my having gone to sea armed with a typewriter! It stood me in good stead when by sheer bad luck I became involved in a seamen's strike. At this point I had written exams and had my coastal mate's licence, along with an inflated opinion of my abilities as a seaman.

I sold a story based on the incident which follows. Our skipper, Bert Backwell, took our tug, the *Prosperative*, and an oil barge alongside a deep sea freighter anchored, and on strike, in Vancouver harbour. I was on the deck of the barge with a heaving line to put lines up to the ship. I noticed a small boat nearing our barge at high speed. I had been warned about strike breakers and dashed to the bridge to turn our searchlight on them. I saw them lash onto our barge and saw that they all carried baseball bats. As there was no time to alert the skipper I seized the high pressure fire hose, called out for the deck hand to turn on the pressure, and scythed a jet of water across the legs of the bat-wielding thugs. After being washed into Vancouver harbour they departed for shore. Our skipper issued a hefty dram of rum to celebrate this lucky caper.

For the next three years I made many trips up and down the coast towing log booms. I kept up with my writing and continued to gather family history information from relatives in Vancouver. During long stretches ashore I worked at other things. I was advance agent for a circus and then for 'The Great Orlando,' an Australian hypnotist. I kept thinking about moving back to Glengarry to live on our family farm. After meeting Muriel and getting married, I persuaded her to move back to Glengarry with me. I was not a great farmer, but liked the semi-independent life, and tried, unsuccessfully, to combine it with my historical pursuits. My interests were in family and local history but it paid no bills. Not having a degree I was in no position to teach and so I sold insurance and other things as well as farming. Muriel taught school between raising and caring for our four children. Without her contribution to family finances I could not have spent the time I did at historical research.

We became involved through Radio Farm Forum and folk schools (a rural adult education idea from Denmark) in helping to start the Glengarry Historical Society. I was elected the first president. This started a pattern in my life. Start a project, get other people involved, and move on to another of the many projects I seemed to dream up. My forte was never to buckle down to the fine detail of running something. Luckily there were almost always others around much better qualified to execute those of my ideas that had lasting merit. Several people will attest to the fact that not all of my ideas had merit!

It took a long time but my family history interest finally found a focus in the field of documents and archives. I began noting collections of papers in Glengarry that were in private hands, often in danger of destruction. I was able to take some of these papers to the National Archives of Canada in nearby Ottawa. They were copied and I began to make use of them for a column I began writing for the *Glengarry News*. I was somewhat naive and ahead of my time in wanting to start a local archives. (My forthcoming book, *The Paper Chaser*, will recount the unusual and bizarre tales of my continuing career searching out papers.) Thanks to the support of a new friend, Donald Fraser McOuat, I was given the opportunity to pioneer in a new job that I helped create: field officer of the Archives of Ontario. Finally I was actually going to be paid to locate and acquire papers. Moving from Glengarry to Toronto in 1963 was not easy as our family had established roots there. I was now in the happy position of being able to convert my hobby to a paying job, which is something few of us are able to achieve. In my case good timing for a change or it may well have been, as Presbyterians would say, preordained.

My agenda for this new and untried line of work commenced with no guidelines or direction from the archives or civil service procedures as to how it could work. I decided (and McOuat reluctantly agreed) that I would proceed to set my own guidelines. I felt these should follow the precepts of any skilled salesman. Keep in close contact with my eastern Ontario history buffs and gradually build a network across the province. I continued to gather family history information in the form of documents, both originals and copies, combined with the recording of oral history. Thus I was able to combine my official work with my hobby. I was most fortunate over the years to have received help from a host of friends too numerous to mention. Information for this book has come from across this continent and abroad.

These papers have been made available to the contributors of this volume. I count myself fortunate that I was able to interest them in this project, which covers aspects of the emigration and its people. We can thank Rae Fleming for suggesting this particular chapter-by-chapter format which makes for a rich and varied book. I can think of no other book which tells the story of a major emigration in this manner and it is my hope that this book will spawn further scholarly research and writing on the subject.

The genealogical charts I published in 1960 never satisfied me, especially as I continued to locate more documents and stories about my Glenpean line that had not been included in Somerled MacMillan's book, *Bygone Lochaber.* Up until three years ago I projected a privately-printed family history of 500 copies, based on my research material. Reviewing this material – the passenger lists particularly – for the three brigs made me realize that Glenpean and Murlaggan had taken to America many families in addition to McMillans.

The writers of these chapters showed interest in the project from the time I first mentioned it to them. I have known Barry Penhale, our publisher, and Rae Fleming for many years. The three of us discussed the idea of the book in some detail. Barry tentatively agreed to publish the book based on my concept of the finished work. It is most unusual for a publisher to agree to a book without a manuscript in hand. Rae decided he would prefer to be editor if I could elicit contributions from various specialists.

Recently I read Al Purdy's riveting autobiography *Reaching for the Beaufort Sea.* A great title and a great book. This well known Canadian poet tells about his career, warts and all, including the often sad, but amusing, frailties of his own family. I wish I could be as disarmingly frank about some of my warts. I mention this because all too often we suppress unpleasant aspects of our own family history.

I end with a selection of stories that relate to Glengarry and our people, exposing some warts in amusing bits of oral history that have been handed down to me. You may want to do the same thing with your family. I hope it helps get you started. For the most part there is no documentary verification for these tales. I have repeated them numerous times to indi-

viduals, party groups and public audiences. They are gathered together for the first time. Family and local history is the unifying theme of this book. As a preamble to these stories the following anonymous statement points up how important this type of history can be for my family and yours:

> We stand to gain a new understanding about ourselves as we learn more about our ancestors and the lives they lived. In today's mobile, often unstable, society it is important for people to have knowledge of their larger family connections, both here and abroad.

•

The following quotation from the 1984 book, *Williamstown, 200 years of Sharing,* shows how insufficient editing can create an anecdote that bears repeating: 'The book contains approximately 200 pages of historical pictures and antidotes [sic] and will be available before Christmas.'

•

Father, who died in 1976 at age 91, had his share of warts as well as virtues. He was rigid, unbending, intolerant of human frailties, but persevered in his beliefs. He went from a prosperous Glengarry farm to preaching the gospel and was still doing that at age 85, without notes. For him the Presbyterian work ethic was real. He could never quite understand why I kept chasing around the country after other people's old papers, much less why I was getting paid. His regular comment after my sessions at trying to mine his extremely retentive, but selective, memory for nuggets of family history was to say 'But Hugh, when are you going to get a real job?' I tried explaining that I was sort of a preacher in travelling around the country talking to people singly or in groups to try and persuade them to preserve our history. He never accepted that idea; it was still not a real job.

•

The only historical relic that was saved in our family is the 'Brown Bess' flintlock musket that was carried

John Roy McMillan's Tower Musket, made ca. 1780, held by his great-great-great-grandson, Malcolm MacMillan. (Photograph courtesy Michael Albano, Rockwood, Ontario)

by my ancestor, John Roy MacMillan, when he served as a yeoman in the Royal Canadian Volunteer Regiment (1797-1802) and later with the Glengarry Militia in the War of 1812. This survived the house cleaning efforts of my two deranged cousins mentioned in the 'Charts' chapter.

Sorting my John from two other John's in the Royal Canadian Volunteer (RCV) Regiment was made easier by a mix-up in the paper work that was part of the process in granting crown land at the time. Alexander McMillan, mentioned in chapter 10, returned from Scotland to Canada in 1793 with a number of young kinsmen including his brother, John Roy. It appears that he recruited them soon thereafter into the army. When the regiment was disbanded in 1802 John Roy would have been in line to receive a grant of 200 acres of land from the Crown. Instead he got 600 acres in the north end of Lancaster township (later Lochiel) in Glengarry County. Normally there would only be two to three items in the file for a lot. The land board somehow granted him 600 acres instead of 200 not knowing there were actually three John McMillan's being granted land. The other two Johns must have been outraged at getting no land. The fortunate result for me as a researcher was that Alexander, Captain of their company, had to supply

an affidavit attesting to the antecedents of our three Johns. Occasionally bureaucratic mix-ups can yield some advantage.

•

Thanks to Mary Beaton of Ottawa the following item was extracted from an article in the Glengarry News of 7 Sept 1894 celebrating the 100th anniversary of the 'Glenelg' settlers:

> Died 1870 at Torbolton [near Ottawa] at 101 yrs late of lot 24, 5th con. Lochiel Glengarry, Mary (Grant) McMillan relict of late John McMillan elder of St Columba, emigrated to Canada in 1791 at 22 years of age. 15 children, 8 survive, eldest is now 80 yrs of age. Leaves 138 grandchildren and 185 great grandchildren.

I am sure the figures on grandchildren and great-grandchildren are in error. I have never been able to come up with such numbers. The rest of the obituary helped prove information I already had recorded. I had assumed that Mary was part of the United Empire Loyalist migration from the Mohawk Valley of New York State. This story established that she had come directly from Scotland and was not therefore a Loyalist, which reduced my loyalist ancestors from four to three. My research had already revealed her link to Cuthbert Grant and I also discovered a connection with Alexander Grant, former Nor'Wester, of Duldregan Hall at L'Orignal on the Ottawa River.

No image of Mary Grant MacMillan survives but she must have been a hardy woman to have gone through fifteen childbirths. My father was told by his father that sometime after John Roy died in 1841 she walked over 100 miles north along the Ottawa river. This trek was to join her oldest daughter Mary who was married to Captain Alexander McMillan (possibly her cousin, son of Lt. Col Alexander). They went north to the Fitzroy Harbour area (my birthplace) at an earlier date. Could they have made their trip easier by a trek to L'Orignal on the Ottawa where they could have boarded the steamer *Shannon* and gone

Archibald Kains (1865-1944), grandson of Mary and Thomas, was a retired banker who spent the last years of his life collecting papers and information about the Kains and the McMillans. In 1942 he journeyed from his home at 9 Rideau Gate in Ottawa (next to the Governor-General's residence) to Washington. The purpose of this jaunt was to return to President Roosevelt some sterling silver that his grandfather had looted from the White House in 1813. I am still searching for items he removed from the Nelson's flagship *Victory* when it was a hospital ship during the Crimean War. He was called back to active service

Captain Thomas Kains (1790-1855), married to Mary McMillan (1798-1865), daughter of Archibald 'Murlaggan' McMillan and Isabella Gray. Kains helped to burn the White House, Washington, during the War of 1812. (Courtesy of Joan Ritchie, Little Silver, New Jersey)

Archibald C. Kains, international banker and historian (1865-1944), son of Thomas Kains and grandson of Archibald 'Murlaggan' McMillan. (Courtesy of Joan Ritchie, Little Silver, New Jersey)

upriver to at least Bytown (Ottawa)? Mary must have known that her late husband's cousin (another Mary McMillan, daughter of Archibald 'Murlaggan') was married to Thomas Kains, captain of the *Shannon*.

•

Thomas Kains was a half-pay officer of the Royal Navy who had been in the party that set fire to the White House in Washington in the War of 1812. I traced his and Mary's portraits and his naval outfit to descendants. They were as far afield as New Jersey and as close by as sixty miles from my home in Guelph.

and served as purser on the ship. His grandson Archibald began his banking career at Brantford. His portrait shows a handsome figure in a MacMillan kilt. In New Jersey I located his letters to Pauline Johnson, the famous Indian poet from Brantford, and it appears he had the good fortune to have been her lover.

•

According to the notes from my father that survived the 1971 fire, the home of John Roy on lot 24, concession 14 (today the 4th of Lochiel) was a meeting place for the emigrants. He would have built a log house around 1802 when he took up his land grant and likely built the stone house ca. 1815-20. This fine old stone house is today set well back from the road on the slope of a hill. Out at the road is a small private cemetery which lends considerable credence to my supposition that it was a central meeting place for the recently arrived emigrants. John Roy in 1802 was just out of the army and would know about his brother Allan and cousin Archibald arriving in Montreal with over 400 relatives and kinsfolk. John Roy, along with the other two Johns, was likely in the forefront of those trying to lure the new arrivals to their area. I could never find the headstone for John Roy in the

cemetery which was on his land. Rumour had it that someone took the stones away. But who? And where did they take them? My grandfather's brother John sold the farm early in this century to a Henry Vogan. The mystery was solved, but not to my satisfaction, over twenty years ago. It turns out Mr Vogan had to rebuild the chimney on the house. He was having difficulty finding flat stones when he thought of the abandoned cemetery at the road. You can guess what happened next. I may try to convince the present owners to take the top portion of the chimney down and retrieve the stones to put them back in the cemetery. Anyone for a cemetery project?

•

There are moments when I think 'Klondike Lily' must have been a figment of my imagination – or my father's. He told me during one of my note-taking sessions (I couldn't get him to go for a taping session) that cousin Lily had a wooden leg and she went out west in the 1890s but no word on how she lost her leg. Given the long skirts of the day the wooden leg would not be visible. At a later note-taking session I asked if she had any nickname. 'Well yes, she was called Klondike Lily!,' he told me. This answer got my full

Stone house built (ca. 1815) by John Roy McMillan, brother of Allan 'Glenpean' McMillan, on lot 24, concession 4, Lochiel Township, Glengarry County. This house and a log house which preceded it were reported to be a meeting place for emigrants. (Oil painting by Stuart McCormick. Hugh P. MacMillan Collection, Guelph, Ontario)

attention but the only extra information I gleaned was his comment that 'she sinned!' 'Most of us have sinned,' I replied, 'so what was her sin?' Silence. A later session with an elderly cousin finally produced an answer after a dram or so of single malt. I was told that 'she was one of those, you know... madams with the gold rush.' Elated at this success, I kept up the questioning but no more information came forth. I told this story to Aunt Grace, who was noted for her total lack of humour as well as delusions of grandeur. She was most indignant when I told her that I intended to record the story in our family history as an unproved legend. I spent a large amount of time and some money researching 'Klondike Lily' with no success to date. Pierre Berton and a few other Klondike experts claim to have heard of her but lack details. Dear aunt Grace did not appreciate my comment that it's not every family who turns up a 'Madam' in the family record.

•

Allan 'Glenpean' McMillan's portrait, on the cover of this book, was likely painted in 1802, around the time he was emigrating to Canada. In 1970 I made my first trip to the west coast on behalf of the Archives of Ontario. One of my self-assignments was to acquire the Archibald 'Murlaggan' McMillan papers in Vancouver. They were in possession of a great grandson, Dr. John MacMillan. His sister Marjorie, wife of Judge Oscar Orr, had photographs and paintings while John had the papers. This was another case where my personal interest combined neatly with my official mandate. I was able to secure copies of all the papers, many of which have been used for this book, but John had willed the collection to the Public Archives in Ottawa. Marjorie had sent the portrait of Allan 'Glenpean' to the Argenteuil County Museum in Quebec. This is a fine old stone building on the Ottawa River twenty miles down river from Archibald 'Murlaggan' McMillan's land near Grenville. The local historical society operates the museum. Strangely, there was no portrait of Archibald, but his wife Isabella Gray's fine portrait was with a

Isabella Gray (1770-1853), wife of Archibald 'Murlaggan' McMillan. The portrait is in the collection of Jack Barker (great-great-great-grandson of Isabella and Archibald), Cowansville, Quebec.

descendant, Jack Barker. While on this same visit in 1970, I sat visiting with Judge Oscar Orr who died recently at almost 100 years of age. We were waiting for Marjorie to find more pictures of relatives. The Judge saw me eying a jagged piece of metal perhaps four inches long mounted on a pedestal. On inquiring as to what it was, I was regaled with this explanation:

That is a piece of shrapnel that hit me above my left eye and lodged in my mouth. Luckily I survived this ordeal, but was left with a tiny open wound above my eye. This resulted in a strange phenomenon that lasted many years before the wound finally healed. When I used my pipe, smoke issued from my forehead. I dined out for years on the following incident that resulted from this oddity: Marjorie and I were riding on an train in England soon after I had sustained this injury in World War l. A very stern looking bishop, complete with all his regalia, got in our compartment. Being a very proper Englishman there was no chit-chat with a colonial soldier. Indeed he buried his head behind the paper he was reading while I lit up my pipe. At one point he happened to lower his paper just as a large puff of smoke escaped from my forehead. The paper quickly went back up but he kept taking a peek. Still not a word from the good bishop but he was seen to be crossing himself as he got off at the next station. No doubt it confirmed his worst suspicions about colonial troops.

Marjorie sent me on my way after dinner with a photograph of Allan's portrait and extensive notes about our family connection. The picture was deposited in the Archives of Ontario. The notes were added to my growing pile of material gathered for this book. Marjorie died soon after this and these notes did not survive our 1971 fire. In 1990 I went to the Argenteuil museum to compare my photograph of Allan with the original portrait. Much to their embarrassment they were unable to find it but we are still searching. Did she send it to some other museum? Was it stolen? The search for the missing portrait continues.

•

In the fall of 1991 I was driving east from Victoria, BC, where we had been visiting our daughter Jocelyne who had moved there with her husband to teach French. My wife Muriel was staying for a longer visit. My eastward trek was to include gathering stories for this book. I stopped at Eureka, Montana, to pick up 'Doc' Smiley, another of my fur trade history friends, at his Tobacco Plains ranch. He was going on with me to the North American Fur Trade Conference at Michilimackinac, Michigan. Here I hoped to garner more information on James McMillan, the

subject of Heather Devine's chapter in this volume. One of Doc's numerous claims to prominence is that he was the last veterinary surgeon of the last US cavalry regiment (Custer's 7th) to have horses. When Hitler's panzer divisions went through Poland in 1939 the regiment switched to tanks and 'Doc' was out of a job. One of Eureka's attractions is a clever replica of an alligator chained to the water pipe of the men's urinal in the Elkhorn bar. It is just dark enough that you don't notice this creature in the swirling water of the trough as you unzip. When you do spot his head with open jaws amidst the foaming water, you have the urge to zip up and leave fast. A second look at this mean-looking critter and you realize you've been had. Many a tourist has made it to the urinal well into his cups but departed sober. The bartender was surprised at my lack of reaction when I came back from the loo and sat at the bar awaiting 'Doc,' who was driving in from the ranch. The bartender, used to having his fun with the tourists, couldn't stand my lack of response. He finally enquired if I noticed anything unusual. 'Not really,' I replied, 'but aren't you afraid that little alligator in your urinal will drown?'

•

Travelling across the vast open grasslands and mountains of Montana, we stopped at Three Forks in the 'Big Sky' country of Madison county with the towering Gallatin Mountains to the east of us. Here we got a great welcome from cousin Catherine McMillan Shirley whom I had last seen in 1949. I was the first relative to visit her father Peter Miles McMillan and his family. He organized a party that lasted for days, with all ex-Glengarrians invited. Peter Miles was a compulsive gambler. When the party ended, he drove me 200 miles west to Bute in his big Frazer car (now a collectors' item). Here we met my partner Harry Dixon who had a contract to sell advance tickets for Seal Brothers circus. At that time Montana did not welcome paper money. Peter Miles went to his bank and got out a bag of silver dollars with about fifty for me. We must have stopped at every bar en route to Bute. By the end of the day, I had just about doubled my stake by playing the slot machines but Peter Miles had several bags of coins. He left Glengarry for Montana about the turn of the century. My father had told me that Peter's brother Archie was given the farm by their father. Peter was given a $100 gold piece as his patrimony then headed west to make his fortune. This he did but lost it several times because of his compulsive gambling.

Gathering even these few stories about family history takes time, patience, and luck. My timing was good – for a change – as Catherine died only a year after she told me the following tale, which she alone knew:

In 1917 father and mother left Goldfield (200 miles west) and headed for this area. The trek took all summer but they were not alone. The slow progress was on account of them driving about 3000 head of sheep. They could only make fifteen to twenty miles a day as the sheep had to graze and find water. Dad must have done well in the short time he had been in the west. He and mother had the two oldest of our family but I was not yet born. Dad had a Model-T Ford for mother and the kids to ride in while he and his French-Canadian sheepherders drove the sheep from horseback with the help of a dozen or more sheep dogs. There is not even one picture to show this strange cavalcade on the move. Dad also had about $25,000 in silver dollars which was some fortune in those days. Within a short time he was near to being broke through his gambling. Lucky for him mother had enough sense to get some money from him and she bought an old house which she named the MacMillan Hotel. Mother

MacMillan Hotel, Harrison, Montana, owned by Peter Miles McMillan and wife. Peter was a great-grandson of John Roy, who was a brother of Allan 'Glenpean.' (Courtesy Allan Campbell, Brockville, Ontario)

grubstaked him many times when his incessant gambling would put him broke again.

•

My grandmother Annie McIntosh McMillan (1860-1942) was a handsome woman judging by her photographic portrait. She was raised on a prosperous farm in Charlottenburgh township, Glengarry. She wrote interesting letters many of which have survived. All her McIntosh relatives moved to the west coast just before World War One. Her most interesting ancestor was Captain Walter Sutherland, a spy for the British during the Revolutionary War. I only wish I had asked grandmother more questions and had written down the answers. Information I did get from her and wrote down has helped make this book. My few notes taken at age fifteen and salvaged years later il-

Hughie Archie Roy McMillan (1853-1914), his wife, Annie McIntosh (1861-1942) with family which included two sets of identical twin girls. Standing on left is John Archie McMillan, father of Hugh P. MacMillan. (Hugh P. MacMillan Collection, Guelph, Ontario)

lustrate the amateur work of a teenage historian who noted that Walter was hidden by a woman whose name was Humiah. As her reward, she asked that if he ever had a daughter to call her Humiah. I thought nothing of this at the time but many years later my official and personal sleuthing paid off. I located a sizeable cache of Sutherland papers in Scarsdale, New York. They were with William G Schram, a Sutherland descendant, who had been in touch with my grandmother in 1911. To my utter amazement, on looking through his detailed genealogical charts which he had worked on for over 60 years, the name Humiah cropped up all over the charts. I even had a first cousin called Humiah, one of the two sisters whom I mention in the introduction to the Glenpean charts in chapter 10. Why would anyone give some poor female child, a strange biblical name unless there was a story behind it? For me this was proof that there really was something to grandmother's story. It also points up the value of oral history and the workings of syncronicity whereby a series of unrelated events led to this discovery. We will likely never know the full story but it is obvious the tale had been widely repeated and by chance survived in my random notes.

Annie told me her great-great-grandfather had been killed at Culloden in 1746. The English were still anathema to her. One time she warned me to never marry a 'Sassenach' when I grew up. Years later, I learned what the word meant, but I did go and marry one anyway. I don't suppose Granny is pleased. In her later years she struck me as a very pious woman. I am left wondering what her reaction was to the following portion of a letter she received on September 12th, 1882, from her cousin Isabella Grant at Cashion's Glen, South Branch, Glengarry:

> Dear friend Annie – I am sorry to tell you that I was up to Crawfords last night and the girl has decided not to go from home at present. I think she is expecting a few husking bees and she don't want to loose the fun the next time John goes for a girl he must do as we were telling him he must sleep with her and she will be sure to stay.

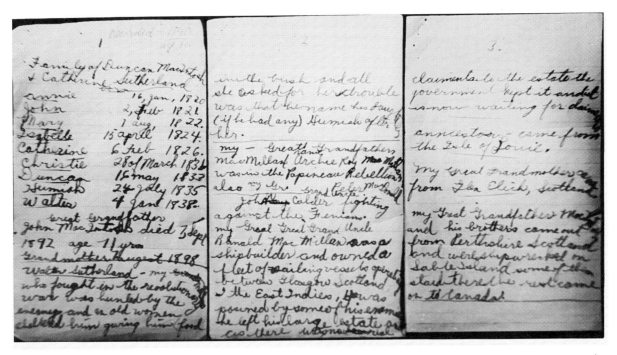

The budding researcher at work – notes made by Hugh P. MacMillan in 1940 at age 15. (Hugh P. MacMillan Collection, Guelph, Ontario)

Well! And some of us thought our elders rarely thought of sex, except of course, for the pleasure of creating us. Annie was twenty-two. Two years later, she married my grandfather. Who was the girl and who was John, and did Isabella or Annie have any experience sleeping with John? He must have had talent as a bed partner. We will never know but it does make Granny and cousin Isabella much more human. Aunt Grace would not have approved of this portion of such a letter being made public notwithstanding the worthy cause of advancing social history.

•

Great uncle John (Archie Roy) McMillan (1851-1917) is one of the more interesting of my grandfather's five brothers. He remained a bachelor, albeit one who, judging by his correspondence, had several admiring and available women. He must have been an indifferent farmer for he also was a part time drover and land speculator. This is documented in some of his papers I managed to salvage from my housecleaning cousins' bonfire (see chapter 10). Uncle

John's business records show him owning almost a block of land and buildings on Greene Avenue between Ste Catherine and Sherbrooke streets in Montreal. Land speculation must have been too slow for him and he sold out before World War One to buy prairie land near Saskatoon. He became overextended and, as we would be said today, he had a cash flow problem. He lost the lots near Saskatoon, along with his grandfather John Roy's stone house and farm in Glengarry. Mr. Vogan the chimney re-builder became the next owner.

John spent his last years with Sandy, another bachelor brother. Sandy owned the farm where we lived from 1952 to 1963. He was a skilled cabinetmaker and according to my father went to the shanty every winter from about 1870 to 1900. He took a crew of men, horses and supplies by train to Saginaw, Michigan. His uncle Miles (brother of Archie Roy) likely lured him to this area. In the 1860s Miles had worked his way up the Ottawa valley and into upper Michigan following the white pine trade. As Ted Cowan points out in his chapter, the Lochaber emigrants were used to the handling of big timber when they came to Canada in 1802. Their part of the Highlands were heavily timbered with streams to raft logs on. We have preserved the cast iron stove he took to the shanty. The door casting reads 'Copps Bros, Hamilton 1879.' A family relic with a story. These two look-alike brothers had lean craggy features. Their faces are clean-shaven except for the handlebar mustaches that go with the slicked back hair parted in the middle. I can remember great uncle Sandy whose frugality extended to cutting hard peppermint candies in half! The following excerpts from two unsigned letters to John indicate that two ladies he knew had very dissimilar problems for him to solve:

> Dear Friend – I have heard you were talking about coming down the time of the fair be sure and call I will be on 171 St. Urbain St [Montreal]. The fair is commencing on the 11 ending on the 19 you come down some of those days if you don't feel to high. I haven't been sick since you came down you know what I mean I didnt tell them at home as they would take a fit. I wish I had some of the stuff you were telling me off. I don't think you deceived me in doing anything wrong. J. A. you will burn this letter as soon as you read it. I think of the last night we were together. I was dreaming about it last night. xxxxx yours ——

There are indications in John's cash books that he was paying to support an unnamed orphan in Montreal. 'Little Jack' McDonald a famous Glengarry fiddler knew J. A., as he was known, when he would stop at the Dalhousie hotel going to and coming from Montreal. This would be an overnight stop (if he was taking his horse and rig) for a room and a tune or two on the fiddle. 'Little Jack' told me once,

> That uncle of yours could step dance, play the fiddle, and sing gaelic songs all night long. He was a caution with ladies and not feared to spend

his money, or pay for his mistakes as when he got Betsy in a fix.

I'm sure I would have liked Uncle John Archie but Aunt Grace would have been disapproving.

The second letter, undated and unsigned, is circa 1895. This is a completely different sort of problem:

> John, Why don't you be smart for yourself and others you have a bill against Mrs M Cameron... she has that house insured at $1,000.00 and that is more than she will ever get for it and if you would watch your chance when there is a storm and set that big shed next to the house in a flame. Set it inside and up near the roof and then we will all get our money and she will not loose everything and of course watch the wind is not hie so not to hurt anyone... or after a rain or towards morning no one in gods world would ever no. Be sure and burn this paper...

For the sake of social history we can be thankful that my uncle J. A. did not put his own papers to the torch. There is no indication that he followed her detailed instructions. Aunt Grace would have objected to letting such terrible things be known, but why not?

•

Lt. Col. Alexander McMillan (ca. 1756-1823) was the first of our 'Glenpean' line known to have arrived in America and it was likely information he supplied his brother Allan and cousin Archibald that aided them in planning the 1802 emigration. His presence in America as early as 1777 was noted along with the following interesting 'snippets' of information I have found regarding his military career. *Neilson's Quebec Almanac of 1796*, page 6, records the following charming description of Alexander by Col. Landemann of the Royal Engineers:

> McMillan was a jolly fat Scotchman, with a very plump, round face, sandy hair and a rosy complexion. In the course of the evening (after dinner at McLean's) he treated us to a tune on two Jews harps, performing on both at once, and as he as-

serted, playing first and second. His Jews harps were great pets, and he kept them in a neat case made for the purpose, well supplied with cotton to protect them from injury.

All my efforts to find these Jews harps have come to naught.

In 1967 I located Donald MacMillan, a great-great-grandson of Alexander, who owned a trucking firm in East Brunswick New Jersey. He had carefully preserved his great-grandfather's hand-made French-Canadian-style arm chair. Family legend had it that

McMillan chair, made ca. 1815 for Lt. Colonel Alexander McMillan of the 2nd Battalion Glengarry Militia. Alexander was the brother of Allan 'Glenpean' McMillan. Chair is now in Nor'wester Loyalist Museum, Williamstown, Ontario. (Photograph courtesy of Philip Shackleton, Pender Island, British Columbia)

the chair was made by the St. Regis Indians near Cornwall, Ontario as a token of regard for having led them on the successful raid on French Mills, New York on 23 November 1812. At that time, he was Lt. Col of the 1st Regiment of Glengarry Militia. I asked Donald to donate the chair to the Nor'Wester & Loyalist Museum in Williamstown, Ontario. As co-founder of the museum, I was searching for pieces with a story. Donald was on hand in September 1967 to present the chair at the opening of the museum. At this time our brigade of three fur-trade canoes arrived from Grand Portage, the old North West Company rendezvous at the head of Lake Superior. I had organized the brigade, and was one of the paddlers. Our piper led us ashore and several of us who were related to a Nor'Wester or had Loyalist connections took turns being photographed in the chair. Artifacts such as this are best left with an institution or collector rather than our attic. They are more likely to survive.

Much of Alexander's military career is documented in a file at the National Archives of Canada (RG 8, C-series, vol. XVII, pg. 793):

> Appointed to DeLancey's Brigade in 1777, served in Revolution, present at the reduction of Savannah and elsewhere. Appointed to the Royal Canadian Volunteer Regiment in 1796 and remained until disbanded in 1802. Later Lt. Col. of the 1st Regiment, Glengarry Militia. From January 1809 commanded the flank companies of the 1st and 2nd Glengarry, was at the Salmon River battle, and was appointed to the Militia Pension Board of Upper Canada.

Alexander had a son who was a Captain in one of the Glengarry Regiments (Fencibles) during the War of 1812. This son was likely Alexander Allan who was married to Elizabeth Crytes, a United Empire Loyalist and the great-grandparents of Donald in New Jersey (the man who donated his ancestors' chair to the Nor'Wester Museum in 1967). Elizabeth was likely a daughter of George Crytes, a soldier in the King's Royal Regiment of New York during the Revolution-

Hugh P. MacMillan and Nor'wester crew running rapids (1970) at Quetico Park, Northwestern Ontario, en route to Winnipeg to celebrate the 300th anniversary of the founding of the Hudson's Bay Company. The route through the park and beyond marks the old fur trade route to Red River. That same route later marked the boundary between the United States and Canada. (Courtesy Mark Stiles, Ottawa, Ontario)

ary war. Alexander Allan is a source of confusion as there were two men by the same name. Captain Alexander Allan McMillan was at the military settlement at Perth, Lanark County, soon after its creation in 1816. He was a half-pay officer from the Glengarry Fencibles with an outstanding record in the War of 1812. He built a stone house there about 1842 and was the first warden of the district. He was better known for having fought a duel with a Dr. Thom at Perth. Apparently Thom neglected to invite McMillan's wife to a New Year's levee, a sign that the Doctor considered her socially inferior. McMillan challenged him to a duel. Pistol shots were exchanged, with no casual-

ties, and presumably honour was satisfied. McMillan received large land grants in the township of Drummond. Sometime in the 1830s, an Alexander McMillan was applying for land at Prescott, Upper Canada, some fifty miles to the south east on the St. Lawrence River. This Alexander was building a brewery on his land and was in the freight forwarding business.

In his father's will of 1819, Alexander Allan is mentioned as a merchant at Prescott. He had been a tinker and a talented Scottish fiddler. Also mentioned in the will are members of his father's second family by Marcella McDonell. Aneas John, a son by Marcella,

178

may have succeeded his father as an Indian agent. Ewan, Anne, Margaret and Janet, brothers and sister of Aeneas John, are also listed but we have no information on them.

Alexander Allan was likely involved in the Battle of the Windmill, fought over three days, from the 14th to 16th of November 1838, one of several clashes along the Canadian-American border during the Upper Canadian Rebellion of 1837-38. With several other citizens of the town, he was on the hit list of the secret 'Hunters Lodges' positioned across the river in New York state, and that list had been published in the 1838 summer issue of the *Sentinel*, Prescott's only newspaper. The Lodges' objective was to bring Canada under American control and McMillan had publicly opposed them. About 200 invaders crossed the St Lawrence river from Sackett's Harbour in two schooners, lashed together and towed by the steamer *United States*. Led by a Finnish soldier of fortune, Nils von Schoultz (1797-1838), they landed at the stone windmill slightly to the east of the heavily defended Fort Wellington at Prescott, then took the stone mill and outbuildings, which are standing today. There were many casualties on both sides during the battle that followed. The British troops and militia finally forced a surrender. John A. MacDonald, a Kingston lawyer, politician and later Prime Minister was unsuccessful in defending von Schoultz and the other ringleaders. Von Scoultz and nine of his men were hanged at Kingston the following month.

In the 1960s I acquired many of the papers (now at the Archives of Ontario) of Duncan Clark (1795-1862), fur trader, militia officer and compiler of historical data such as the battles at Lundy's Lane and Queenston Heights in the War of 1812. He would have known Alexander Allan McMillan, a fellow militia officer. Clark lived at Cardinal, a few miles downriver from Prescott. In 1969 I wrote an article about him, which appeared in *Canadian Antique Collector* under the title, 'Canada's Paul Revere.' In 1813 Clark rode horseback along the St. Lawrence river from Cardinal to warn the British troops of Wilkinson's American army moving downriver in bateaux. The next day the British troops defeated the much larger American force at the Battle of Crysler's Farm.

Duncan Clark also fought in the Battle of the Windmill, and wrote an article about it for the *Sentinel*:

The vessels sheared off a little, intending to land at Pryors wharf, as would appear from their movements. The wind blowing strong down the river at the time the schooners fell below Pryors wharf and passed so near to McMillan's wharf that a man could have jumped ashore... the schooner's had fallen down owing to a strong south wind opposite the yellow storehouse of Alex McMillan Esquire.

It is possible that Alexander Allan and his wife Elizabeth sold out in Prescott soon after 1838, and moved some fifty miles north to the military settlement at Perth. This is one more family mystery to be solved.

•

Lt. Col. Alexander McMillan, father of Alexander Allan, lived at Williamstown and Lancaster. He was a founding member of the Highland Society of Canada in 1818 and died in 1823, the same year as his brother Allan. In 1823 his nephew James, a former Nor'Wester, then employed by the new Hudson's Bay Co., came to the village of Williamstown by canoe very much as I was to do 144 years later in our re-created cross-Canada canoe brigade of 1967. With him in 1823 he had two of his Métis children, Margaret and Allan, to be baptized at St. Andrew's Presbyterian Church, Williamstown. (In her chapter, Heather Devine also mentions this episode.) Imagine taking two children 5,000 kilometres by canoe from the Columbia river on the west coast. Allan may have stayed in the east with relatives, for he next appears in 1836 as an apprentice clerk hired to go from Lachine to Red River.

It is of interest how this information came to light. My fur trade history friends often exchange leads.

Professor Jennifer S.H. Brown, a fur trade academic at the University of Winnipeg, showed me an unpublished manuscript by Henry Conolly, a Hudson's Bay Company trader, son of William Conolly, a North West Company partner. Henry had died on a steamship en route to Labrador in 1910 with the unedited manuscript of his father's memoirs. Jennifer had this copy on loan from Jim Morrison, another of my researcher friends. It was an exciting moment when I came on the reference to Allan and his 1836 trek from Montreal to the Red River settlement partly by snowshoe. On contacting Jim, I discovered the original copy of the manuscript was with the Robert Bell papers in the National Archives. Robert Bell of the Geological Survey of Canada was a renaissance man who carried on a correspondence with everyone from Charles Darwin to a Hudson's Bay Company clerk in the Arctic. It is not surprising that he would have such an item in his papers. Bob Douglas's mother, who was Bell's daughter, tried to get the memoirs published in New York while living there in the 1920s. Jim Morrison plans to edit and publish this important material. I had missed acquiring this huge collection of papers in 1965 when I foolishly refused them. They were with Robert Douglas, grandson of Robert Bell, and had been earlier refused by the National Archives. I reasoned that if the National Archives didn't want them, why should I take them? In the 1970s the National Archives had to buy most of the papers they could have had earlier for free. My missed opportunity illustrates how synchronistic coincidences can be of great benefit if we only have the wit to take advantage of them.

In 1966 I acquired a transcript copy of an 1801 journal of a canoe voyage from Fort George on the Niagara river to Fort Malden on the Detroit river. The writer was Lt. Miles McDonell of the Royal Canadian Volunteer regiment. He was stationed at Fort George while Alexander McMillan was at Fort Malden. I assume my ancestor, John Roy, was there too. Miles, who was later an agent to Lord Selkirk and the first governor of the Red River colony, was from

Glengarry. He commented at length on what a fine visit he had with his old friend McMillan. 'We gathered for dinner with my old friends Capt's McMillan and McLean. We drank toasts and Alex entertained us.' Likely Alexander played his Jews harps.

As I mentioned earlier, Alexander was a member of DeLancey's Brigade for seven years during the American Revolution. The entry on Col. James DeLancey (1746-1804) in volume V of the *Dictionary of Canadian Biography* (238-9) gives a vivid account of the guerrilla-type warfare of DeLancey's Brigade:

> James DeLancey then made his way to New York City, where in 1777 he raised a picked force of horsemen drawn from his own county. The company was to harass the enemy near New York City and to procure supplies for the British army from the so-called 'Neutral Ground' between the British and American positions. General William Tryon of New York commented, "This Troop is truly [the] 'Elite' of the Country... I have much confidence in them for their spirited behaviour." Over the next five years, DeLancey's 'Cowboys,' as they were called, became one of the best known and feared of the loyalist units. The many exciting adventures of the 'Outlaw of the Bronx' (DeLancey had his headquarters near the Bronx River), gave him a glamorous image among both loyalists and patriots in New York. Although taken once, he was exchanged, and he continued to harass the enemy throughout the war; even George Washington was well aware of his activities and much desired his capture.

Alexander must have had some scalp-tingling experiences during this period of his career, but I have been unable to locate more about him after years of searching. I would still like to find those Jews harps!

•

In 1962 I had the pleasure of meeting, for the only time, Mrs. Charles MacMillan at the home of her grandson Jack Barker in Cowansville, Quebec. Then in her 90s, the sprightly widow had many stories to

Duncan McMillan (1812-1901), son of Archibald 'Murlaggan' McMillan, said to resemble his father. (Hugh P. MacMillan Collection, Guelph, Ontario)

money belt and headed east by train through the western states to Chicago, then to Montreal. Somewhere in Montana the train came to a halt in a narrow rock cut. Word spread through the cars – train robbers! It was a certainty they would be searched and all valuables taken. Mary, like most women of the period, had hair to her waist but it was coiled in a large bun on top of her head. Many around them were trying to hide valuables in their shoes and skirts – all the places the bandits would be sure to look. Mary had a better idea. She had Charles take his money belt from under his shirt and extract the large denomination bank notes then pitch the belt out the window. She kept a few dollars in her purse and had Charles keep some money in his pocket along with his watch. Her nimble fingers soon had the $100 banknotes in tight little rolls, which she kept shoving in the mass of hair atop her head. When the bandits arrived in their car, the search began. Her wedding ring, his watch, and their money was taken. At this point Mary burst into tears exclaiming, 'But we have no money to get us back to Montreal!' One of the bandits felt sorry for her and tossed her a $5 gold piece. Mary was still chuckling sixty years later at how she fooled those Montana bandits.

•

tell. Her late husband Charles was a grandson of Archibald 'Murlaggan.' I taped several hours of tales about the family. Unfortunately these were lost in our 1971 fire. Only one of the stories stayed in my memory bank. About 1890 Charles and his bride, Mary Armentrot, decided to leave the Grenville, Quebec, area and move to Oregon. They had some money and established a business which they ran for about ten years. In 1901, Charles' father,

Duncan, died and on inheriting the family property, they decided to move back east. They sold their business, stashed the proceeds (about $20,000) in his

Another family story (confirmed by my father's notes) concerns Ranald and his nephew Alexander who went to the West Indies. I have mentioned Ranald in my introduction to the 'Charts' chapter. This concerned his being captured on the way to Jamaica in 1805 by a French privateer. A second letter from Archibald McMillan of Murlaggan, 27 April 1805, to his cousin Captain Alexander Cameron in Surinam states that 'My cousin Ronald McMillan came here in October last and resided 'twixt this and friends in Glengarry and Lancaster all winter.' He likely stayed for a time with his brother John Roy (my great-great-grandfather) and with his brothers Allan and Alexander. Somerled MacMillan, our late bard/historian, states on page 74 of *Bygone Lochaber*, 'We have good reason to believe that Ronald was released and found his way to Jamaica where some of his descendants are living.' A further note from my father adds the following to what he heard from his father about Ronald visiting in 1805: 'The French pirates released Ranald (Ronald) because many of the crew on the pirate ship were Gaelic-speaking Highlanders.' This is not surprising given the close connection between France and Scotland in that period.

I made contact with Robert MacMillan and his sister Judy Ann who own an advertising business in Kingston, Jamaica. Robert, in a recent phone conversation, stated that he thinks they may be descended from Ranald but that they have no proof. This exciting development came through a chance encounter that I had with an Anglican rector who is a native of Jamaica and knew these MacMillans. Synchronicity at work again. Last year Margaret LaRue of Keswick, Ontario got in touch with me as a result of my advertising for descendants of the Glenpean and Murlaggan line. She is a descendant through John, son of Allan 'Glenpean'. I knew nothing of this line before she contacted me nor did she know anything about our West Indian connection. She, along with her husband Roger and friends, have been going to Grenada for several years with a volunteer church group building low-cost housing. I put her in touch with some of our West Indian cousins in Grenada. On 12 February 1993 she had a taped interview with Sylvia (McMillan) Sargent at Belle Vue, St. Davids, Grenada. Sadly, Sylvia died a few months after the interview. The rambling transcript has a charm all its own, including several reference to 'Outside Children,' the charming euphemism for illegitimate children, of which the McMillans, there as here, had their share. The following dialogue from the interview has a tie in with Jamaica, which helps confirm family contacts, through the islands, and back to Glengarry:

Margaret: 'Now that is Alexander's father, that's Allan McMillan and he came from Scotland.'

Sylvia: 'To where, to Canada?'

Margaret: 'Yes, I've brought you a book by Marianne McLean. It's wonderful history. Now this is Allan's picture, and on this chart, that is John, Alexander's brother. He is my ancestor. The man who gave me this information is Hugh MacMillan and he's a descendant of John Roy, Allan's brother.'

Sylvia: 'And I'm telling you now we have a Hugh McMillan, and he had an uncle Hugh. And they have one fault – a terrible fault – drinking whisky.'

Margaret: 'Oh my God! my father drank and he died a young man.'

Sylvia: 'And my father too – and stealing horses – old MacDonald McMillan, the one in Canada and Jamaica, yes, Grandma told me he had a son but she was a very young person. There wasn't a lot of transportation. It'd be horse riding, and she comin' from Carriacou... I suppose she didn't know much about who he was. Anyway she fell in love with this McMillan man and he gave her this little son and he went to Jamaica to get horses for the estate and he got drowned there. He didn't come back and she brought up the child. She lived to be 83. She never married or anything.

Margaret: 'What was her name?'

Sylvia: 'Clare Carolyn MacGillivray, and you saw him and one of his daughters. As I tell you he had a lot of outside children. I am the 13th child but the only child of his marriage... but they're not alive, you know. One was a doctor, one a lawyer, one a soldier, one a farmer, another to Venezuela.'

This points up the complexity of West Indian genealogy – combined with a scarcity of documents. It would be a fascinating project for a historical or anthropological team, but it would take months, years, to sort this ethnic mix. Between 'Outside Children', drinking whisky, and stealing horses, we McMillan menfolk have a lot of warts to choose from and perhaps to live down.

•

As stated earlier, the Métis and West Indian branches of our Glenpean line make for an exciting addition to our family and the emigration story. I suspect, judging by the Highland names among the West Indian connection, that there were many more than McMillans venturing to the Indies with Ranald, Archibald and their nephew Alexander. This does not appear to be the case with the fur trade. James was the only McMillan in the North West Company. Two anecdotes about William (son of James) and his family bear repeating. If you look closely at the picture of William and his wife Margaret Dease (page 96), you will notice that his right hand is withered. In her chapter, Heather Devine has already mentioned the story of the gun that misfired and blew part of his hand away. William's father, James, had a similar experience in 1813 on the Columbia River.

The family spoke Cree in the home as well as French intermixed with Gaelic and English. Journeys took him as far afield as Kentucky to buy horses in order to improve his buffalo runners. At age 70 he went to the newly-opened Mayo Clinic at Rochester, Minnesota for eye surgery but came back nearly blind. Métis such as William were in constant danger travelling through hostile Sioux territory. The Mankato massacre of 1862 occurred near the little town of Rochester about the time William was on his journey. In 1968, his grandson Joseph gave me these tales, but refused to talk into my tape recorder. He ended the interview by bringing in his cousin to play me the Red River Jig on the fiddle, which he said was composed by William. More recently Orval McMillan, a Toronto businessman and grandson of Joseph, told me more about his grandfather's father and also about Joseph (1849-1922), son of William. He was a close friend of Donald A Smith (Lord Strathcona). Orval recounts how he was born in St. Boniface, Red River and was married to Polly Bruce, also Métis. He and his family crossed the Assiniboine River in 1860 settling on what was known as the Strathmillan Estate which extended one mile north. While great-grandfa-

ther was not involved with Donald Smith in his railway ventures, there is no doubt he benefited from Smith's land dealings. He was a farmer who taught at St. Boniface college. Conservative politics was his great passion. He was Reeve of Assiniboia, now incorporated into Winnipeg, from 1906 to 1912, and I have his massive armchair which he sat in as reeve. In Long Beach, California, Joseph owned a winter home, located on the beach. From Donald Smith, he rented a railway car for the family trips to California. The house was torn down in 1966.

It is instructive to note how one branch of an extended family can progress. From a tacksman (Allan) in the Highlands of Scotland helping move over 400 of his kinsmen to America, to his son, a North West Company fur trader (James), to his free trader and buffalo hunter son (William), to his son Joseph with his private rail car to take his family to Long Beach California for the winter. In the meantime another branch went south to the West Indies, while the rest of us were felling trees and farming in Glengarry. If you have a Glenpean/Murlaggan connection, examine the charts in chapter 10 to see where you fit in our extended family.

•

This final potpourri of stories came from my father's memory storehouse. Had I not persisted, the stories would have been lost. It is remarkable how such stories, albeit subject to error, were handed down through four generations of collective memory, this despite the loss of the Gaelic, which would have improved them.

Alex Willie MacMillan from Lochiel was a well-known undertaker in Alexandria whose ancestor came out in 1802 with the other emigrants. He had a wicked sense of humour. He once said to me, 'The first decision that a Glengarry lad gets to make is choosing his father's coffin.' There is some truth to this, as given half a chance, many Highland males fit easily into the role of a patriarchal autocrat. My own father had such leanings. Alex Willie once stopped my father on the street for a little chit chat. Father enquired as to Alex Willie's health and his business.

Alex Willie's succinct comment was, 'Well, Rev J. A., it would be tolerably better if you could fix me some funerals real quick.' In the 1930s, Alex Willie and a friend were driving back to Alexandria on a cold winter day with a corpse sitting up in the back seat of his old touring car. They had to get out and shovel as the road was not ploughed. Another car caught up to them and two men got out to help push them through the worst drifts. It was getting dark and one of the men noticed the man in the back seat so he called out to Alex Willie, 'What's the matter with your friend in the back seat? Why isn't he out here pushing?' Alex Willie's quick answer was 'Seems he had too much of the grog and fell to sleep, but reach in and give him a shake.' The stranger's comment was not recorded.

Grandfather Hughie Archie Roy died in 1914 at age 61 of pneumonia, possibly brought on by an overly lengthy stay in a snow bank on a cold winter's night. I suspect this may have been the result of an overly lengthy stay at the Quigley Hotel a short distance from the farm. The ledger kept by the 'Wildcat' Chisholms for their store & hotel has frequent entries for 'Wee Hughie' taking home a jug of 'high wines'. This was a lethal mix of overproof alcohol mixed with snuff, hot peppers and fruit juices. These entries commence in the 1860s when he would have been a lad of ten or so. Father refused to comment on the possible cause of his father's pneumonia except to say:

> My grandmother served food and drink from the time she married and came here in the 1830s as a bride of Archie Roy. This farm was the place the 'stage' from L'Orignal on the Ottawa River to Lancaster on the St Lawrence stopped to change horses. She would need these spirits for the travellers. I can just remember her smoking her clay pipe which she kept on the mantel. Once a traveller picked it up to smoke it, so before she used it next she broke a piece of the stem. I heard that when she died in 1893 she left $20,000 in her will – all of it money made from the sale of food and drink.

**Photograph of oil portrait of Margaret Grant (1815-1893), wife of Archie Roy McMillan. The oil portrait itself was destroyed by fire in 1971. Margaret ran a mid-point change station for the stage from L'Orignal on the Ottawa River to Lancaster on the St. Lawrence. (Hugh P. MacMillan Collection, Guelph, Ontario)**

Margaret Grant was of Loyalist stock from the 'South Branch' of the Raisin River near Williamstown. The photograph of her portrait shows a handsome woman. Despite her missing dentures (they fitted badly in those days), she had fine features with a sharply chiselled nose and piercing blue eyes. Not someone you would want to get on the wrong side of. Father commented, 'Grandfather Archie Roy dressed up once for me in his top hat and tailcoat to show me how he looked when he went to see lawyer McLennan in Cornwall about his uncle Ranald's estate in the Indies.' When I pressed father for more details he changed the subject. It is all part of the recurring story first told me by my grandmother about Ranald (Ronald) and ships, money and poison. It is unlikely we

Archie Roy McMillan (1803-1899), son of John Roy McMillan and nephew of Allan 'Glenpean' McMillan. Archie Roy owned and farmed over 1200 acres in Lochiel Township, Glengarry County. (Hugh P. MacMillan Collection, Guelph, Ontario)

will ever solve this mystery. I have had British chancery court records checked, but to no avail. Most of such stories have some basis in fact but with no records, they are usually impossible to verify.

•

My last-note taking session with father gave me these bits of family lore:

My great grandfather carried that old musket you are so proud of in the army after he came to Canada, then my grandfather had it in the Papineau Rebellion. I went to Illinois in 1906 when I was 21 to buy a Percheron stud horse. My father gave me the money and I took the stud back by train. That was how I made some money to be a preacher. It was the year father got one of the first

phones at Lochiel. I see his name on that 1907 list of subscribers you found some place. That old bill you found dated 1893 proves that it cost $252.03 to roof our barn with a slate roof. Father McMillan, whose church was next to our farm, was proud of the slate roof on his own house. He thought it the only slate roof around till he was told that Hughie Archie Roy McMillan put a slate roof on his barn years ago. It was around this time that the Orange Lodge people needed a white horse for their July twelfth parade as the one they had used in past years had died. A lodge member commented, 'Why not ask Father McMillan if we can borrow his white horse for the day?' This seemed like an unlikely prospect but ask him they did. He told them he would like to help them but his parishioners would not be pleased at him aiding this Protestant group; however, he said he would be away that day and the horse would be in the barn. They understood and before daylight on the 12th, they were leading the horse down the road. At first light they were shocked to find someone had gone and painted the horse green. This is the only recorded instance of an Orange Walk that had King Billy riding a green horse.

The business records to do with the slate roof were in the wooden chest of documents I found at my uncle's house in 1971, the year he was killed in a car accident. It was while looking after his estate that I was pleasantly surprised to find that my housecleaning cousins had missed the chest. There is a fine collection of nineteenth century letters and business papers that will be deposited with the Glengarry Historical Society. The 1907 Glengarry telephone book consists of only one page listing nineteen subscribers with grandfather being one of them. The rules on the reverse page are interesting. The subscriber is instructed to read the rules 'before and after eating' and to 'always hang the receiver on hook with ear down to keep out dust.' Furthermore, 'outsiders will not be permitted to run in and use the telephone a minute,' and '3 minutes is a goodly time to talk business and should also satisfy those socially inclined.' Imagine how such rules would go over today!

•

Donald John MacGillivray, a first cousin of my father, was a veteran of the Boer War. His great-grandfather came to Glengarry with the 'Glenelg' settlers in 1794. Donald John told me about his father courting Isabella, my grandfather's sister. Finally he drove down to Lochiel with his horse and buggy to see her father, Archie Roy. Archie Roy considered the marriage proposal and answered, 'No, you can't marry Isabella cause she is keeping house for her two brothers Sandy and John, but you can marry my other daughter Henrietta.' Donald claims his father left in a fine rage and headed back for Kirkhill. When he cooled off, he thought 'Well, they are sisters and they look alike – so why not?' Donald John made many fine cedar chests which he gave to certain select women in Glengarry, those who allow their husbands to have a dram in the house. Muriel was grateful when she got her cedar chest many years ago.

My great-grandfather Archie Roy was among the first generation born in Canada. I heard much more about him from my father, than I did about his son Hugh Roy, my grandfather. It would seem that Hugh Roy could have been overshadowed by his father who may well have assumed the role of patriarchal autocrat. Although Hugh Roy's barn was roofed with slate in 1893, his new house only rated a tin roof. Perhaps some sort of nineteenth-century one-upmanship? Or perhaps he was proclaiming his independence?

Archie Roy born in 1803 was age 38 when his father died in 1841. During the course of his 96 years, he bought in excess of 2000 acres of land for six sons. He likely accumulated his first capital by going to the shanty (lumber camp). Father did recall that he worked for Hamilton Bros. on the Grand (Ottawa) River opposite Grenville, where his cousin Archibald Murlaggan McMillan was located. Father also recalled that he imported the first dual-purpose (milk and beef) short horn cattle into Glengarry.

By 1838 he settled on lot 28, concession 14 of Lochiel and moved from a log house to a frame house soon after. By 1882 his son Hugh Roy had built a six-bedroom brick house complete with a veranda on three sides, an ornate curved staircase in the front hall, with the requisite summer kitchen to keep the main kitchen cool during the summer heat. I recall the log house which had been converted to a pig pen, while the frame house served as a granary. These were good times for shrewd farmers. Father recounted that while he was growing up, the family of eight, in addition to two or more hired hands, were employed on the farm. A hired girl worked in the house. Succeeding generations in our family, including mine, were less successful as farmers. A small number of the descendants of these Lochaber folk are still on the same land, while the rest of us are scattered across this country and abroad.

Archie Roy's travels as a young man probably took him no farther afield than the shanties up the Ottawa or to Montreal. He and other settlers would have walked through the dense bush between their homesteads at Lochiel to Hamilton's Mill, now Hawkesbury. Cash income attracted to the sawmills or shanty. This sixty-mile trail became the 'Military Road' which evolved into the present day Highway 34 from Hawkesbury on the Ottawa River to Lancaster on the St. Lawrence. Archie Roy and his wife Margaret Grant were ideally located to operate their stage coach stop at the midway point between the Ottawa and the St. Lawrence.

Archie Roy and his father were likely among Glengarry farmers who supplied produce such as salt pork and butter to the fur traders. His first cousin James would have been his contact. Since these men left so few records, we can only speculate. The subject deserves more detailed research.

# BIBLIOGRAPHY

Anderson, Marjorie O., ed., *Early Sources of Scottish History* (Stamford: Paul Watkins 1990).

— *Kings and Kingship in Early Scotland* (Edinburgh: Scottish Academic Press 1980).

Anson, Peter F., *Underground Catholicism in Scotland 1622-1878* (Montrose: Standard Press 1970).

Barrett, Stanley, *Paradise: Class, Commuters and Ethnicity in Rural Ontario* (Toronto: University of Toronto Press 1994).

Black, George F, *The Surnames of Scotland* (New York: The New York Public Library 1946).

Boswell, James, *Journal of a Tour to the Hebrides With Samuel Johnson, LL.D.* (London: Oxford University Press 1924).

Brown, Jennifer S.H., *Strangers in Blood: Fur Trade Company Families in Indian Country* (Vancouver: University of British Columbia Press 1980).

Buchanan, R.M., *Notes on the members of the Buchanan Society* (Glasgow: Jackson, Wylie & Co. 1931).

Buchanan of Auchmar, *An Inquiry into the Genealogy... of the Ancient Scottish Surnames* (Glasgow: John Wylie & Co. 1820).

Bumsted, J.M., *The People's Clearance* (Winnipeg: University of Manitoba Press 1982).

Cameron, Duncan, 'A Sketch of the Customs, Manners, Way of Living of the Natives in the Barren Country About Nipigon,' in L.R. Masson, *Les Bourgeois de la Compagnie du Nord-Ouest* (New York: Antiquarian Press Ltd. 1960).

Campbell, J.G., *Gaelic Ghosts* (London: Bodley Head 1972).

Carmichael, Alexander, *Carmina Gadelica*, Vols. I-V (Edinburgh: Oliver & Boyd 1940).

Chadwick, Nora K., *Celtic Britain* (London: Thames & Hudson 1963).

Chambers, Robert and William, *The Gazetteer of Scotland* (Edinburgh: 1832).

Coues, Elliot, ed., *The Manuscript Journals of Alexander Henry and David Thompson 1799-1814*, Vols. I and II (Minneapolis: Ross & Haines, Inc. 1965).

Devine, Heather, 'Roots in the Mohawk Valley: Sir William Johnson's Legacy in the North West Company,' in Brown, Jennifer S.H., William J. Eccles and Donald P. Heldman, eds., *The Fur Trade Revisited: Selected Papers of the Sixth North American Fur Trade Conference* (East Lansing, Michigan: Michigan State University Press 1994).

Dorge, Lionel, 'The Metis and Canadien Councillors of Assiniboia, Parts I-III,' in *The Beaver* (Summer, Autumn and Winter, 1974).

Dwelly, Edward, *The Illustrated Gaelic-English Dictionary* (Glasgow: Alex MacLaren & Sons 1901).

Forsyth, Rev. W., *In the Shadow of Cairngorm* (Inverness: Northern Counties Publishing Co. 1900).

Grant, Rev. John, *Old Statistical Account of Abernethy and Kincardine*, Vol. XIII (1794).

Haldane, A.R.B., *The Drove Roads of Scotland* (London: Thomas Nelson & Sons 1952).

Harkness, John, *Stormont, Dundas and Glengarry* (Cornwall: Facsimile edition 1972).

Hunter, James, *The Making of the Crofting Community* (Edinburgh: John Donald 1976).

Hurst, James Willard, *Law and Economic Growth; the legal history of the lumber industry in Wisconsin 1836-1915* (Cambridge, Mass.: Harvard University Press 1964).

Johnson, Samuel, *Journey to the Western Islands of Scotland* (London: Oxford University Press 1924).

Laing, David, ed., *Andrew of Wyntoun, Orygynale Cronykil of Scotland*, Vol. III (Edinburgh: William Paterson 1879).

Lang, Andrew, ed., *The Highlands of Scotland in 1750* (Edinburgh: William Blackwood & Sons 1898).

Laurence, K.O., *Immigration into the West Indies in the 19th Century* (Kingston, Jamaica: Caribbean Universities Press 1971).

Lower, A.R.M., *Great Britain's Woodyard: British North America and The Timber Trade, 1763-1867* (Montreal and Kingston: McGill-Queen's University Press 1973).

MacCulloch, Donald B., *Romantic Lochaber* (Edinburgh: Oliver & Boyd 1948).

Macdonell, J.A. (Greenfield), *Sketches Illustrating the Early Settlement and History of Glengarry* (Montreal: W.F. Brown 1893).

MacDonell, Margaret, *The Immigrant Experience* (Toronto: University of Toronto Press 1982).

McGillivray, Robert and George B. Macgillivray, *History of Clan Macgillivray* (Thunder Bay: Privately Published 1973).

McGillivray, Royce, and Ewen Ross, *A History of Glengarry* (Belleville: Mika Publishing 1979).

MacGregor, Alexander, *Highland Superstitions* (Stirling: Aeneas Mackay 1937).

Mackay, William, *Urquhart and Glenmoriston* (Inverness: Northern Counties Publishing Co. 1914).

Mackenzie, Alexander, *History of the Camerons* (Inverness: A. & W. Mackenzie 1884)

— *The History of the Highland Clearances* (Glasgow: Alex MacLaren 1883).

Mackintosh, Charles Fraser, 'The Camerons of Letterfinlay,' in *Transactions of Gaelic Society of Inverness*, Vol. XVII, 1892.

— *Minor Septs of Clan Chattan* (Inverness: John Mackay, 1898).

McLean, Marianne, *The People of Glengarry* (Montreal and Kingston: McGill-Queen's University Press 1991).

MacLeod, Donald, *Gloomy Memories of the Highlands of Scotland* (Toronto: Privately Published 1857).

Macmillan, Hugh, *The Clan Macmillan* (London: Macmillan & Co. 1901).

MacMillan, Rev. Somerled, *Bygone Lochaber* (Glasgow: K. & R. Davidson 1971).

MacMillan, Somerled, *The Macmillans and their Septs* (Glasgow: Private Publication 1952).

McMullen, Christopher W., *The MacMillan Endeavour* (Bruceton Mills West Virginia, 1990).

Merk, Frederick, ed., *Fur Trade and Empire, George Simpson's Journal* (Cambridge, Mass.: The Belnap Press of Harvard University Press 1968).

Mitchell, Joseph, *Reminiscences of My Life in the Highlands*, 2 Vols. (London: Gresham Press 1884).

Moncrieffe, Sir Iain, *The Highland Clans*, (London: Haarlem Press 1967)

Murray, Norman, *The Scottish Hand Loom Weavers 1790-1850, A Social History* (Edinburgh: John Donald Publishers Ltd. 1978).

Newman, Peter C., *Caesars of the Wilderness* (Markham: Penguin Books Canada Limited 1987).

Pine, L.G., *The Highland Clans* (Newton Abbot, Devon: David & Charles 1972).

Prebble, John, *Glencoe: The Story of the Massacre* (Harmondsworth: Penguin Books Ltd. 1986).

— *Culloden* (Harmondsworth: Penguin Books Ltd. 1986).

— *The Highland Clearances* (Harmondsworth: Penguin Books Ltd. 1986).

— *Mutiny: Highland Regiments in Revolt, 1743-1804* (Harmondsworth: Penguin Books Ltd. 1975).

— *The King's Jaunt* (London: Fontana Paperbacks 1988).

Ramcharan, S., *Racism: Nonwhites in Canada* (Toronto: Butterworths 1982).

Rich, E.E., ed., *Simpson's 1828 Journey to the Columbia*, Vol. X (London: Hudson's Bay Record Society 1947).

Richardson, Bonham C., *Caribbean Migrants*, (Knoxville: The University of Tennessee Press 1983).

Robertson, James, *General View of the Agriculture in the County of Inverness* (London: Board of Agriculture 1808)

Satzewich, V., *Racism and the Incorporation of Foreign Labour: Farm Labour Migration to Canada Since 1945* (London and New York: Routledge, Chapman and Hall 1991).

Skene, W.F., *ed., Celtic Scotland, The Book of Deer*, 3 Volumes (Edinburgh: The Spalding Club 1969)

— *The Highlanders of Scotland* (Stirling: The Sentinel Press 1902).

Smout, T.C., *A History of the Scottish People, 1560-1830* (London: Collins Fontana 1972).

Sprague, D.N. and R.P. Frye, eds., *The Genealogy of the First Metis Nation* (Winnipeg: Pemmican Publications 1983).

Stanley, George F.G., Thomas Flanagan, and Claude Rocan, eds., *The Collected Diaries of Louis Riel.* Vol. V (Edmonton: University of Alberta Press 1985).

Stanley, George F.G., *The Birth of Western Canada* (Toronto: University of Toronto Press 1992).

Stewart of Ardvorlich, John, *The Camerons* (Glasgow: The Clan Cameron Association 1974).

Thomson, Derick, *An Introduction to Gaelic Poetry* (London: The Camelot Press 1974).

— ed., *The Companion to Gaelic Scotland* (Oxford: Basil Blackwell Ltd. 1983).

Tyrrell, J.B., ed., *David Thompson's Narrative, 1784-1812* (Toronto: Publications of the Champlain Society, no. 40, 1962).

Van Kirk, Sylvia, *'Many Tender Ties': Women in Fur-Trade Society 1670-1870* (Winnipeg: Watson & Dwyer Publishing Ltd. 1983).

Watt, D.E.R., ed., *Walter Bower, Scotichronicon*, Vol. VIII (Aberdeen: Aberdeen University Press 1987).

Whitaker, R.. *Double Standard: The Secret History of Canadian Immigration Policy* (Toronto: Lester and Orpen Dennys 1987).

Williams, Glyndwr, ed., *Hudson's Bay Miscellany 1670-1870* (Winnipeg: Hudson's Bay Record Society 1975).

# INDEX

The following index is composed of two parts, A and B. Thanks to David Anderson, the ships' lists of the Lochaber immigrants of 1802 (chapter 1) has its own index (pages 12-13), an alphabetized list of passengers. That list, reduced to heads of household and place of residence in Scotland, is included here as Part A.

Part B here is a nominal index of places and people connected with the Lochaber-Glengarry story. The variety of spellings of the Gaelic names presents challenges. There are 160 known versions of McMillan, including variants such as Bell, the English version, and Cameron, since Lochaber Macmillans associated with Cameron of Lochiel were sometimes called Cameron. To make matters even more complicated for genealogists, historians and indexers, most of the early Lochaber residents, as was the Gaelic custom, rarely used the surname, preferring to be known by their first name plus a physical characteristic and/or their residence and/or as son of the first name of their father. Often residence alone designated a person.

Readers will soon discover that even today Allan 'Glenpean' McMillan and his first cousin, Archibald 'Murlaggan' McMillan, are often named by their region in Scotland – Glenpean and Murlaggan; and that Lochiel sometimes means 'Cameron of Lochiel.'

For more details on the earliest known McMillans, the reader is invited to refer to Graeme Mackenzie's genealogical tree on page 34. For details on the fur trader, James, son of Allan 'Glenpean' McMillan, and James' three Métis families, readers should refer to Heather Devine's family trees on pages 95, 97 and 98.

The over 1700 names in Duncan MacDonald's Glenpean and Murlaggan charts (chapter 10) are not included in either Parts A or B. These charts are remarkable for their rich detail, and for the ease that descendants will have in finding their nuclear families. John MacMillan of Glenpean's offspring have merely to look for their names in the appropriate generation of descent from John MacMillan. Thus an index would seem redundant.